unio mystica

A Rebel Book

www.osho.com

Printing: Lightning Print Inc.

A Rebel Book

Publisher: Osho International, 570 Lexington Avenue,
New York, NY 10022

Previously published as *Unio Mystica*, Volume I

Osho ® is a registered trademark of Osho International Foundatioi
used under license.

ISBN 0-88050-998-8

UNIO MYSTICA

Poetry of the Sufi Master, Hakim Sanai

Spontaneous talks given
to disciples and friends
at Osho Commune
International, Pune, India

osho

contents

I Polishing the Mirror of the Heart

Hakim Sanai: this name is as sweet to me as honey, as sweet as nectar. Hakim Sanai is unique, unique in the world of Sufism. No other Sufi has been able to reach to such heights of expression and such depths of penetration. Hakim Sanai has been able to do almost the impossible.

If I were to save only two books from the whole world of the mystics, then these would be the two books. One would be from the world of Zen, the path of awareness: Sosan's *Hsin Hsin Ming*. I have spoken on it; it contains the quintessence of Zen, of the path of awareness and meditation. The other book would be Hakim Sanai's *Haqiqa'ul Hadiqa*: *The Walled Garden Of Truth* – in short, *The Hadiqa*: The Garden. This is the book we are entering today.

The Hadiqa is the essential fragrance of the path of love. Just as Sosan has been able to catch the very soul of Zen, Hakim Sanai has been able to catch the very soul of Sufism. Such books are not written, they are born. Nobody can compose them. They are not manufactured in the mind, by the mind; they come from the beyond. They are a gift. They are born as mysteriously as a child is born, or a bird or a roseflower. They come to us, they are gifts.

So first we will enter into the mysterious birth of this great book *The Hadiqa*: The Garden. The story is tremendously beautiful.

The Sultan of Ghazni, Bahramshah, was moving with his

great army towards India on a journey of conquest. Hakim Sanai, his famous court-poet, was also with him, accompanying him on the journey of this conquest.They came alongside a great garden, a walled garden.

That is the meaning of *firdaus*: the walled garden.And from *firdaus* comes the English word 'paradise'.

They were in a hurry; with a great army the Sultan was moving to conquer India. He had no time. But something mysterious happened and he had to stop; there was no way to avoid it.

The sound of singing coming from the garden caught the Sultan's attention. He was a lover of music, but he had never heard something like this. He had great musicians in his court and great singers and dancers, but nothing to be compared with this.The sound of singing and the music and the dance – he had only heard it from outside, but he had to order the army to stop.

It was so ecstatic. The very sound of the dance and the music and the singing was psychedelic, as if wine was pouring into him: the Sultan became drunk. The phenomenon appeared not to be of this world. Something of the beyond was certainly in it: something of the sky trying to reach the earth, something from the unknown trying to commune with the known. He had to stop to listen to it.

There was ecstasy in it – so sweet and yet so painful, it was heart-rending. He wanted to move, he was in a hurry; he had to reach India soon, this was the right time to conquer the enemy. But there was no way.There was such strong, strange, irresistible magnetism in the sound that in spite of himself he had to go into the garden.

It was Lai-Khur, a great Sufi mystic, but known to the masses only as a drunkard and a madman. Lai-Khur is one of the greatest names in the whole history of the world. Not much is known about him; such people don't leave many footprints behind them. Except for this story, nothing has survived.

But Lai-Khur has lived in the memories of the Sufis, down the ages. He continued haunting the world of the Sufis, because never again was such a man seen.

He was so drunk that people were not wrong in calling him a drunkard. He was drunk twenty-four hours, drunk with the divine. He walked like a drunkard, he lived like a drunkard, utterly oblivious of the world. And his utterances were just mad. This is the highest peak of ecstasy, when expressions of the mystic can only be understood by other mystics. For the ordinary masses they look irrelevant, they look like gibberish.

You will be surprised to know that the English word 'gibberish' is based on a sufi mystic's name, Jabbar. It is because of Jabbar's utterances that the English word 'gibberish' has arisen. But even Jabbar was nothing compared to Lai-Khur.

To the ignorant, his utterances were outrageous, sacrilegious, against tradition and against all formalities, mannerisms and etiquette – against all that is known and understood as religion. But to those who knew, they were nothing but pure gold.

He was available only to the chosen few, because only very few people can rise to such a height where he lived. He lived on Everest – the Everest of consciousness, beyond the clouds. Only those who were fortunate enough and courageous enough to climb the mountain were able to understand what he was saying. To the common masses he was a madman. To the knowers he was just a vehicle of God, and all that was coming through him was pure truth: truth, and only truth.

He had made himself deliberately notorious. That was his way of becoming invisible to the masses. Sufis do that; they have a very strange method of becoming invisible. They remain visible – they remain in the world, they don't escape from it – but deliberately they create a certain milieu around them, so that people stop coming to them. Crowds, curious people, stupid people, simply stop coming to them; the Sufis don't exist for them, they forget all about them. This has been an ancient method of the Sufis so that they can work with their disciples.

You can see it happening here. You are my Sufis. I am almost invisible to the people who live in Pune. I am here and not here: I am not here for them, I am here only for you. I am invisible even to the neighbors here. They see and yet they don't see, they hear and yet they don't hear.

Lai-Khur had made himself deliberately notorious. Now, can you find a more notorious man than me? And it is so good: it keeps the foolish away. He was now visible only to the perceptive. A master, if he really wants to work, if he means business, has to become invisible to those who are not authentic seekers.

That is what Gurdjieff used to do. Gurdjieff must have learnt a few things from Lai-Khur. Gurdjieff had lived with Sufi masters for many years before he became a master in his own right. And when I have finished this story you will see many similarities between Gurdjieff and Lai-Khur.

Lai-Khur called for wine and proposed a toast "to the blindness of the Sultan Bahramshah."

Now, first the great mystic called for wine. Religious people are not supposed to drink wine. It is one of the greatest sins for a Muslim to drink wine; it is against the Koran, it is against the religious idea of how a saint should be. Lai-Khur called for wine and proposed a toast "to the blindness of the Sultan Bahramshah."

The Sultan must have got mad. He must have been furious – calling him blind? But he was under the great ecstatic impact of Lai-Khur. So although he was boiling within, he didn't say a thing. Those beautiful sounds and the music and the dance were still haunting him, they were still there in his heart. He was transported to another world. But others objected, his generals and his courtiers objected.

When objections were raised, Lai-Khur laughed madly and insisted that the Sultan deserved blindness for embarking on such a foolish journey. "What can you conquer in the world? All will be left behind. The idea of conquering is stupid, utterly stupid. Where are you going? You are blind! Because the treasure is within you," he said. "And you are going to India; wasting time, wasting other people's time. What more is needed for a man to be called blind?"

Lai-Khur insisted: "The Sultan *is* blind. If he is not blind then he should go back to his home and forget all about this conquest. Don't make houses of playing-cards, don't make castles of sand. Don't go after dreams, don't be mad. Go back! look within!"

The man who has eyes looks within, the blind man looks without. The man who has eyes searches for the treasure within. The man who is blind rushes all over the world, begging, robbing people, murdering, in the hope that he will find something that he is missing. It is never found that way, because it is not outside that you have lost it. You have lost it in your own being: light has to be brought *there*.

Lai-Khur insisted that the Sultan was blind. "If he is not, then give me the proof: order the army to go back. Forget all about this conquest, and never again go on any other conquest. This is all nonsense!"

The Sultan was impressed, but was not capable of going back.

It must have been the same situation as had happened before, when Alexander the Great was coming to conquer India, and another mystic, Diogenes laughed at him. And he said, "Why? For what are you going on such a long journey? And what are you going to gain by conquering India, or by conquering he whole world?"

And Alexander said, "I want to conquer the whole world so that finally I can rest and relax and enjoy."

And Diogenes laughed and said, "You must be a fool – because I am resting now!" And he was resting, relaxing on the bank of a small river. It was early morning and he was taking a sunbath, naked on the sand, He said, "I am resting and relaxing *now*, and I have not conquered the world. I have not even *thought* of conquering the world. So if you are conquering the world and trying to become victorious just to rest and relax, it looks absolutely meaningless, because I am resting without conquering anything. And the bank of this river is big enough, it can contain us both. Rest here. Throw away your clothes and take a good sunbath and forget all about conquering!

"And look at me: I am a conqueror without conquering the world. And you are a beggar."

The same must have been the situation with the Sultan Bahramshah, and Lai-Khur must have been again the same type of man. In this world there have been only two types of people: those who know, and those who don't know. It is the same drama played again and again, the same story enacted again and again. Sometimes it is Alexander the Great who is playing the blind person and it is Diogenes who tries to wake him up. Some other time it is Lai-Khur who is trying to wake Sultan Bahramshah.

Alexander said, "I am sorry. I can understand your point, but I cannot go back. I have to conquer the world; without conquering it I cannot rest. Excuse me. And you are right, I concede it."

And the same happened with Bahramshah. He was sad, ashamed, shy. But he said, "Excuse me, I have to go, I cannot go back. India has to be conquered. I will not be able to rest or sit silently until I have conquered India."

Then a toast was called "To the blindness of Hakim Sanai" – because he was the next most important person with Bahramshah. He was his adviser, his counselor, his poet. He was the wisest man in his court, and his fame had penetrated into other lands too. He was already an accomplished poet; a great, well-known wise man.

Then a toast was called "to the blindness of Hakim Sanai," which must have given the great poet a considerable jolt.

There were even stronger objections to this on the grounds of Sanai's excellent reputation, his wisdom, his character. He was a man of character, a very virtuous man, very religious. Nobody could have found any flaw in his life. He had lived a very very conscious life, at least in his own eyes. He was a man of conscience.

More objections were raised. Because maybe the Sultan was blind, he was greedy, he had great lust, he had great desire to possess things, but that could not be said about Hakim Sanai. He had lived the life of a poor man, even though he had been in the court. Even though he was the most respected man in Bahramshah's court, he had lived like a poor man – simple, humble, and of great wisdom and character.

But Lai-Khur countered that the toast was even more apt, since Sanai seemed unaware of the purpose for which he had been created; and when he was shortly brought before his maker and asked what he had to show for himself he would only be able to produce some stupid eulogies to foolish kings, mere mortals like himself.

Lai-Khur said that it was even more apt because much more is to be expected from Hakim Sanai than from Sultan Bahramshah. He has a greater potential and he is wasting it, wasting it in making eulogies for foolish kings. He will not be able to face his God; he will be in difficulty, he will not be able to answer for himself. All that he will be able to produce will be this poetry, written in praise of foolish kings like this blind man, Bahramshah. He is more blind, utterly blind.

And listening to these words and looking into the eyes of that madman, Lai-Khur, something incredible happened to Hakim Sanai: a satori, a sudden enlightening experience. Something died in him immediately, instantly. And something was born, something utterly new. In a single moment, the transformation had happened. He was no longer the same man. This madman had really penetrated his soul. This madman had succeeded in awakening him.

In Sufi history, this is the only case of satori. In Zen there are many cases; I have been talking to you about those cases. But in the world of Sufism this is the only case of satori, sudden enlightenment – not methodological, not gradual; in a shock it happened.

Lai-Khur must have been a man of tremendous insight. Hakim Sanai bowed down, touched the feet of this madman and wept tears of joy that he had arrived home. He died and was reborn. That's what a satori is: dying and being reborn. It is a rebirth.

He left the Sultan and went on a pilgrimage to Mecca. The Sultan was not willing, he was not ready to allow him to go. He tried in every way to prevent him: he even offered his only sister in marriage, and half the kingdom, to Hakim Sanai. But now all was meaningless. Hakim Sanai simply laughed and he said, "I am no longer a blind person. Thank you, but I am finished. This madman has finished me in a single stroke, in a single blow."

And he went on a pilgrimage to Mecca. Why? Later on, when he was asked he said, "Just to absorb, just to digest what that madman had given me so suddenly. It was too much! It was overflowing, I was overwhelmed; it had to be digested. He had given me more than I was worthy of."

So he went to Mecca on a pilgrimage, to meditate, to be silent, to be a pilgrim unknown to anybody, to be anonymous. The thing had happened, but it had to be absorbed. The light had happened, but one has to get accustomed to it.

And when he became accustomed to the new gestalt, to the new vision, he came back to Lai-Khur and presented him this book, The Hadiqa. That's what he wrote on the way back from Mecca.

He poured his experience, his satori, into this book. These words are saturated with satori. This is how this great book was born, like a child is born, mysteriously; like a seed becomes a sprout, mysteriously; like a bird comes out of the egg, mysteriously. Like a bud opens early in the morning and be-comes a flower, and the fragrance is spread to the winds.

Yes, this book was not written. This book is a gift from God. This book is a gift from God, and a gratitude from Hakim Sanai to that strange madman, Lai-Khur.

Now the sutras.

> WE TRIED REASONING OUR WAY TO HIM:
> IT DIDN'T WORK;
> BUT THE MOMENT WE GAVE UP,
> NO OBSTACLE REMAINED.

Hakim Sanai was a man of character, a religious man. He had tried hard, he had tried all the possible ways to reach God. And he was a very intelligent man, knowledgeable, and was known as a wise man. He was a very capable, rational person. He had tried in every possible way to reach God through reason.

But nobody has ever reached God through reason. That is not the door to him, that is the wall that prevents you. Reason is perfectly capable of knowing the superficial, but it cannot dive deep into the depths. It knows only how to swim on the surface. Reason is perfectly good as far as the journey *outwards* is concerned, but it is utterly impotent as far as the journey inwards is concerned.

Reason is good and adequate if you want to know about matter. But it is utterly incapable if you want to know any-thing about consciousness. Reason can measure, but conscious-ness is immeasurable. Reason can weigh, but consciousness has no weight. Reason can see, but consciousness is invisible. Reason has the five senses as its servants, but consciousness is *behind* the five senses. You cannot touch it, you cannot smell it, you cannot taste it, you cannot hear it, you cannot see it: it is *behind* the five senses. You cannot touch it, you cannot smell it, you cannot taste it, you cannot hear it, you cannot see it: it is behind these five windows of the senses which open towards the outside.

You can see the sunlight, but you cannot see your inner light with your eyes. You can hear the birds singing, but you cannot hear your own heart singing.

Reason is capable of measuring. That's how the word 'matter' came into existence. 'Matter' means that which can be measured; 'measurable' is the meaning of the word 'matter'. Reason measures, so whatsoever can be caught in the trap of reason is matter.

But there are things which are immeasurable. How to measure love? How to measure consciousness? The immeasurable is there. But if you insist that you will use only reason to know it, then you will remain ignorant of the immeasurable. Then you will remain ignorant of God.

Hakim Sanai says:

WE TRIED REASONING OUR WAY TO HIM:
IT DIDN'T WORK...

It cannot work, it is intrinsically inadequate. Logic cannot conclude about the unknowable. Logic moves into the world of the known; logic cannot take a quantum leap into the unknown.

Have you not observed it? Your mind can think only about the known. How will you think about the unknown? If it is unknown, there is no way to think about it. Thinking is based on the known. That's why thinking is repetitive, it moves in a circle. Yes, it can go on refining the known – it can go on refining it more and more, it can go on polishing the known – but it can never come to know the unknown.

At the most, it can guess about the unknown. But guesswork is guesswork; it can never become a certainty. It will never give you faith, it can't become trust, because deep down you know it is a guess: it may be so, it may not be so. It cannot become a rock on which the temple of life can be raised. No, it remains doubtful.

Every guess is rooted in doubt: perhaps it is so, perhaps it is not so. And there are three layers of existence. One is the known: a very small, lighted part; a lighted spot, very small, that we have come to know. Then surrounding it is the infinite unknown, a great night of darkness. But about the unknown we can have a few guesses, we can infer, because the known and the unknown are not qualitatively different. That which is known today was unknown yesterday, and that which is unknown today may become known tomorrow. So the known and the unknown correlate; they are of the same family.

Science lives in these two worlds, the known and the unknown. You base your reasoning, your guess, your inference, on the known, so you can deduct something of the unknown and you can reach into the darkness and make a little more territory lighted. But there is something else, the third realm: the unknowable. Logic can function perfectly in the known; it functions only partially in the unknown as guessing; it cannot function in the unknowable at all. The unknowable is beyond logic, beyond reasoning, beyond knowledge, beyond the mind. And that unknowable is God.

Remember, God is not unknown. If God is unknown, then science one day will know him. God is unknowable. yes, God can be experienced and lived but cannot be known, cannot be reduced to knowledge, cannot be reduced to a hypothesis, cannot be reduced to a formula like H2O.

God remains a mystery. Even to those who have experienced him, God remains a mystery. In fact the deeper you go into him, the deeper becomes the mystery. The more you penetrate into him, the more and more you disappear. One day, God is not known; on the contrary, the knower disappears. Just like a dewdrop slipping into the ocean, the knower dissolves.

In the world of science the unknown is constantly transformed into the known. And it is hoped that one day the unknown will disappear completely and all will be known.

In the world of religion it is just a totally different story, diametrically opposite. The unknown does not disappear, but the knower disappears.And one day *all* becomes unknowable, and the known also becomes unknowable.Then the mystery is total and absolute.

WE TRIED REASONING OUR WAY TO HIM:
IT DIDN'T WORK; BUT THE MOMENT WE GAVE UP,
NO OBSTACLE REMAINED.

God happens in a state of let-go, in surrender.You cannot seek and search for God.All searching will remain rational, all seeking will be based in the mind. The mind is the great seeker. And all search, inquiry, seeking, is based in curiosity.

And deep down behind all your search is the ego:"I want to become a knower." It hurts not to know, it hurts to remain ignorant. The ego wants to gratify itself. And the ego cannot know God, because ego is the barrier. We are not separate from existence, and the ego has given us the illusion of being separate. The ego simply means the illusion of being separate from existence.

Surrender is dropping the illusion of separation. Let-go means "I am no more." Let-go means "I dissolve." Let-go means "I drop all searching, seeking, inquiring." Let-go means "I will be just passive and available."And then it happens.

That's how it happened to Sanai. Looking into he eyes of that man, Lai-Khur, listening to his strange words, listening to his strange music, feeling his presence, it happened. And Sanai had worked his whole life and hadn't reached any closer. And then out of nowhere, in the presence of the master, Lai-Khur, it just happened of its own accord.

He must have been in shock when Lai-Khur said, "Hakim Sanai, you are blind!" Nobody had said that to Hakim Sanai. He was respected and thought to be wise; even kings and emperors used to ask his advice. And this madman, a beggar, calls him blind! He must have been shocked. In that shock his mind stopped. It was almost like an electric shock.

If you are available to the master's energy, it is an electric shock. It can shatter your mind. It can create a chaos — a beautiful chaos, a chaos out of which stars are born. And such a chaos was created by the impact of Lai-Khur.

Sanai disappeared. For a moment he was not there. Only the master and his presence, and those great waves coming from the master...he was drowned. It was a moment of let-go. And God came in the form of Lai-Khur. God came through the flute of Lai-Khur.

...BUT THE MOMENT WE GAVE UP,
NO OBSTACLE REMAINED.
HE INTRODUCED HIMSELF TO US...

When you are in a let-go, god comes. It is never man who reaches God. This is one of the fundamentals of Sufism: it is always God who reaches man.

God is constantly trying to reach you but you don't allow him. You are so closed, you never leave your windows open. You are very tightly closed, nothing can enter you; you are closed airtight. God is trying in every way to reach you, like a mother searches for the child. But you are not available, you are not present. You are so afraid and so defensive.

It happens almost every day. When I initiate you into sannyas I try to reach you. But very rarely does somebody turn up who is available, very rare. Very rarely can I find a way to reach your heart. But whenever it happens, immediately you are no more the same. It happens sometimes, a person *is* available and open, is not defending, drops the armor that we all carry always.

We are so afraid of people, we are so afraid of love, we are so afraid of others, that we keep a distance. That becomes a habit. When you come to a master, that habit is there.

Just two nights ago, there was a young sannyasin going back home. I asked him, "When are you leaving?" and he would not answer. And I asked him, "When will you be coming back? And he would not answer. Then I asked him to come close, "So I can touch your head." He wouldn't even come close to me – utterly closed, he did not give me any opening.

These are just ways to find an opening. It does not matter when you are leaving, today or tomorrow. I ask you only so that you can give me a little opening. I start communication so that I can change it into communion.

But he was not ready to say anything. Nothing is wrong if you don't want to say anything; it is perfectly good. Silence can be immensely beautiful. But silence has to be open, only then is it beautiful; otherwise it is the ugliest thing. He was afraid to say a thing, he was afraid to utter a word, because if he said a word, I would find and entry. At least to utter that word he would have to open himself a little bit.

It would not have been so wrong if it had been an open silence; it would have been tremendously beautiful. But it was not an open silence, otherwise he would have come close. I was calling him to come close, and he wouldn't come. I wanted to touch him – because if words cannot reach him, maybe my presence can. But he would not allow that either.

God is trying to reach you. And when you are in the presence of a master, God is trying very hard to reach you. HE INTRODUCED HIMSELF says Sanai TO US OUT OF KINDNESS...

Because Sanai was not going to search for God, he was going on a journey of conquest with the king. It happened from nowhere, out of the blue. That singing, that dancing, Lai-Khur's music – he was caught unawares. Just see it: there were many people there. The Sultan was there but he missed; he was not open. Hakim Sanai *got* it. He was open, he allowed it to happen, he did not resist.

HE INTRODUCED HIMSELF TO US
OUT OF KINDNESS...

Remember it: God does not come to you because you are worthy. What worth can you have? Not because you have earned it, not because you deserve it, but only because he is kind. He is Rahim, he is Rahman, he is compassionate. These are the Sufi names of God. Rahim means compassionate, Rahman again means compassionate, merciful, kind. he comes to you out of his kindness. It is not out of your efforts that he comes; he comes out of your surrender.

...HOW ELSE COULD WE HAVE KNOWN HIM?

Sanai says: now I can say that there was no way to know him. I had tried hard in every possible way; in every rational way I had searched for him. If you cling to reason, you are bound to become and atheist sooner or later. Or you will become a hypocrite. These are the people around you.

Those who are trying to reach towards God through reason and the mind are bound to fall into these two categories: either they become hypocrites, the so-called religious – these people you will find in the churches, temples, mosques and *gu - rudwaras*, reading the Koran and the Gita and the Bible. These are the so-called religious, the hypocrites. They are dishonest; they have not found anything, but they are not even ready to accept that they have failed. They are not ready to accept the failure of their ego, hence they have started believing. They have not found anything, but they still believe. This belief is false; this makes a person pseudo.

That's why all so-called religious people are pseudo people, ugly – something on the surface, and something totally different deep down. Deep down, a thousand and one doubts, and on the surface just a painted belief. It does not come out of their being, it is not part of their life. It has not grown in them, it is not based in existential experience. It is out of fear that they have believed, it is out of frustration that they have believed. It is because they could not carry the inquiry further. They were tired, they lost courage, they were disheartened. And neither are they authentic enough to say, "We tried and we have not found him. So maybe he is not."

That is the other category, the atheist. The atheist is at least true; he is at least sincere and honest. The theist is not even honest. The theist is in a double-bind: he believes in honesty, but he is based in dishonesty.

Now all around the world, your churches, your priests, go on teaching you: Be honest, and believe in God. And have you ever thought that these two things are not possible together? Be honest, and believe in God. And have you ever thought that these two things are not possible together? Be honest, and believe in God: this is a double-bind, you are creating a contradiction. If the person has to be honest he cannot believe in God, because what will belief mean to an honest person? Either you know or you don't know. If you know, there is no need to believe; you know it already. If you don't know, how can you believe?

If the person has to be honest, he cannot believe, he *need* not believe. And if the person has to believe, he cannot be honest. Now you have created a contradiction in the person's being. This is what reduces everybody to a hypocrite. Then you become two or even many. Then you lose integrity. You become dual: you say one thing, you do another; you do one thing, you mean another. You are never one. And when you are not one, you are never blissful. Bliss is the by-product of oneness.

Reason cannot find him. Reason is not the only door in your being, there are deeper doors in your being. Are you not aware of the heart? Can't you feel the beat of the heart? Have you not seen anything happening through the heart? When you look at a lotus flower and you feel the beauty, is it reason?

Can reason prove that the flower is beautiful?

Reason has not even been able to define what beauty is. For the rational mind there is no beauty. But you know that beauty exists, and when you see it you are overwhelmed by it. The rational mind says there is no beauty, this is just an illusion, a projection, a dream.

The full-moon night: is it just an illusion? The hypnotic splendor of it: is it just a projection of your mind? It can't be so, because even the ocean, which has no mind, is affected. It can't be so. When the sun rises even birds are affected – it can't be just the mind and its projection.

Beauty exists. But reason has no way to approach it, it is felt from the heart. Have you not felt beauty? Love exists: that too is not through reason, that too is felt from the heart. When you fall in love can you justify it rationally? Can you say what love is? Nobody has yet been able to.

God is all these experiences together: the experience of beauty, the experience of good, the experience of love, the experience of truth. All these experiences happen: don't try to reach them through reason, they happen through the heart. All these experiences that come through the heart, the totality of them is called God. God is not a person somewhere sitting high in heaven.

Satyam, shivam, sunderam: in the East, that has been the definition of God. *Satyam*: he is truth. *Shivam*: he is good. *Sunde - ram*: he is beauty.

These are the experiences that stir your heart. And God is the ultimate experience through the heart. Knowing the real through the heart is the meaning of experiencing God. Knowing the real through the mind is the experience of matter. The reality is one.

Never fall into the fallacy of thinking that there are two realities – matter and consciousness, God and the world. No. The reality is one; that which is, is one. But that one can be approached in two ways. You have two approaches possible.

You can reach it through the head: then it is matter, then the interpretation of reality comes in materialistic terms. Or you can reach it through the heart, and then it is consciousness or God.

These are our interpretations.and certainly the interpretation that comes from the heart is higher, is deeper, is more profound. And it transforms your life: it transports you into another dimension of bliss, of benediction.

> HE INTRODUCED HIMSELF TO US OUT OF
> KINDNESS: HOW ELSE COULD WE HAVE KNOWN
> HIM? REASON TOOK US AS FAR AS THE DOOR;
> BUT IT WAS HIS PRESENCE THAT LET US IN.

And remember one thing more: Sufism is not against reason. That is the difference between the Zen approach Zen is irrational, it says: Drop reason, drop it utterly. Sufism is not irrational, it is suprarational. It says: Use reason, but it takes you only to the door. It cannot take you inside the temple, it takes you up to the door. Use reason, but don't be caught by it, don't be stuck with it.

That's how it happened to Sanai. he had used his reason to its ultimate potential. In fact that's why it was possible for Lai-Khur to take him inside the temple. The Sultan missed, because he had not even used reason to its optimum. Others were also there, they all missed the point. Only Sanai got it. He had used his reason to its optimum – he had seen that it comes to a certain extent, it takes you to a certain point, and then it is stuck, then it is exhausted. And reality goes on spreading beyond it, so reality is bigger than reason. Use reason as far as it can take you, but then don't remain there. Go beyond it.

Zen is irrational, Zen is absurd, that is its beauty. Sufism is supra-rational, it is not absurd, that's *its* beauty. Both are right doors to the divine. But Zen is negative, it says: Drop reasoning.

Sufism is positive, it says: Use reasoning but always remember there is something beyond it. Never forget the beyond.

Zen is *via negativa*, Sufism is *via positiva*. Sufism is utterly positive. So people who have a leaning towards positivism will find it easier to have an affinity with Sufism, and people who have a negative approach and are attuned to and enjoy the negative, they will find it easier to follow the path of Zen. One has to decide. One has to watch one's leanings, one's characteristics.

REASON TOOK US AS FAR AS THE DOOR;
BUT IT WAS HIS PRESENCE THAT LET US IN.

Use reason, reach the door, remember that the real is still to happen. Wait. Wait in tremendous openness, remain vulnerable. Don't become closed, don't start making a conclusion. A conclusion means you are becoming closed. If reason can give you a conclusion, this way or that, for or against God, you are finished; then there is no beyond.

See the point that reason is inconclusive, and remain non-conclusive and wait. You have come to the door, now his presence will take you in.

That is the meaning of the great maxim that when the disciple is ready, the master appears. It is possible that Lai-Khur was singing, dancing, and playing music only for Hakim Sanai. The ways of existence are mysterious. The trap was ready for Hakim Sanai: that man was ready, he had come to the door.

The same happened to Omar Khayyam, another great Sufi. He was a mathematician, a great mathematician, a genius. He had used his reason to its uttermost, and then he was taken in. And the great mathematician became a drunkard, and the great mathematician started talking of wine, of drunkenness, and the great *Rubaiyat* was born.

One cannot believe, reading Omar Khayyam's *Rubaiyat*, that he was a great mathematician. One cannot conceive of what kind of mathematician he was, because his poetry is so pure. How can a mathematician attain to such purity of poetry? A mathematician is a logician, he functions through syllogism. He is very practical, he is very objective. He does not allow his subjectivity to enter into his observations; he is very detached. And mathematics is the only perfect science in the world. All other sciences are so-so; mathematics is the only perfect science. How can a perfect scientist become a sufi?

But now you can understand how it happened. When you come to the extreme point of your reason, and if you are still available, not closed – if you have not concluded, this way or that way, if you have not yet become a theist or an atheist, if you still have the awareness that reason remains inconclusive – then you will be taken in by his presence. He will appear as a master and will take you in.

And then it can happen in a single moment. When one is standing on the boundary, then in a single moment one can enter into the unknowable.

BUT HOW WILL YOU EVER KNOW HIM, AS LONG AS YOU ARE UNABLE TO KNOW YOURSELF?

God can only be known if you have known yourself. And where are you? You are not in your head, you are in your heart. The head can fall into a coma, you will still be alive. There are people who fall into comas and remain in comas for years.

Once a woman was brought to me; for nine months she had been in a coma, utterly unconscious. The mind was not functioning any more, she was almost vegetating. But she was alive, because the heart was still beating. Once the heart stops then all stops.

So your life is somehow rooted in the heart, not in the head. The heart seems to be the contact point between you and the universe. It is through the heart that you are plugged in with the universe. And one has to know one's heart: that is self-knowledge, that is the meaning of "Know thyself." Because it is only by knowing your heart that you will know the contact with the universe. Entering into your heart, you will become able to enter into the ultimate.

ONCE ONE IS ONE, NO MORE, NO LESS: ERROR
BEGINS WITH DUALITY; UNITY KNOWS NO ERROR.

You have many minds but you have only one heart. Have you observed this fact? You don't have one mind; you are multipsychic, you have many minds. They constantly change – every moment your mind changes. One moment it is full of doubt, another moment it is full of belief, and another moment again it is full of doubt. One moment you are so full of love, another moment so full of anger and hate.

Watch it: you have a thousand and one minds and they go on rotating. There is a kind of rotation system in your head. for a moment one mind becomes the master, and in that moment you decide something and you think you will be able to do it. You will not be able to, because next moment the monarch is gone. It is a rotation system: another mind has come up, now another spoke of the wheel has come up. And this mind knows nothing of the decision that the other mind has taken.

This self knows nothing of the other self; it will destroy whatsoever you have decided. One moment you decide never to smoke again, another moment you are pulling out your cigarette packet. And you are surprised – just a moment ago you had decided, and the decision seemed so total, so *trustable*. And now it is all gone, gone down the drain, nothing of it is there. And you are perfectly willing to smoke again. And again that old mind will come back and torture you, and you will repent and think that you are guilty.

But this will go on changing. Mind is a flux, it is a continuum of many minds. And that's why those who live in the mind live a disintegrated, fragmentary life.

The heart is one, it is always one. The heart means the watching consciousness in you. Who is the watcher of the head? Try to meditate over it. Anger comes: who is watching? You know perfectly well that there is anger; you know perfectly well that it is coming and growing, you know perfectly well that soon you will be overwhelmed by it. And then it is going, receding, disappearing, you know it is gone. Gone, gone, gone, it is no more there. Who is watching?

Love comes and goes. Misery comes, happiness comes, everything comes and everything goes. Who is watching? The watcher remains.

Only one thing in you is constant, and that is the watcher. Everything changes, only the watcher abides. It is always there – even while you are deeply asleep it is watching the dreams; even when there are no dreams it is watching the deep sleep. When you are awake it is watching the world, when you are asleep it is watching your inner world, but the watching continues. Not even for a single moment does the watching stop. That is the eternal thing in you, non-temporal: your heart.

Sufis call it the heart. And it is one. And to know the one is to go beyond all errors.

ONCE ONE IS ONE, NO MORE, NO LESS: ERROR
BEGINS WITH DUALITY; UNITY KNOWS NO ERROR.

This unity is called *unio mystica*. This is the mystic unity. This is the integration, the individuation, the centering of the soul. And then you can remain centered even when there is a cyclone raging around you. Then you are the center of the cyclone.

Then you can remain in the world and be not of the world. All errors arise out of duality. And you are not only dual, you are a multiplicity. So, errors and errors and errors – you have become divided into so many fragments. You are a crowd, that's your problem, and the crowd is constantly fighting. It goes on fighting. You are a civil war. And hence your life loses all joy, all bliss, all grace.

Be one, and suddenly grace is attained. And suddenly you become elegant, with no effort. Then your life has a beauty of its own. It is exquisite. It is no more that ordinary life – ugly, vulgar, mundane. Now it is the holiest of the holy. It is sacred, it is divine.

THE ROAD YOUR SELF MUST JOURNEY ON LIES IN POLISHING THE MIRROR OF YOUR HEART.

What is the meaning of "polishing the mirror of your heart"? More and more, make your heart your center. Fall into your center more and more. Whenever you remember, move to the heart, come down from the head. Be watchful, be wakeful.

But your wakefulness has to be very loving, otherwise you wakefulness can also become only a part of the mind. It if is loving wakefulness, if it is heart-wakefulness, then it will be from the center of your being.

So when you are aware, be loving too. Let love and awareness meet and mingle; let your awareness be suffused with love. You can watch a flower without love: watchfulness will be there, but without love it will be a dry phenomenon. This watchfulness is possible even through the head; then it will not polish the mirror of your heart.

Watch and yet be loving. Watch lovingly. Slowly slowly, your watchfulness and your lovingness become one – they are two aspects of the same phenomenon. Then it is polishing the heart. Love is the method of polishing the heart. Awareness helps you to reach the heart, and love helps you to polish it. And the more it is polished, the better it reflects reality.

THE ROAD YOUR SELF MUST JOURNEY ON LIES

IN POLISHING THE MIRROR OF YOUR HEART.
IT IS NOT BY REBELLION AND DISCORD...

You need not fight with yourself, you need not force anything upon yourself, you need not be in conflict. You have to fall into accord, not discord.

Hence Sufism knows nothing of asceticism. The ascetic is a masochist; he is not a really religious person. He does not love himself, he hates himself.

The Sufi loves himself, the Sufi loves all. The Sufi is love.

IT IS NOT BY REBELLION AND DISCORD THAT THE
HEART'S MIRROR IS POLISHED FREE OF THE RUST
OF HYPOCRISY AND UNBELIEF...

Remember, I told you the possibilities are two if you act from the mind. One is hypocrisy, the so-called religious person. Hindu, Mohammedan, Christian, Jaina, Jew: the so-called religious person, the hypocrite. That is one possibility. The other possibility is unbelief, atheism:"There is no God. I have searched, I have searched to the very limits of my reason, and I have not found God. There is no God."

Both are foolish attitudes. One should remain non-conclusive. One should remain on the border of reason without any conclusion, just silent, passive, available. Then the presence of god takes you in.

...YOUR MIRROR IS POLISHED BY YOUR CERTITUDE
BY THE UNALLOYED PURITY OF YOUR FAITH.

There is certainty that is arrived at through reason, but that certainty is always based on doubt. Doubt cannot be destroyed by reason because reason feeds on doubt, reason begins in doubt. Reason begins in questioning, reasoning is basically skeptical. So even if it comes to a conclusion it is only hypothetical. it is only for the time being. If some new facts are revealed the conclusion will have to be changed.

That's why science can never say, "This is the truth." Science can only say, "Up to now, whatsoever we know, this seems to be the truth." It can only say, "Hitherto, up to now, this appears to be the truth. We cannot say anything about tomorrow. New facts will be coming, new facts will be revealed, then we will have to change.

Now Newton is out of date. Soon Albert Einstein will be out of date. But Buddha is never going to be out of date, Lai-Khur is never going to be out of date, Jesus is never going to be out of date. Because whatsoever they have said is not based in doubt. It is not through reasoning, it is concluded through the heart. And the heart knows the eternal because the heart is in contact with the eternal. The head only contacts the temporal, the momentary.

So there is a certitude that is arrived at through love, not through logic. There is a certitude that is arrived at not by the head, not through the head, not by any syllogism, but by a singing heart, a dancing heart.

Have you ever felt any conclusiveness, certainty, certitude, arising out of your love? Then you will understand the meaning. When you say "I love this woman" have you arrived at this conclusion through reason? If you have arrived at it through reason, it may disappear any moment.

That's why, in the West, love has become a very momentary phenomenon. Even love is arrived at through the head. You conclude: "This seems to be the most beautiful woman amongst the women I have known up to now. Who knows about tomorrow? A woman with a longer nose, a woman with more beautiful hair, a woman with deeper shining eyes...who knows? Nothing can be said about tomorrow. This woman may become out of date; you can always come across a better person.

If the conclusion is through the head, then love will never

become deep and intimate. Then it will be momentary, then it will be just arbitrary. That's what is happening in the world. Love has become very arbitrary, for the moment; it is just an arrangement for the moment.

But this is not the way to grow deep into love. Love needs intimacy. Love needs a certitude that is not arrived at by the head but through the heart. When certitude is arrived at through the heart, it is for ever and for ever. It knows no change.

Blessed are those few people who can still have some certitude from the heart in their love. Very rare they are now on the earth; that tribe is disappearing, that species is disappearing. And that is a great calamity.

Now, if you come to me, and listening to me, finding me logical, appealing to your logic and your reason, you become a disciple, that is not going to go very far. Tomorrow I may say something that may contradict, that may puzzle your. That will create doubt.

But if it is a heart relationship – not hearing what I say but seeing what I am, not listening only to my words but listening to my silences, not listening to the philosophy that I teach but the presence that I shower upon you – then there is a certitude which is faith, which is trust, which is for ever.

If you arrive through your reason, it is just arbitrary. And you will never be in a let-go. You will always be there, watching from the corner of your eye: if something goes against your head then I am not for you. Then I have to be always fulfilling your expectations – which I cannot do, which no master can ever do. And whatsoever I say, you will always interpret it in your own way.

Just a few days ago, a woman was here. She was very serious, and she asked me, "What to do about my seriousness?" And I talked to her, saying that seriousness is a kind of illness. "You are serious because you think seriousness is something valuable. It is not, it is just stupid. Be playful."

Ad what did she conclude, do you know? She took sannyas, went back, and wrote from there, "I have listened to you, and I am trying to follow you in my own way. I have dropped sannyas, because I think one should be playful – although I have not been able to drop any other thing, I am still serious."

Now look: she could drop only one thing, and that was sannyas. If she had dropped all seriousness, then it would have been okay to drop sannyas too. But the mind is cunning. So now she has interpreted it in her own way, that one should not be serious about sannyas;about everything else she is the same. She has not understood me. In fact to be a sannyasin simply means that you will take your whole life playfully. Dropping sannyas means you have dropped the idea of playfulness.

But this is what is going to happen to many people who only connect through the head. Beware of it. The heart MIRROR IS POLISHED BY YOUR CERTITUDE – BY THE UNALLOYED PURITY OF YOUR FAITH.

> BREAK FREE FROM THE CHAINS YOU HAVE FORGED
> ABOUT YOURSELF; FOR YOU WILL BE FREE WHEN
> YOU ARE FREE OF CLAY.
> THE BODY IS DARK – THE HEART IS SHINING
> BRIGHT; THE BODY IS MERE COMPOST – THE
> HEART A BLOOMING GARDEN.

Become *disidentified* from your head and become disidentified from your body. Remember that you are nothing but your watchfulness. And this does not mean that you have to be against the body. Sufis are not against the body either; they love the body, because the body is the compost. It can become fragrance: it has to be transformed.

> ...THE HEART A BLOOMING GARDEN.

The body has to function as compost in the garden of the

heart. One has not to be against the body or against the head. Use the head up to the door, use the body so that it becomes the soil.

But remember always, the flower of heartfulness, the flower of heart-wakefulness, has to bloom in you. And it can bloom any moment.All that is needed is to drop the chains that you have forged around yourself – your defenses, your armor, your protections.

BREAK FREE FROM THE CHAINS YOU HAVE FORGED
ABOUT YOURSELF; FOR YOU WILL BE FREE WHEN
YOU ARE FREE OF CLAY.

We have to become too much identified with the earth, with the body, with the clay. We have become too much iden-tified with matter, we have forgotten that we are nothing but a witnessing. That witnessing is your ultimate reality. Let it also become your immediate reality, and you will become the gar-den of the heart. And you will bloom.

And unless you bloom into a great lotus, into a great golden lotus, your life is in vain.

That's what Lai-Khur told Sanai: "Don't waste your life in writing eulogies to foolish kings. God will soon encounter you, and you will not be able to answer him. Don't remain blind any more Do something: open your eyes!" Sanai lis-tened and was transformed. Listen to me: you can also be transformed.

2 On the Altar of the Real

The first question:

TODAY IN LECTURE I LOOKED AT YOU AND I FELT
MYSELF SO SHALLOW AND PHONY AND FALSE.
THERE DOESN'T SEEM TO BE ANYTHING DEEPER
INSIDE OF ME. DO THESE FEELINGS SHOW THAT I
DON'T HAVE A CENTER YET? IT ALSO SHOCKS ME
THAT THIS SEEMS TO BE MY FACE AT THE MOMENT.

Bhagavato, nobody can exist without a center. Life is impossible without a center – you may not be aware of it, that's another matter. It has not to be created but only rediscovered. And remember, I am not saying 'discovered', I am saying 'rediscovered'.

The child in the mother's womb remains perfectly aware of the center. The child in the mother's womb *is* at the center, vibrates at the center, pulsates at the center. The child is the center in the mother's womb, he has no circumference yet. He is only essence, he has no personality yet.

Essence is the center, that which is your nature, that which is God-given. Personality is the circumference, that which is cultivated by society; it is not God-given. It is by nurture, not by nature.

As the child comes out of the womb, he comes for the first time in contact with something outside of himself. And that contact creates the circumference. Slowly slowly, the society initiates the child into its own way. The Christian society will make the child a Christian, and the Hindu, a Hindu, and so on and so forth. Then layer upon layer of conditioning is imposed on the child.

Basically, if you enter into a well-developed personality you will find these three things. First, a very thin positive layer – positive but phony. That is the layer which goes on pretending; that is the layer where all your masks are contained. Fritz Perls used to call that layer the "Eric Berne layer". It is where you play all kinds of games.

You may be crying within, but on that layer you go on smiling. You may be full of rage, you may want to murder the other person, but you go on being sweet. And you say "How good of you to come. I am so happy, so glad to see you." Your face shows gladness; that is phony.

But to exist in a phony society you will need a phony layer. Otherwise you will be in as much difficulty as Socrates was, Jesus was, I am. That phony layer keeps you part of the phony society; you don't fall apart. It is a false world, what in the East we have called 'maya'. It is illusory, it is all false and phony.

The other person also is smiling as falsely as you are smiling. Nobody is really smiling. People are carrying wounds – but they have decorated their wounds with flowers, they are hiding their wounds behind flowers.

Parents are in a hurry to give this layer to the child. They are in a hurry because they know the child has to exist as a member of a false society. It will be difficult for the child to survive without it; it functions as a lubricating agent.

This is a very thin layer, skin-deep. Scratch anybody a little and suddenly you will find that the flowers have disappeared; and rage and hatred and all kinds of negative things are hidden behind it. That is the second layer – negative but still false.

The second layer is thicker than the first. The second layer is the layer where much work has to be done. That's where psycho-therapies come in. And because there is a great negative layer behind the positive, you are always afraid to go in, because to go in means you will have to cross that ugly phenomenon, that dirty rubbish that you have gathered, year in and year out, your whole life.

From where does the second layer come? The child is born as a pure center, as innocence, with no duality. He is one. He is in the state of *unio mystica*: he does not yet know that he is separate from existence. He lives in unity; he has not known any separation, the ego has not arisen yet.

But immediately the society starts working on the child. It says, "Don't do this. This will not be acceptable to the society: repress it. Do this, because this is acceptable to the society and you will be respected, loved, appreciated.

So a duality is created in the child; on the circumference a duality arises. The first layer is the positive that you have to show to others, and the second layer is the negative that you have to hide within yourself.

The child is innocent. He is innocent in his love, he is innocent in his anger. He does not make a distinction. When he is in love he is in love, and he is totally in love. And when he is angry he is totally angry, he is just pure anger. Hence the beauty of the child. Even when he is angry he has a superb beauty, grace – even in his anger, because the totality is there. Grown-ups even when they are in love are not so beautiful, because the totality is missing.

We create a division in the child in each child. Our society has lived up to now in a kind of schizophrenia. The real humanity has not yet been born. The whole past has been a nightmare, because we divide the person into two: the positive and the negative, yes and no, love and hate. We destroy his totality.

These two layers are our split. The first layer is positive and false, the second layer is negative and false. They are false because only the total can be real. The partial is always false, because the partial denies something, rejects something, and the denied part makes it false. Only in total acceptance does reality arise.

Bhagavato, the center is there in you, but you will have to go digging through these two layers, the positive-and-phony and the negative-and-phony. And then you will fall into that oceanic oneness, the total, the whole. Then suddenly great bliss arises: that is satori. It is not to be created, it is already there. It is not even to be discovered, it has only to be rediscovered. You have known it before, hence the search – otherwise the search would be impossible.

Why do people go on searching for bliss? Because they must have known it. Somewhere deep down, the memory still persists of those sweet moments in the mother's womb when all was quiet and still, when all was one, when there was no worry, no responsibility, when there was no other. It as paradise.

It is the meaning of the symbol of the Garden of Eden. The womb is the Garden of Eden. But you cannot live in the womb for ever, sooner or later you have to come out of the womb. And the moment you come out of the womb, the society is bound to educate you. The society and its education is not yet human. it is neurotic, it is very primitive, because it does not help the child to grow in his center. It does not help the child to grow remaining alert of the center. On the contrary, it tries in every way to make the child forget the center and become identified with a false personality that the society provides for him.

The society is not interested in the child, the society is interested in its own structure persisting. The society is not interested in the individual; it is against the individual, it is all for the collective. And the collective has been neurotic and ugly. But the society is past-oriented and the individual is future-oriented; the individual has to live in the future and the society knows only the past in which it has lived. The society has no future, the society consists of the past. And it goes on imposing that past on the child.

In my vision, in a real human society, nothing will be imposed on the child – nothing at all. Not that the child will be left all alone to himself. No, he will be helped but nothing will be imposed. He will be helped to remain whole, he will be helped to remain rooted in the essence. He will not be forced to shift his consciousness from the essence to the personality. The future education will not be an education in personality, it will be an education in essence.

And that is the meaning of a religious education. Up to now, there has been no religious education. And whatsoever you call religious education is either Christian, Hindu or Mohammedan; that is indoctrination, not religious education. Religious education will help the child to remember what is already there in him, not to forget it.

The real education will make the child more meditative, so that he never loses contact with his inner being. There is every possibility of losing that contact, because he will be moving with others: he will start imitating others, he will have to learn many things from others. Let him learn, but let him become aware that he is not to become an imitator.

But that is just what is being done, and has been done, down through the ages. We teach children to become imitators: "Be like Jesus. Be like Socrates. Be like Buddha." The child can only be truly himself and never anybody else. And whatsoever he tries to become will be false and phony.

Bhagavato, you ask me: TODAY IN LECTURE I LOOKED AT YOU AND I FELT MYSELF SO SHALLOW AND PHONY AND FALSE.

It is good. It is immensely beautiful that you felt it. This is the beginning. If you become aware of the phony, you cannot remain unaware for long of that which is real – because to be aware of the phony means that somewhere you have started becoming aware of the real. Maybe it is very vague, cloudy, not yet clear, not yet transparent, muddy. But the beginning has started.

To know the false as false is the beginning of knowing the real as real. This is a good beginning, an auspicious beginning.

You say: THERE DOES NOT SEEM TO BE ANYTHING DEEPER INSIDE ME.

To become aware of this, that "There is nothing deeper inside me" is the first step towards depth. Millions of people go on thinking that their shallow personality is their soul. Their shallow personality has depth they think. They go on believing in it and believing in it they go on missing their reality.

My function here is to make you aware of the false and the phony and the unreal and the superficial. And when for the first time it dawns that you are phony it hurts, because you have always believed the opposite. You have always remained with the idea that you are very very real and deep, that you have heights and depths. And you have nothing.

Right now as you exist, you don't have any depth, you don't have any height. You exist as *persona*; you are not yet aware of the essence. And only the essence can have heights and depths. But to become alert that "I am shallow" is good, tremendously important, significant. Don't forget it again: remember it. It will hurt, it will become a pain in the heart, it will become a wound. It will be like an arrow going deeper and deeper, and it will become more and more painful.

That it is the journey that every seeker has to go through. That is the pain which is needed for your rebirth. Don't forget it, and don't start believing again in the old phony personality.

You are not that which up to now you have been thinking you are. You are something totally different. You are not this body: you are in the body but not the body. And you are not this mind either; the mind is there, but you are far beyond the mind. You are the witness.

Bhagavato, you say: I FELT MYSELF SO SHALLOW...

Who has felt it? Remember that. Shallowness itself cannot

feel that it is shallow. It will have no idea of depth – how can it feel it is shallow? Misery itself cannot feel that it is misery. Somebody else is needed, somebody who has known states of bliss. Only such a one can become aware of misery.

Disease cannot feel itself as disease, only health can feel disease as disease. Remember that.

Who has become aware that "I am shallow, I am false and phony and there seems to be no depth in me"? Who is this? This witness is you. This is your center; your center is arising out of the chaos of your personality. This is a great moment, a moment of great blessings: don't lose track of it. Howsoever painful the journey, one has to go through it, because the end is utterly blissful.

This is the sacrifice that each sannyasin has the make; the sacrifice of the phony on the altar of the real.

The second question:

WHY IS IT SO DIFFICULT TO BE SILENT?
MY WORDS ARE SO MECHANICAL AND USED,
A CONTINUOUS REPETITION OF HISTORIES,
THE SAME OLD PAST WHICH DOESN'T EXIST
ANY MORE. HOW AM I STILL NOT TIRED OF IT?

Pratito, it is difficult to be silent because in silence one disappears. You can exist as an ego only in noise. Noise is the food for you to exist as an ego; you live on it, you thrive on it. Hence the difficulty of becoming silent.

When people start thinking of becoming silent, they have the idea that when silence comes they will be there and they will enjoy the silence. That idea is utterly wrong; you don't have any notion of real things. When silence comes, you will not be there; you and silence cannot exist together. You are the noise. So when silence comes there is only silence.

UNIO MYSTICA

There is nobody who is silent, there is nobody who can be there enjoying silence. Silence is not an experience, because there is no experiencer. It is utter silence; there is nobody.

Sufis call if *fana*: dissolution. Buddha has called it nirvana: extinguishing the candle. All is gone and there is only nothing, a kind of nothingness.

You will not be able to find yourself as a self. Hence the difficulty. You will have to die to become silent — wand who wants to die? We want silence also as a decoration, as a medal, so we can brag that "Not only have I got money, I have also got meditation." So that we can brag that "Not only am I rich outwardly, I am rich inwardly too.". The first interest in search-ing for silence arises out of the ego. And the ego itself is the barrier.

So when you come in contact with a master or with an energy-field, with a school where things are being done — *really* being done, not only thought about — then the fear arises. Then you become aware of the phenomenon that with the noise disappearing you will also disappear. Are you ready to risk that much?

You say, Pratito: WHY IS IT SO DIFFICULT TO BE SILENT? Because you are invested in noise.

MY WORDS, you say, ARE SO MECHANICAL AND USED, A CONTINUOUS REPETITION OF HISTORIES, THE SAME OLD PAST WHICH DOESN'T EXIST ANY MORE.

Mind is nothing but the past. It is just the records of the past; it is a recording mechanism. It is your history, it is that which is no more, it is memory. But that memory keeps you alive as an ego. And you have to go on repeating that memory again and again; that helps, that supports the ego. You have to go into your past again and again to revive your ego: this is the way you nourish it.

If you drop your past completely.... Just think for a mo-ment: if by a magic wand your past is dropped completely,

45

this moment, who will you be? Will you be able to say 'I'?. With the past disappearing, the 'I' will have disappeared with it. You will be, but you will not be able to say 'I'. You will be just a silence, and empty canvas, a meditation. A peacefulness, a stillness, but there will be no 'I'.

Just think: slowly slowly, in a minute, drop your past. Drop your past and then think: what remains? Nothing remains. Or, only nothing remains. That nothing is you. That nothing is your reality, your essence.

So this is a mechanism to keep the ego going. You will have to repeat it: you will have to go again through the same words and the same memories and the nostalgia, again and again. And you will improve and polish on those memories. You will invent things which have never been; you will make your past look very beautiful and golden, which it was not. You will drop all that is ugly and you will go on and on pro-jecting. People go on inventing their past too. They make it as beautiful and rich as possible, because that is where their ego exists.

Everybody thinks that their childhood was very beautiful. The childhood *was* beautiful, but that childhood you don't re-member at all. The womb was beautiful, but that you don't remember at all. And after birth, the first two or three years were beautiful, but that too you don't remember at all.

The childhood that you remember is after the fourth year, and that was not beautiful at all. That was one of the most dif-ficult times in your life, because you were being forced, pulled and pushed into the social structure. You were cut this way and that, you were being adjusted to the machine. You were almost destroyed. You were manipulated. No child likes it. Every child resists, becomes angry, rebels, but is helpless. And finally the parents win and the society wins.

Those days were ugly, remember again. There is nothing golden in them. But later on, everybody thinks those days were beautiful. That is your invention. People not only project the future, they project the past too: they go on coloring it, polishing it, retouching it again and again.and, slowly slowly, they make a fairyland of their past. And then they feel very good; the ego is supported by their beautiful past. The ego becomes beautiful through a beautiful past.

Just look into the autobiographies that people write. In autobiographies you will not find anything truthful. Or if sometimes you find something truthful it will be about others, not about the person who has written the autobiography. It will be about others but not about himself.

All autobiographies are a species of fiction. People invent them. Autobiographies should be counted as fiction, nothing else, because you write about your childhood later on. That childhood is just an invention: with all your experiences, with all your knowledge, with your whole life lived, you create a childhood. The childhood you would have liked to live, you create it. It is a beautiful fiction.

And one has to repeat it, remember one thing. Lies have to be repeated again and again, otherwise you will forget them. That's why it is said that if you want to lie you need a good memory. A man who speak the truth need not have a good memory. There is no need; the truth is the truth. The person who is constantly lying will really need a good memory. Lies have to be repeated, only then can they live; otherwise they disappear.

You ask me, Pratito, "Why do I go on mechanically into the same past again and again, repeating old habits? " Because this is the way you can keep it alive. Otherwise it will disappear on its own.

And this is something to be understood. If you stop participating with your past – if when the past repeats like a mechanical habit you watch it, you don't cooperate with it – you will see, you have taken the energy out of it. Slowly slowly, watching it, it starts dropping. Once your watching has become total, the past disappears.

And the disappearance of the past is satori. Because in the past exists your personality, your I, your ego, your self. With the past they all disappear and you are thrown back into the very center of your being. Again you are innocent, again you are a child. That's what Jesus means when he say, "Unless you are like small children you will not enter into my kingdom of God."

What kingdom is he talking about? He is talking about the kingdom that is within you: the center, the essence, or you can call it whatever you want. A rose is a rose is a rose, it doesn't matter by what name you call it. The childhood can be regained, rediscovered. That innocence, that beautiful innocence, can be yours again. And it will be far richer than it was, because now you will be fully alert of it. You will be conscious too. To be consciously a child is to be a saint.

There is a story of the little boy of six years of age together with his girlfriend of five year of age who approach his mother with the news that they are going to get married.

"And what are you going to do for money?" the mother asked.

"Well," said the little boy, "I get ten cents a week allowance and Mary gets five cents a week allowance."

"And where will you and she live?"

"Well, we thought that one week we would live at our house and the next week we would live at Mary's."

"What," asked the mother, "are you going to do when you have children?"

"Well," the little boy replied, "touch wood – so far we have been very lucky!"

That innocence is still somewhere in you. That totality, that beautiful ignorance, is still somewhere in you, hidden behind so many layers of the personality. And those layers go on repeating themselves.

Watch the repetitiveness of your mind. Even if sometimes it changes words, it goes on repeating the same thing. Even if sometimes it changes habits – you may stop smoking, then you start chewing gum. It is the same thing, the same game played with different toy. Watch the utterly unoriginal nature of your mind. Consciousness is original, mind is always repetitive and unoriginal.

A telegram arrived at the army barracks. Corporal Jones' mother had died. That evening on the parade ground the sergeant-major bellowed at the men, "Attention! Jones, your mother is dead. Okay, men dismissed."

Poor Corporal Jones collapsed, distraught. Next morning the commanding officer called the sergeant-major to his office. "Now, Sergeant-major, a word about death. When one of the men's parents passes on, goes beyond to meet his maker as it were, I think it would be better for morale if you broke the news with a little more kindness. Be a bit more subtle – know what I mean? different approach – know what I mean? There's a good chap, off you go now."

Now it happened that one month later, poor Jones' father also passed away. The sergeant-major, remembering what his officer had said, thought, "Right, now – different approach, subtle, bit of kindness!"

That evening he called to the men, "Attention! All those with father take one pace forward. Jones, where the hell do you think you are going?"

It does not make much difference. Mind is repetitive, mind is just an old gramophone record. You can change words, you can change habits, it remains the same. The worldly man becomes the other-worldly, but it remains the same.

I have watched so many of your saints, and I have not seen any difference at all. They are still in the marketplace, although they live in the monastery. They have only changed forms, superficial forms, but their mind is exactly the same with no difference at all. They are playing the same games with new names, and they are utterly satisfied.

I have always felt deep compassion for your so-called

saints; they are really pitiable. Whenever I see a so-called saint, deep down I say "Poor man" – because he is thinking he is a changed being. He is not. First he was running after money, now he is running *from* money, but the running continues. First he was continuously hankering for this woman and that, now he is continuously afraid of women. But he remains obsessed with the same idea; for or against makes no difference. He is focused on the same target. First he was in lust, now he is anti-lust, but the object of lust or anti-lust is the same.

So whether you desire the world or you renounce the world will not make much difference, unless you understand the ways of your mind, how it functions repetitively. Watch. Nothing else has to be done: just watch. Watch all the subtle ways how the mind moves into old grooves; just go on watching. Slowly slowly, the watcher arises, the watcher on the hills. And the mind is left far behind.

Deep down in the valley it continues; it goes on playing the tape. But you are no more it, you are no more in it. You can use it whenever it is needed, and you can forget all about it whenever you don't need it.

Talking to you, I have to use the mind; there is no other way. But the moment I have gone into my room I put it off. It is just a question of putting it on and off. It is a good mechanism, it can be used beneficially. The problem arises only when it becomes the master and it starts using *you*.

And that's what is happening, Pratito. The mind has become the master, and consciousness is completely lost. Regain your consciousness, become more alert and attentive. And the best thing to be attentive of is your own mind. Just watch its subtle and delicate methods, how it goes on playing games. And I am not saying to change those games – because if you become interested in changing, you will forget watching. That's why I don't say to my sannyasins, "Leave the world." I say, "Live wherever you are." Sometimes it even looks very strange...

Just a few months ago, there was a French prostitute here.

She wanted to take sannyas but she was also afraid — she was afraid that if I came to know that she was a prostitute I might not give her initiation. But she was really a sincere soul, she could not hide it. And that's what I call saintliness. She said, "I should not hide it from you, I have to tell you that I am a prostitute. Can you still initiate me into sannyas?"

I said, "I might have rejected you before, but now I cannot reject you. Your innocence, your sincerity — nobody was asking you, you have told it on your own. This is beautiful. I will initiate you."

Then another problem arose in her mind. When after a few months she was going back, she asked, "Now what am I supposed to do? I am a prostitute and that is the only profession I know. Now what am I going to do? Will you give me some indication?" I said, "Who am I to give you any indication? Just go, and go on doing whatsoever you have been doing. Just be watchful from now onwards."

She said, "Do you mean that I can continue to be a prostitute?" I said, "That is not the point, whether to continue as a prostitute or not to continue as a prostitute. Even if you leave and you become a nun, your mind will be the same as that of the prostitute. It is not a question of where you are — in a monastery as a nun, or in the marketplace as a prostitute. That is not the point at all. The point, the whole point, consists of one thing, and that is: wherever you are, watch your mind. Now become alert. Let this light of watching always be there. And if some transformation happens through that watching, that is another thing."

And it *did* happen. But that is not renunciation, that is not renouncing anything. Something simply withers away, something becomes utterly stupid and drops. Something simply falls; you cannot hold it any more because it is so stupid.

My sannyasins have to remain in the world as they are. All that I teach is: become more alert, aware, watchful. And if something happens out of that watchfulness, it is good. It is not your choice, it happens choicelessly.

Pratito, you say: WHY IS IT SO DIFFICULT TO BE SILENT?

Because you are still clinging to your ego, afraid to die.

You say: MY WORDS ARE SO MECHANICAL AND USED. Everybody's words are mechanical and used.

You say: A CONTINUOUS REPETITION OF HISTORIES, THE SAME OLD PAST WHICH DOESN'T EXIST ANY MORE.

Yes, that is the case with everybody. Don't be worried about it, you are not suffering from anything special. It is just the ordinary disease of man, the ordinary disease called 'mind'; very ordinary and normal.

You say: HOW AM I STILL NOT TIRED OF IT?

Because you are still inventing it. How can you be tired? You go o improving upon it. You go on painting it here and there, decorating and refining it a little bit more. You are still working on it; this is your creation. The painting is not finished yet, it is on the way. That's why you are not bored with it.And you will not be bored if you continue working on it, improving o it, refining it, making it more and more delicate and beautiful' you will never be bored.

Stop cooperating with it.And the way to stop cooperation is to become alert – then immediately cooperation disappears.

Just try. There is anger: become aware of the anger. I am not saying to stop anger, drop anger; just become aware. See that the anger is there and watch that it is arising, that you are surrounded by it, that it is clamoring all around like a cloud and you are suffocated by it. Go on watching, without doing a thing.

The moment you do something you have lost your watchfulness. Doing means you become engaged, doing means you become cooperative. And there are two types of cooperation: you can either be for, or you can be against. Both are cooperative. In both ways you become entangled.

Avoid being for or against. Don't be for anger, don't be against anger. It is there, a fact. Just watch without any judgment and you will be surprised: soon you will have found a golden key. Watching, slowly it disappears. And it disappears without leaving a trace on you. Then you have the key; then use it for all kinds of thoughts.

One day you have become alert to the secret process of watching, that watching destroys the mind, disconnects you from the mind. Watching puts the mind off. And once you have risen above the mind like a Himalayan peak, you are the master. That is the goal of being a sannyasin.

The third question:

HOW IS ONE TO KNOW THAT SANNYAS IS GOOD?

Sir, the proof of the pudding is in its tasting. Become a sannyasin: there is no other way. It is an experience; you have to know it through your own experience. And it is such an interior experience that nothing can be said about it from the outside. And it is of such depth that no word is capable of expressing it.

It is as if you have a pain in the heart: only you know. Or you have a headache: only you know. You may have come across people who have no experience of headaches...

I know one person. He is sixty years old and he has never had a headache. It is impossible to explain to him what a headache is. The more you explain to him, the more he seems puzzled. he has never had any experience – how can you convey it?

Sannyas is a very deep experience. It goes to your very roots. it shakes you out of your sleep, it starts transforming you from within. It is not something on the outside. The orange clothes and the mala and the new name – that is not sannyas.

That is just an indication, a gesture; that is just a beginning, the first step. And everything else that happens then is very interior.

And you say: HOW IS ONE TO KNOW THAT SANNYAS IS GOOD?

The mother ran into the nursery when she heard her five-year-old son howling. His baby sister had been pulling his hair.

"Don't mind the baby," his mother said. "She doesn't know that it hurts you."

A few minutes later, the mother ran back to the nursery. This time it was the baby doing the screaming.

"What's the matter with the baby?" the mother asked.

"Nothing much," her five-year-old son replied. "But now she knows."

But that is the only way to know. So please let me pull your hair! Become a sannyasin and you will know: it *is* good. It is immensely good, there is nothing like it.

The fourth question:

OSHO, WHEN I DROPPED MY JOB AS A POLITICAL
REPORTER IN ORDER TO COME TO PUNE, SOME OF
MY FRIENDS WHO ARE ENGAGED IN THE STRUGGLE
AGAINST ATOMIC WAR, ATOMIC POWER,
DESTRUCTION OF THE ENVIRONMENT, THE
DISMANTLING OF DEMOCRATIC FREEDOMS,
ETCETERA, CALLED ME AN ESCAPIST. SOMETIMES I
WONDER IF THEY ARE RIGHT. ARE THEY?

Satyananda, they are right, but they are right in a totally different sense of which they are not aware.

Once can escape from reality, one can also escape *to* reality.

And the second is the case. When you move into meditation or into sannyas it is escaping *to* reality, not *from* reality.

Because the most real thing in you is your own center. The farther away you are from your center, the farther away you are from reality.

And the struggle that they are continuing AGAINST ATOMIC POWER, DESTRUCTION OF THE ENVIRON-MENT, THE DISMANTLING OF DEMOCRATIC FREE-DOMS, ET CETERA is not going to succeed in their way – it is not possible to succeed that way.

We are not struggling against anything like that here, because we are cutting the very roots. They are struggling only against the leaves. From where does atomic power come? Who has created it, and why? From where does war come, and why? Who has destroyed the environment, and why? From where does all this destructiveness come?

Why is there no democracy in the world? Why is there no individual freedom in the world? Who has done all this? Do you think you can make some party, some class, some section of the society, responsible for it? Then you will be utterly wrong.

It is the human mind that is responsible. The way the human mind has existed up to now is somehow wrong. The human mind has not yet learned how to be creative, hence there is destruction. And there *will* be destruction, unless we change the very foundation of the human mind.

Struggling against war is not going to help, because that is again another war. Have you not seen the pacifists and their processions, and how they howl and scream and how angry they are? And they are pacifists. And every pacifist procession ends in destruction: they start looting the shops and burning the buses and throwing stones at the police. And they had come to propagate peace.

This is an old stupidity. All wars are fought in the name of peace, all the wars have *always* been fought in the name of peace. Can't you see he point? Man wants to fight, any excuse will do. And peace is a beautiful excuse.

All politicians talk about peace and prepare for war. And if you ask them why, they will say "how can we protect peace? We have to be strong, otherwise peace will be destroyed. So we have to prepare for war in order to have a peaceful world." And when the preparation has gone on for long then you have to do something, because otherwise the preparation becomes heavy.

For example, a person has been continuously exercising and preparing himself, just in order to be ready to fight. Then one day he is ready. Now he hankers to fight; now his whole preparation forces him to fight. And he was not exercising alone: the neighbor was also going to the gym, and also getting muscular, and also becoming a Muhammad Ali. And both walk before each other's house in a very aggressive way, and both are afraid of each other. And then finally somebody has to begin to fight.

Machiavelli said the best way to defend is to be offensive, the best means of defense is to be offensive. Then somebody has to start it, because it becomes heavy. it becomes a tension, and the tension has to be released.

Now, when you go on piling up arms and bombs, how long can you go on piling them up? One day you have to start selling them; it is dangerous to go on accumulating them. Then, somewhere or other, there has to be a war: it becomes an economic necessity.

Big world wars are fought once in a while, and between two big wars small wars go on – sometimes in Israel, sometimes in Korea, sometimes in Vietnam, sometimes Bangladesh, Kashmir...they go on. Because the great powers are creating bombs and the Pakistanis will fight; they will become the market. Then the Israelis and the Arabs will fight, and they will become the market.

Just see the whole point. If Israel gets arms from America, then the Arabs will get arms from Russia: both need a market. If India gets arms from Russia, then Pakistan gets arms from

America: they both are in need. And they are improving their arms every day – so what to do with out-of-date arms? They are useless. You can destroy them, dump them in the ocean, but then all that you have put into them is lost.

Sell them to backward countries. For them they are great things. For Russia and America they are out of date, useless, but for India and Pakistan they are just the last word. They are primitive as far as American technology and Russian technology are concerned; they are of no use. If Russia and America go to war they will not be of any use; there is no point in keeping them.

So this whole game continues. We go on talking of peace, and we go on creating war.

We have to understand the human mind; the human mind has to be changed from the roots. If the human mind remains ambitious then there is no possibility of a world without war: ambition is war. If the human mind remains sectarian – Christian, Hindu, Mohammedan – there is no possibility of any peace. Because those sects will divide people, and any division is the beginning of war.

Satyananda, you have not escaped *from* reality, you have escaped *to* reality. We are not talking about peace; there is no point in talking about it. We are creating the foundation of it. We are not pacifists and we are not marching on the streets and going on a long walk – to the capital – a pacifist procession with slogans and shouting. We are not doing all that nonsense, it is pointless! It simply helps a few people to throw out and cathart their destructiveness, that's all. They enjoy it.

I know those people, they are always in every protest march. I lived in Jabalpur for many years, and I was watching every kind of thing that went around. So whenever there was a protest march or anything, I would go and watch. I was surprised: I found one man in *all* protest marches, all kinds – communist, socialist, *Jansanghi*, Hinduites, *Arya Samajis*, anybody! He was always there. I was puzzled: he is congressee, he is a communist, he is a socialist, he is a *Jansanghi*....

One day I caught hold of him and I asked him, "You puzzle me very much. I see you in every procession, every protest, and you shout the best!"

He said, "I am also puzzled, because I see you always watching, and you never participate! How do you manage it? And I was afraid that one day or other you were going to ask me," he said, "because you see me in every protest. I enjoy shouting. I don't care for whom I am shouting or against whom I am shouting. I enjoy shouting! It is such good exercise, and I feel so thrilled and excited, and it always gives me a good appetite. And it brings some excitement; otherwise life is a boredom."

If you don't believe me, you can ask Astha. Her father and mother have both been of this type their whole life, just protesting. It does not matter against whom — who cares? Those are just excuses.

We are not doing anything like that here. So those who are doing such things will think that this is an escape from reality, because they think what they are doing is reality. It is not. And naturally, sitting silently here — meditating, dancing, with closed eyes doing *Vipassana*, watching, being alert — certainly, for them it is an escape. It *is* an escape, but in a different sense.

You are going, Satyananda, to the very root of all diseases. And we are trying to cut that very root. We are trying to create a new kind of human being — without ego, without ambition, without any desire to succeed in the world. We are trying to create a human being who wants to dance, sing, love, who wants to celebrate life. We are trying to create a creative human mind.

And remember, only a no-mind is a creative mind. When the so-called mind disappears and there is just pure emptiness, virgin emptiness, out of that virgin emptiness arises creativity. A thousand and one flowers bloom in that emptiness.

That is the garden Hakim Sanai is talking about: the *hadiqa*, the garden. We are trying to create that garden. We will make our bodies a compost, we will make our minds a compost, so that the golden flower can bloom in us. This is not an escape from reality, this is escaping *into* reality.

The fifth question:

OSHO, IN SO MANY WAYS YOU MAKE US
UNDERSTAND, BUT STILL WE DO NOT
UNDERSTAND. OSHO, WHY DO WE NOT
UNDERSTAND?
WHEN WILL WE UNDERSTAND?
HOW WILL WE UNDERSTAND?

Chaitanya Bodhisatva, understanding is not something that knows any 'when'. It is not of time, so it is not predictable. I cannot say 'today' or 'tomorrow' or 'the day after tomorrow'. It can happen right this moment, it may not happen for lives together. It is unpredictable. It is unpredictable because it cannot be caused. It happens when it happens; understanding comes to you. All that you can do is not to create it – you cannot create it. And the understanding that is created by you will not be much of an understanding, either. So don't ask 'how'; there is no 'how' to it.

'How' means some technique, some method, so that we can create understanding. Understanding is not a thing that can be manufactured. Then what is it? It is already the case. You understand, but the understanding goes against your investments. Whatsoever I am saying is so simple that it is impossible not to understand it. I am not talking about difficult things, I am not talking about philosophy. I am making simple statements, just like "two plus two is four": you need not be a great genius to understand it.

And you understand it perfectly well. It is not that you don't understand it; it is a question of something else. You don't want to understand it. You understand it, but you don't *want* to understand it. You want to avoid it, you want to postpone it, hence you ask "When? How?" Those are tricks, strategies, to postpone until tomorrow.

I say: Now! Don't ask when. And don't ask how, because 'how' brings the future in. Then you say "I will practice; it can't happen just now. I will practice tomorrow, the day after tomorrow, and slowly slowly, gradually, one day it will happen." : And meanwhile you remain the same. It is a trick.

What I am saying is so obvious, but it goes against your investments. You have invested too much in your ignorance. Your whole life up to now has been lived by an utterly wrong kind of mind, and you have invested all that you had, your whole life. Now suddenly you see the point: you become afraid. Seeing it means that you have been a fool up to now. Seeing it means that up to now all has been futile, that up to now you have not really lived. This is too much, you cannot swallow it. You create a new trick: you say "I will try to understand."

Bodhisatva, you have understood. It is already there. Now please, don't play games. and remember, if you cannot live this understanding that is happening to you today, you will not be able to live it tomorrow either, because tomorrow the investment will have become even more. One day more you will have invested in your wrong attitudes, wrong structures; it will become more and more difficult. That's why it becomes difficult. The older you are, the more difficult it becomes.

Why do you see so many young people coming to me? The reason is, their investment is not so big. They can still hope to change their life and *live*. When old persons come, their investment is too big. Unless they are very courageous and really young inside, they will not be able to take the jump. Their whole life they have lived in one way; now suddenly I am showing them a different path to be followed. It is so new: it will be uncomfortable, inconvenient, insecure. And now not much is left – they are getting old, death is coming. To risk in such a moment becomes difficult. They understand perfectly well, but they don't *want* to understand. They want to go on dreaming, they want to continue the dream.

Mulla Nasruddin one night dreamt that Khidr, the Sufi hidden master, was standing before him and asked him, "What do you want, Nasruddin?"

Poor Nasruddin could not ask much. That's how people are. If God suddenly appears and asks you, "What do you want?" – just think, what comes to your mind? A house, a car, a bank balance...you cannot even ask for something worthwhile. Mulla said, "A hundred-rupee note." Poor man, that was the best thing that he could imagine.

But Khidr is also something; he said, "I will give you one rupee. Two." Mulla said, "No, a hundred!" "Three."

And this way it continued, this haggling continued, in the dream. It came to ninety-nine, and Khidr was very adamant. He said, "I will not give a single pai more. Ninety-nine? Take it or leave it!"

And Mulla said, "I will take a hundred! And how miserly you are! Just for one rupee? Why not make it a hundred?"

And the fight became so hot that Mulla woke himself up. He opened his eyes, Khidr disappeared, the notes disappeared. The wife was sitting by his side, because he was talking so loudly that she had become awake and was listening. Great haggling was going on and talk about money, and she was also interested. And she did not want to disturb him; something great was happening. "Eighty, eighty-one, eighty-two..." and it went on "...ninety-nine." And Mulla said, "Ninety-nine, no! A hundred! I will take only a hundred."

And then suddenly he opened his eyes, and the wife said, "What is happening?" And Mulla said, "You keep quiet!"

He closed his eyes again and said, "Okay, give me ninety-nine." But now the dream is gone; now there is no Khidr, nobody.

And he said, "Okay, ninety-nine I say! Where are you?

Ninety-eight! Ninety-seven!" And he started coming down but now there was nobody and not even one rupee. And he was very angry and said, "How foolish I am! I should have accepted ninety-nine. Just for one rupee.... This Khidr is a miser. And I am also a foolish man; now I cannot find him."

That's the situation. If you understand me, the dream will be broken. And you are always nearabout ninety-nine. It is just going to happen tomorrow – one more day, a little more effort.... And the hundred-rupee note is just hanging there in front of you like a carrot.

You say to me, "Wait, Osho. Just let try a little more. And you can go on telling me, you can go on teaching me, but tell me *when* and *how*." And you go on working hard to get this hundred-rupee note which is always there around the corner but is never in your hands. It will never be in your hands. And you are not ready to awaken from your sweet dream.

It is not a question of understanding; it is so simple. But you have lived a certain life, your habits have become fixed, your structure has become frozen. Even when you understand, your mind is cunning enough to distort it, to create meanings in it which are not there. It can project its own ideas into it.

What I am saying is simple, utterly simple. Anybody with an innocent mind can understand it. But the problem is you have prejudices, you have your own ideas. You would like to understand it accordingly, according to your own prejudices.

The good Father came upon Pat, the town disgrace, in a highly inebriated condition, tacking skillfully from telephone post to gate, and back again. "Pat, Pat, drunk again?" "Are ye? So'm I, Father."

"Tut, tut, this is no time for levity. You in this beastly condition, Pat, after faithfully promisin' me, two weeks ago, that you would never more drink again – an' after takin' the pledge. It's a burning shame to you, an' a sin against God an' the Church, and sorry I am to be obliged to say so."

"Father Daly," said Pat, in a tone half tipsy, half laughing, "do ye say ye are sorry to see me so?" "Yis, indade I am." "Are you sure y're very sorry?" "Yis, very very sorry."

"Well, thin, Father Daly, if you're very very sorry, I'll forgive you."

This is how it goes on. I say one thing, you manage to make it mean something else. And you are doing it, and you know that you are doing it. It is not a question of when and how: either now or never.

A young Scotsman of good family and good social position had a great fondness for drink. His family and his friends had done almost everything to break him of the habit, with no success. A friend suggested that they try giving him a severe shock. As a means to this end, they procured a coffin, and the next time he came home under the influence, they dressed him like a corpse, darkened the room, placed a few lighted candles around the coffin, and put a friend there to watch him.

He awoke shortly and appeared greatly puzzled by the surroundings, when, catching sight of somebody in the room, he remarked, "Whaur am I?" "Ye're deed," was the solemn reply. "Deed?" he exclaimed. "Hoo lang ha'e I been deed?" "Three days." "Weel, weel," he mused. "Are ye deed as weel?" "Aye, I'm deed as weel," said his companion. "That funny. Hoo lang ha'e ye been deed?" "Three weeks," replied the other sadly. The bibulous one brightened up considerably and said, "Weel, if ye've been deed three weeks, and I've nad I've only been deed three days, ye must know the place better than I dae: whaur can we gang an' get a drink?"

The old mind, the old structure, the old habits, they go on persisting. They will follow you even in your death. That's exactly what happens: you only change your body, your mind continues. Your mind enters into another womb, with all its rotten past. And again you start living the same repetitive life.

Don't ask me when you are going to understand me: you *have* understood me. Now please don't postpone it any more.

It has already happened! It is such a simple thing; I am not giving you puzzles, I am giving you bare, naked truths. And there is no question of *how*.

Listening to me, not interfering with what I am saying, not distorting what I am saying, the understanding will arise on its own – it *is* arising. But it is going to be against your investments, that is true. And unless you dare, you will not be able to come out of your old past, you will not be able to come out of your old ego.

Great daring is needed; not understanding – understanding is already happening – but courage. And what is courage? Courage simply means a readiness to risk the known for the unknown. If the known has not given you anything, why be afraid of the unknown? Let us try it. You are not going to lose anything, because you don't have anything. Why not try it? Either you get something or you don't lose anything; any way you are not going to be a loser.

But people think they *have* something. They think they have lived a tremendously beautiful life, a life of richness. These are just your beliefs. You have been only dragging along. Your life has been drab and flat; no poetry has ever happened in it, no dance. You have not known anything of the beauty and the grandeur of existence. You have not even for a moment touched the divinity of this beautiful universe.

You have not known anything of God, and only that matters. Only that gives richness, only that means life. If you have not touched the divine, if you have not been touched by the divine, if you have not been moved by the divine, if you have not been penetrated by the divine, if you have not allowed God to happen to you, all that has happened is just a dream.

Seeing it, one jumps out of the dream. This is courage, to jump out of the known dream into the unknown. It is a risk. Who knows what is going to happen in the unknown? But one thing is certain; by changing from the known to the unknown you will have grown, you will have become richer.

The last question:

OSHO, WHAT WOULD YOU DO IF, BY SOME CRAZY
TWIST OF FATE, YOU BECAME PRIME MINISTER OF
INDIA?

Ashok, I will resign immediately.

3 Crying for the Light

A Sufi story:

The philosophers, logicians and doctors of law were drawn up at court to examine Mulla Nasruddin. This was a serious case, because he had admitted going from village to village saying: "The so-called wise men are ignorant, irresolute and confused." He was charged with undermining the security of the state.

"You may speak first," said the king.

"Have paper and pens brought," said the Mulla.

Paper and pens were brought. "Give some to each of the first seven savants." They were distributed.

"Have them write separately an answer to this question: 'What is bread?'" This was done.

The papers were handed to the king, who read them out: The first said: "Bread is a food." The second: "It is flour and water." The third: "A gift of God." The fourth: "Baked dough." The fifth: "Changeable, according to how you mean 'bread'." The sixth: "A nutritious substance." The seventh: "Nobody really knows."

"When they decide what bread is," said Nasruddin, "It will be possible for them to decide other things. For example, whether I am right or wrong. Can you entrust matters of assessment and judgment to people like this? Is it or is it not strange that they cannot agree about something which they eat each day, and yet are unanimous that I am a heretic?"

Yes, that is the situation of your so-called philosophers, theologians, doctors of law: the learned people. They are parrots. They have not even known themselves yet – what else can they know? They are not even acquainted with themselves – how can they be acquainted with others? They have not unraveled the mystery that they are.

The closest is your own mystery. If even that is not known, how can you know the mystery of others? Those mysteries are farther away from you, they are distant. The easily approachable, the most easily approachable, is your own mystery. The journey has to begin from there.

The learned people – the pundits, the scholars, the professors – they are only better informed. But information makes no one wise. Yes, it helps you to pretend wisdom. It becomes a camouflage; it is a facade behind which you can hide your ignorance. But the ignorance is not destroyed by it – on the contrary, it is protected.

Your knowledge becomes a defense; it is a security for your ignorance. It is nourishment. You become fully unaware that you are ignorant: that is the purpose of your so-called knowledge. And this is dangerous. If you are unaware that you are ill, then there is no possibility of searching for health. If you become oblivious to the fact of your fundamental ignorance, how are you ever going to become enlightened?

If you have forgotten that your interior is full of darkness, you will not search for light. You will not work to create light. If you have already accepted that you know, then what is the point of going on an adventure of knowing? And that's what your so-called knowledge goes on doing. It does not change the ignorant person into a knowing person; it only gives an illusion of knowledge. It is a mirage. It is a dream in which you become wise. But in reality you remain the same.

The difference between the ignorant and the so-called learned is only of quantity. No qualitative difference at all exists between them. The ignorant is less informed, less polished, less educated. The learned is more informed, more educated, has read more, has listened to more people. The difference is of language. The learned is more articulate, knows many more words. But they are mere words, remember. There is no meaning in it, there cannot be any meaning in it, because meaning comes through experience.

You can learn all the great words there are in the dictionaries. That's how you go on using words. When you use words like 'god' do you know what you are saying? Do you know what you mean? What is God? It is a mere word for you, and it will remain a mere word. But behind the word there is a danger: you may start believing that you know because you know the word.

Knowing the word 'god' is not knowing God. Knowing the word 'love' is not knowing love. Knowing the word 'fire' is not knowing fire. Remember, words are mere symbols. Unless you pour existential meaning into them they will remain empty. There is no meaning in words, the meaning is in the individual and his experience.

If Krishna uses the word 'god' it is not a mere word. It is meaningful, it has significance. The significance comes from Krishna's life, the significance is poured from Krishna's consciousness.

When Jesus uses the word 'god' it is of utter import, it is pregnant with great meaning. The meaning is in Jesus, not in the word 'god' – because the word 'god' had been used by rabbis, down the ages, with no meaning at all. Jesus poured meaning into it. He transformed an empty word into a significant, meaningful, *alive* thing: it started pulsating.

When Buddha touched any word it became alive, it grew wings. Suddenly there was a metamorphosis.

But the learned is only full of dust, the dust that he has gathered from books and scriptures. Beware of such learning, it is more dangerous than simple ignorance. Why is it more dangerous than ignorance? Because ignorance has a purity; it has innocence in it and it has an authenticity. It is true – and from truth there is a possibility to go further. Knowledge, the so-called knowledge, is untrue. From untruth you cannot go on a journey of truth.

Remember, there is no actual difference between the learned and the ignorant, except that the learned believes that he knows, and the ignorant knows that he does not know. But then the ignorant is in a better position.

An American lady who speaks no French takes her little daughter to the Paris zoo. They stop in front of a cage with porcupines inside and read a sign that says: Porcupi Africain, Porcupi Australian. This puzzles them, because the porcupines all look just about the same. So the mother goes up to the guard who is standing nearby and says, "Monsieur, do you speak English?"

The guard touches his cap and says, "Madame, I speak... only a very leetle of English.... Wat ees eet Madame weesh to know?"

"Would you tell us please what is the difference between the Australian porcupine and the African porcupine?"

"Eet eez thees, Madame: zee prick of zee African porcupine, she is longair zan zee prick of zee Australian porcupine."

The lady is horrified and rushes off with her daughter until she finds the superintendent of the zoo. "Monsieur," she says, "Do you speak English?"

"Madame," says the superintendent, "I am speaking English for many years. I have studied at Oxford and in fact I can speak as well as you. What does Madame wishes to know."

So she tells him with great indignation the awful thing that the guard has just said in front of her and her little girl.

"Madame must not be offended," says the superintendent. "You see, what the guard is trying to say is that the quill of the African porcupine is longer that the quill of the Australian porcupine – for, as a matter of fact, Madame, their prick is of the same size."

There is not much difference between the so-called learned and the unlearned. Maybe the difference is of words, of language, but not of any quality. Their inner quality remains the same.

This is one of the fundamentals of Sufism to be understood: knowledge is futile if it has not arisen in your own experience. Knowledge is an utterly unnecessary burden if it is not part of your own life. If it is added to you from the outside, drop it. Don't unnecessarily carry it. It is useless, it is harmful, it is poisonous, and a burden. It will not allow you to move quick and fast. And the more you gather knowledge, the less is the possibility of your movement.

Hence your learned people live like stagnant pools: They are no longer rivers. Learned people go on talking about beautiful words, spinning and weaving great philosophies around them. But if you go into their words and penetrate deeply, you will always find emptiness and nothing else.

Great books are written about God by people who have no inkling. Great books are written about heaven and hell, maps of heaven and hell have even been drawn by people and they don't know a thing. They have not even penetrated their own world of emotions and feelings; they have not contacted their own inner consciousness. And they are talking about distant things: the afterlife, life after death....And they are clever people; they know how to talk, they know how to prove, they know how to argue. And they argue in such a beautiful way that anybody can be deceived.

If you go into their argument you will find it very valid. But the validity of the argument is irrelevant. The question is of whether the person knows or not. Sometimes it happens that a person knows but cannot argue, or argues faultily. A person sometimes knows but has no language to express it, or uses wrong language. But what he says is still true. His argument may be false, his language may not be adequate, but what he says is still true.

And at the other extreme there are people whose language you cannot find fault with, whose argument is perfect, who are accomplished logicians. You cannot argue with them, they will immediately silence you. But still, what they are saying is utterly stupid. It does not make any sense. It is just in their minds; their hearts are utterly untouched by it. They themselves are not moved by what they are saying. When they talked about God there is no juice flowing in their being. When they talk about love you will not see any sign of it in their eyes, and when they talk about poetry there is no poetry in their presence. They talked about grace but you will not see any grace anywhere.

But they can create a great turmoil of words, they can create a great smoke of words. And if you also live in words there is every possibility you will be deceived. That's how million of people are lost. The blind are leading the other blind. The articulate blind are leading the inarticulate blind, the informed blind are leading the uninformed blind.

And whenever a man of eyes is born – a Jesus, a Buddha, a Bahauddin, a Hakim Sanai – all those scholars and learned people are immediately in agreement about one thing, that Jesus is wrong. They may not agree about what bread is, they may not agree about anything else, but about one thing they immediately agree, that Jesus is wrong.

They may be Hindus, they may be Mohammedans, they may be Jews, they may be somebody else. But when there is a man like Jesus they immediately all fall into agreement, because they all see the risk. If Jesus is right, then they are all wrong. Jesus has to be proved wrong. And if they cannot prove him wrong – and they *cannot* prove it – then Jesus has to be destroyed. If they cannot prove it then the only way is to remove Jesus from people's lives.

And once Jesus is killed. the same people who killed Jesus will become Jesus' followers, popes, bishops and priests. Again they are there to philosophize.

With Jesus there is trouble. But with Jesus' words there is no problem. They can spin and weave around any word; whether it is of Moses or Jesus makes no difference to them. Now Jesus becomes their center of philosophizing.

Buddha becomes the greatest source of philosophers: a strange phenomenon, unbelievable – because Buddha was utterly against philosophy. His whole life he remained absolutely anti-philosophy. He never talked about any philosophical subject; he was down to earth. He was a pragmatist, a practical man. If you had asked him about god he would have immediately pushed the question aside and would have said to you, "How is it going to transform you? Talking about god is meaningless – don't waste time. Think about meditation, think about compassion. Think about things which can transform you. What can god do?"

If you had asked him about the afterlife he would have immediately stopped you: "Don't talk nonsense. You are alive, and you don't know what LIFE is, and you are thinking about the afterlife! You don't know what you are right now, and you are asking, 'What will I be after death?' This is utter stupidity."

Rather, go into yourself and see who you are. And if you have known yourself then there is no problem. When you die you will know whether you survive or not – why make much fuss about it right now? And how can it be decided? There is no way of deciding. Even if the whole world says that you will survive the bodily death, the doubt will still persist. Who knows? Everybody may be wrong – because the whole world used to believe that the earth was flat, and the whole world was wrong. The earth was not flat; now we know. The whole world has believed, down the ages, that the sun moves around the earth. Now we know, the earth moves around the sun, not vice versa.

So it is not a question of how many people believe in it. Truth is not decided by the majority, it is not a question of voting. Even if a single man knows truth, and the whole world is against him, he is still true and the world is still wrong.

You cannot be convinced that you will be when you are dead; there is no way of convincing you. You can believe it if you want to; if you want to believe, you can believe anything. But is because you want to, not because you are convinced.

You are afraid of death, so you would like to remain after death: you want to believe it, so you believe it. But you know that it is your belief; it may not be so. Deep down, the doubt will persist.

And Buddha would not have answered any question that you could think belonged to philosophy. He used to say, "If I say something about the beyond, you will misunderstand it. You don't have any experience of the beyond; communication is not possible."

And you can see how difficult it is to communicate. I say one thing, you will understand another. People will understand according to their level of understanding.

A playboy who had squandered a fortune was asked what he had done with all his money. He answered, "Some went for liquor and fast automobiles, and most went for women. The rest I spent foolishly."

Words don't mean the same thing to everybody. It is according to your understanding.

"Your continual unfaithfulness proves that you are absolutely worthless!" yelled the outraged man who had just caught his wife for the tenth time with another man.

"Quite the contrary," came the cool reply. "It merely proves I am too good to be true." It all depends on you.

On a foreign business trip, a man found himself hampered after working hours by the fact that he didn't know the language. He was delighted, therefore, when a gorgeous woman sat down at his restaurant table. "Can you speak English?" he ventured hopefully. "Jus' a leetle," she said with a smile. "Just a little, eh?" he repeated. "How much?" "Twenty-five dollars," was the prompt reply.

Communication is one of the most difficult problems in the world. When you use a word you give it your meaning. When it reaches the other person it is bound to take his meaning. And between the transfer everything is lost.

So Buddha said, "I will not talk of the beyond. And don't ask anything about the beyond. Be more scientific and realistic: go into that which is. Don't talk about truth. Go into that which is, go into that which you are, and that is the way to know the truth.

But once Buddha died, great philosophical schools arose. It had never happened in the whole world as it happened in India after Buddha. The man who for his whole life was against philosophy and philosophizing, became the source of the greatest philosophical endeavor ever. Thirty-six schools of philosophy were born when Buddha died. And the people that he had always condemned all gathered together to philosophize about him.

And see the beauty, the irony of it all! They started philosophizing about why Buddha kept silent. Why he did not say anything about the beyond: that became their philosophy! They started talking about why he kept silent about the beyond. And there were as many answers as possible.

Somebody said, "Because there is no beyond." Now one philosophy has taken roots. Another said, "The beyond is, but it is inexpressible. That's why he kept silent." Now another school, and so on and so forth.

Even the silence of Buddha became a problem, and people started discussing the silence. Nobody tried to become silent; people started talking *about* the silence.

Beware of this trap, the mind is very cunning. If I say something about meditation, I am saying it so that you can meditate. But you start thinking about meditation, what meditation is. "How many kinds of meditation are there in existence? What is the difference between them? Why are they antagonistic to each other?

And then you can go on ad infinitum, and there will not be any time when you will ever meditate. You will become more and more confused. You will become so confused finally that you will not know how to start meditation. because there are so many directions opening. Where to go? What to choose? You will simply be paralyzed.

The mind always does that. And only a few people who are really alert are capable of getting out of these traps of the mind. The mind is a great philosopher. And life is not a philosophy, life is a reality. Philosophy is an escape from reality; philosophy means thinking. Life is – there is no question of thought. You can simply jump into it. The ancient pond a frog jumps in the sound

Just like that, you can jump into this ancient pond of life. You can know it only by jumping into it. There is no other way to know life; thinking about it is the surest way you miss it.

The sutras:

HE DOESN'T KNOW HIS OWN SELF:
HOW SHOULD HE KNOW THE SELF OF ANOTHER?

But this is what everybody is doing. You think you know the woman you love? You think you know your husband? You think you know your child? Just because you carried the child in your whom for nine months. do you think you know him? You only believe that you know him. The child is a mystery; you don't know a thing about him. The child is as mysterious as the whole existence.

You don't know the woman you love. How can you know the woman? – because you have not yet known yourself. The woman may be close to you, but she can never be as close as you are to yourself.

Hence I say if you don't love yourself you will not be able to love anybody else in the world. And if you don't know yourself you will never be able to know anybody else in the world. Love or knowledge, all start from your own center. The first ripple has to arise there, then it can go on spreading. Then it can go on spreading to the unbounded boundaries of existence. But first it has to start at the very core of your being.

HE DOESN'T KNOW HIS OWN SELF:
HOW SHOULD HE KNOW THE SELF OF ANOTHER?

And what is the problem? Why don't you know your own self? This should be the easiest thing in the world, and it has become difficult, the most difficult. This has become almost impossible, to know oneself. What has gone wrong? You have the capacity to know. You are there, the capacity to know is there. Then what has gone wrong? Why cannot this capacity of knowing turn upon itself?

Only one thing has gone wrong, and unless you put it right you will remain ignorant of yourself. And the thing that has gone wrong is, a split has been created in you. You have lost your integrity. The society has made you into a divided house, divided against yourself.

The strategy is simple; once understood, it can be removed. The strategy is, the society has given you ideals of how you should be. And it has enforced those ideals so deeply in you, that you are always interested in the ideal "how I should be" and you have forgotten who you are. You are obsessed with the future ideal and you have forgotten the present reality.

Your eyes are focused on the distant future. Hence they cannot turn inwards. You are constantly thinking of what to do, how to do it, how to be this. Your language has become that of shoulds and oughts, and the reality consists only of *is*. Reality knows no should, no ought.

A roseflower is a roseflower, there is no question of its being something else. And the lotus is a lotus. Neither does the rose ever try to become a lotus, nor does the lotus ever try to become a rose. Hence they are not neurotics. They don't need the psychiatrist, they don't need any psychoanalysis. The rose is healthy because the rose simply lives its reality.

And so it is with the whole existence except man. Only man has ideals and shoulds. "You should be this and that" – then you are divided against your own IS. Should and is are enemies.

And you cannot be anything other than you are. Let it sink deep into your heart: you can only be that which you are, never anything else. Once this truth sinks deep, that "I can only be myself" all ideals disappear. They are discarded automatically. And when there is no ideal, reality is encountered. Then your eyes are herenow, then you are present to what you are. The division, the split, has disappeared. You are one.

This is the beginning of being one with god. First be one with yourself. This is the first step of *Unio Mystica*: be one with yourself. And then the second step, and the last, is: be one with existence. The second is easy. The first has become difficult because of so much conditioning, so much education, so many civilizing efforts. The first has become difficult.

If you have taken the first step of just accepting yourself and loving yourself as you are, moment to moment... For example, you are sad. This moment you are sad. Your whole conditioning says to you "You should not be sad. This is bad. You should not be sad. You have to be happy." Now the division, now the problem. You are sad: that is the truth of this moment. And your conditioning, your mind says, "You should not be like this, you have to be happy. Smile! What will people think of you?"

Your woman may leave you if you are so sad, your friends may desert you if you are so sad, your business will be destroyed if you remain so sad. You have to laugh, you have to smile, you have to at least to pretend that you are happy. If you are a doctor your patients will not feel good if you are so sad. They want a doctor who is happy, jolly, healthy, and you are looking so sad. Smile – even if you cannot bring a real smile, bring a false smile, but smile. At least pretend, act.

This is the problem: you pretend, you act. You can manage to smile, but then you have become two. You have repressed the truth, you have become phony.

And the phony is appreciated by the society. The phony becomes the saint, the phony becomes the great leader, the phony becomes the mahatma. And everybody starts following the phony. The phony is your ideal.

That's why you are unable to know yourself. How can you know yourself if you don't accept yourself? You are always repressing your being. What has to be done then? When you are sad, accept the sadness: this is you. Don't say "I am sad." Don't say that sadness is something separate from you. Simply say, "I am sadness. This moment, I am sadness." And live your sadness in total authenticity.

And you will be surprised that a miraculous door opens in your being. If you can live your sadness with no image of being happy, you become happy immediately, because the division disappears. There is no division any more. "I am sadness" and there is no question of any ideal to be anything else. So there is no effort, no conflict. "I am simply this" and there is relaxation.

And in that relaxation is grace, and in that relaxation is joy.

All psychological pain exists only because you are divided. Pain means division. and bliss means no-division. It will look paradoxical to you: if one is sad, accepting one's sadness how can one become joyous? It will look paradoxical, but it is so. Try it.

And I am not saying try to be happy; I am not saying that, "Accept your sadness so that you can become happy" – I am not saying that. If that is your motivation then nothing will happen; you are still struggling. You will be watching from the corner of your eye: "So much time has passed and I have accepted even sadness, and I am saying 'I am sadness'", and joy is still not coming. "It will not come that way.

Joy is not a goal, it is a by-product. It is a natural conse-
quence of oneness, of unity. Just be united with this sadness,
for no motivation, for no particular purpose. There is no ques-
tion of any purpose. This is how you are this moment, this is
your truth this moment. And next moment you may be angry:
accept that too. And next moment you may be something else:
accept that too.

Live moment to moment, with tremendous acceptance,
without creating any division, and you are on the way towards
self-knowledge. Self-knowledge is not a question of reading
the Upanishads and sitting silently and reciting, "Aham Brah-
masmi, I am God." These are all foolish efforts. Either you
know you are God, or you don't know it. You can go on for
your whole life repeating, "Aham Brahmasmi, I am God." You
can waste your whole life in repeating it, but you will not
know it. If you know it, there is no point in repeating it. Why
are you repeating it? If you know, you know. If you don't
know, how can you know by repetition? Just see the whole
stupidity of it.

But that's what is being done in this country and in other
countries also, in monasteries and ashrams. What are people
doing? Parrot-like repetition.

I am giving you a totally different approach. It is not by
repetition of the Koran or Bible or Vedas that you will become
a knower, no. You will only become knowledgeable. Then how
does one come to know oneself?

Drop the division: the division is the whole problem. You
are against yourself. Drop all ideals which create this antago-
nism in you. You are the way you are: accept it with joy, with
gratitude. And suddenly a harmony will be felt. The two selves
in you, the ideal self and the real self, will not be there to fight
any more. They will meet and merge into one.

It is not really sadness that gives you pain. It is the inter-
pretation that sadness is wrong that gives you pain, and that

becomes a psychological problem. It is not anger that is painful; it is the idea that anger is wrong that creates psychological anxiety. It is the interpretation, not the fact. The fact is always liberating.

Jesus says, "Truth liberates." And that is of tremendous import. Yes, truth liberates, but not *knowing* about truth. Be the truth, and it liberates. Be the truth, and there is liberation. You need not bring it, you need not wait for it: it happens instantly.

How to be the truth? You *are* already the truth. You are just carrying false ideals; they are creating the trouble. Drop the ideals: for a few days be a natural being. Just like trees and animals and birds, accept your being as you are. And a great silence arises. How can it be otherwise? There is no interpretation: then sadness is beautiful, it has depth. Then anger too is beautiful it has life and vitality. Then sex too is beautiful, because it has creativity.

When there is no interpretation, all is beautiful. When all is beautiful, you are relaxed. In that relaxation you have fallen into your own source, and that brings self-knowledge. Falling into one's own source is what is meant by "Know thyself." It is not a question of knowledge, it is a question of inner transformation.

And what transformation am I talking about? I am not giving you any ideal that you have to be like; I am not saying that you have to transform from what you are and become somebody else. You have simply to relax into whatsoever you are, and just see.

Have you hears what I am saying? Just see the point: it is liberating. And a great harmony, a great music is heard. That music is of self-knowledge. And your life tarts changing. You then have a magic key which unlocks all the locks.

If you accept sadness, sadness will disappear. How long can you be sad if you accept sadness? If you are capable of accepting sadness you will be capable of *absorbing* it in your being; it will become your depth.

And how long will you be able to be angry if you accept anger? Anger feeds on rejection. If you accept it, you have absorbed the energy. Anger has great energy in it, vitality, and when that energy is absorbed you become more vital. Your life then has a passion to it, it is a flame. It is not a dull insipid life; it has intelligence and passion and sharpness.

And if you have accepted sex, one day sex disappears too. And it releases great creativity in you, because sex is the potential of creativity. And then you become a creator. Great paintings may arise through you, great poetry may come, great sons may be born, or music. Anything and everything is possible then; you participate with God.

Sex is the lowest form of creativity, just the seed of creativity. Once the seed has broken, has dissolved, has been absorbed, your whole being comes creative. And to be creative is to be blissful, to be creative is to be one with God. When you become a creator you participate in God.

And I am not saying that unless you paint and write poetry you will not be a creator. Buddha did not paint, did not write any poetry, but his whole life was of creativity. Whosoever he touched was transformed. Whosoever was courageous enough to come close to him was reborn. He created a great energy-field, a buddhafield, and whosoever entered that field was never the same again. That is his creativity. He did not write any visible poetry. But the way he walks is poetry, the way he looks at people is poetry. He never danced. But if you watch, silently sitting underneath the bodhi tree there is a great dance happening in him. It is an invisible dance; it is subtle, it is not gross. It is not of the physical, it is a spiritual dance.

He is not separate from existence. So he is dancing with the trees in the wind, and he is dancing with the stars, and he is dancing with the whole. He is not separate any more.

Do you understand the difference? If you try to drop sex, all creativity will disappear from your life.

That's what happened in this unfortunate country. People

tried to drop sex, people tried to somehow impose celibacy on themselves. And they all became uncreative; they all became dull, they lost intelligence. You can go around and look at Indian mahatmas, and you will not see such dull and stupid people anywhere else in the world. Their whole life consists of living in a very uncreative way; they are praised for uncreative things.

Somebody fasts, that's why he is praised – not for any dance. Somebody sleeps on a bed of thorns, that's why he is praised. Now, he has not done anything creative in the world. He has not made the world a little more beautiful than he found it. He will leave the world as ugly as it was before, or even uglier. But he is praised because he lies on a bed of thorns. What is the point of it?

If you repress sex, creativity disappears. If you accept sex, sex is transformed into creativity. If you accept anger, it releases great vitality and passion in you. Your life becomes a passionate life. It is then a life of involvement, commitment and participation. Then you are not just a spectator, then you are in the thick of things, in the dance of life, part of it. Your every moment is of involvement. Then you are not an escapist; you live joyously and totally. Then you contribute something to existence. Then you are not futile, you have some meaning. But anger has to be accepted, then anger's energy is absorbed.

Whenever you reject something, you have rejected some energy. You have said, "I don't want to absorb *this* energy." But this is your energy. And the rejected energy will keep you poor. Reject anger, and you have rejected the possibility of being vital. Now you will be dull. Reject sex, and you have rejected the possibility of being creative. Now no poetry, no song, no dance, is going to happen in your life. You will be just a walking dead man. Your life will be an empty gesture, impotent.

If you have rejected sadness then you will not have any depth. You will remains hallow. Your laughter will also be shallow, because it will not have any depth; that can only be released by sadness through acceptance. Your laughter will be just on the surface.

That's what I mean when I see people and call them phony. A phony person is one who is only pretending to live but not really living, one who is afraid of life. And this phoniness comes through rejection. Go on rejecting everything. Keep an ideal in the mind that you have to become a Buddha, that you have to become a Jesus. You will never become one; on the contrary, you will lose all possibilities of ever becoming anything.

Forget all about Buddhas and Krishnas and Christs, they are not ideals to be imitated. Don't have any ideals, be an ideal-destroyer. This is rebellion and this is religion too. And when there are no ideals haunting you, torturing you, you fall into harmony with yourself. And when you don't reject anything, all energies are yours, you are enriched. Then you have tremendous energy. And that tremendous energy is you, that energy is delight.

Falling into your own source, you become a knower. And the moment you know yourself, you have known all, because it is the same. That which is in me is in everybody. Only forms are different, houses are different. It is the same consciousness.

That in me which says, "I am" says the same in you also: "I am." This I-amness is one. It is the same in the tree, unspoken. It is the same in the rock, fast asleep. But it is the same I-amness. And to know this is to know the meaning of *aham brahmasmi*. I am God.

HE DOESN'T KNOW HIS OWN SELF:
HOW SHOULD HE KNOW THE SELF OF ANOTHER?
HE KNOWS ONLY HIS HANDS AND FEET,
HOW SHOULD HE KNOW ABOUT GOD?

You know only your hands and feet. This is the abode, this

is the house. You are acquainted with only the temple: when are you going to be acquainted with the deity of the temple? Who is this who lives in this house? Who is embodied in the body? What is this consciousness?

You are listening to me, you are listening through the ears. You are seeing me, you are seeing through the eyes. Certainly you are not the ears and you are not the eyes. Eyes and ears are windows – somebody is hidden behind, standing behind the windows.

Just watch: your eyes are windows. When you are looking at me you are looking through the eyes. But who are *you*? Who is this who is looking at me? Who is this who is hearing? What is this consciousness?

Don't reject anything, otherwise you will never be able to know this consciousness. Accept all that you are. If you reject anything you recoil from your own energies. You create fragments. Don't recoil from your energies. When anger is there, accept it. When sadness is there, accept it. This is your energy, this is God's gift. Absorb it, digest it, it is you.

And when you are not recoiling from anything, when you don't have any interpretations of good and bad, when you don't condemn anything, when you forget all about judgment, when you are not a constant judger, assessor, condemner, evaluer, when all these things have disappeared and you are simply a tremendous acceptance of all that is, knowing happens. And in that knowing, God is known.

THIS IS BEYOND THE SAGE'S GRASP: YOU MUST BE A FOOL IF YOU THINK THAT YOU KNOW IT.

Even the so-called sages find it beyond their grasp. So the learned people, the pundits and the scholars, if they think that they know God, that they know themselves, they must be fools.

God is beyond any grasp; even the grasp of the sage is not

capable of holding God in the hands. Because God is never the sought, but the seeker. God is not out there, so that you can grasp him. God is the one who is trying to grasp: how can you grasp the grasper? That will be absurd.

That's why you cannot see your own face. You cannot see your own eyes; you can see them in a mirror but you see only the reflection of your eyes, not your eyes. The eyes cannot see themselves.

How can God grasp himself? If I try to grasp my hand with the same hand, it is going to be maddening. It will drive you crazy. It will be like a dog trying to chase its own tail.

THIS IS BEYOND THE SAGE'S GRASP...

Because it is beyond grasp. Why is it beyond grasp? Not that it is far away, but because it is the very energy that is trying to grasp it. The knower is the known. The knowledge is not going to be of something else, it is self-knowing. There is not going to be any object of knowledge that you will grasp. You are the subject and you are the object. You are all that is. Consciousness is all.

WHEN YOU CAN EXPOUND ON THIS,
YOU WILL KNOW THE PURE ESSENCE OF FAITH;
TILL THEN, WHAT HAVE FAITH AND YOU IN
COMMON?

You can't know what faith is; what you call faith is only belief. Belief is of the head, it is part of knowledge. Belief is false and phony. Belief means somebody else has said something and you have believed it; it is borrowed. Belief is never original. Faith is always original. It arises in you: it is the growth of your own consciousness.

...YOU WILL KNOW THE PURE ESSENCE OF FAITH

only when you have known yourself;

TILL THEN, WHAT HAVE FAITH AND YOU IN
COMMON?

So don't deceive yourself that you are a believer. Don't pretend, and don't think that you know, and don't think that you think original thoughts. No thought is ever original. Only experience is original.

After little Lori had a tussle with a neighborhood friend, the girl's mother scolded her. "Remember, Lori," said the mother, "that it was the devil who suggested to you that you pull little Alice's hair."

"I suppose so," said Lori. "But kicking her in the shin was my own idea."

People go on thinking that something "is my own idea" – it gives a good feeling to the ego. But no idea is yours. Only consciousness is yours. Alfred Tennyson says: But what am I? An infant crying in the night? An infant crying for the light? And with no language but a cry!

Knowledge is not going to help. A cry may be of more help. Weeping, crying, tears, love – something authentic, something true, something that arises in your being in this moment, may be of more help. It will give you some taste of reality. Otherwise your faith is only borrowed, dead.

That's how there are so many Mohammedans and Hindus and Christians and Jews, but you don't find religious people anywhere. Religious people have disappeared from the earth. Yes, Christians are there, Hindus are there, but where are the religious people?

Religion consists of faith, not of belief. Behind the belief there is always doubt. Belief is rooted in doubt. It is because of the doubt, it is to repress the doubt, that you put a belief upon yourself. It is as if you hide a wound behind a roseflower, but the wound remains there.

Mr. and Mrs. Mandelbaum decided the only solution to their marital problems was in divorce. So they went to see the rabbi.

The rabbi was concerned about the three children and was reluctant to see the family broken up. He thought that if he could stall the couple maybe they would work it out together.

"Well," said the rabbi, "there's no way of dividing three children. What you'll have to do is live together one more year. You'll have a fourth child, and then it will be easy to arrange a proper divorce. You'll take two children, and he'll take two."

"Nothing doing," said Mrs Mandelbaum. "Rabbi, if I had depended on him, I wouldn't even have had these three!"

Just on the surface, things appear in one way. Deep down it is totally different. On the surface, people show trust and confidence in each other. Deep down, there is doubt. On the surface, love; deep down, there is hatred. On the surface, people are so nice; deep down, they are really bitter and poisonous.

This duality has to be dropped. Faith arises only when you have become one. Faith is the fragrance of oneness, of integration, of individuation.

> IT IS BETTER TO BE SILENT THAN TO TALK
> NONSENSE LIKE ONE OF THE LEARNED;
> FAITH IS NOT WOVEN INTO EVERY GARMENT.

It is better to be silent, says Hakim Sanai, because at least in silence you will not be lying to anybody. And you will not be lying to yourself either. In silence at least you will be ignorant; you will not pretend knowledge.

If a person can remain silent for a few hours every day he will become aware of his whole phoniness, because he will see his real face again and again. If you continuously talk and continuously relate with people you forget your original face, because you have to wear masks continuously. For twenty-four hours you are talking, using words. And when you continu-ously use words, slowly slowly you start believing in those words, in the sound of those words.

Words have a hypnotic power. If you use a certain word again and again, it hypnotizes you. If you use the word 'god' again and again, slowly slowly you start thinking that you know what you mean, that you know what God is. It is very dangerous to repeat words.

But people go on talking. They don't give any gap in which they can simply be silent and be. If you are silent for at least one hour every day, you will be aware continuously that your talk is nonsense. And then ninety-nine percent of your talk will start disappearing. What is the point of talking nonsense?

But why do people talk then? They talk just to hide them-selves behind the noise. Whenever you are nervous you start talking.

Now it is a known fact: if people are forced to live in soli-tude, after three weeks they start talking to themselves. They cannot *bear* silence, it becomes intolerable, so they start talking to themselves. They have to talk; words somehow keep them clinging to their personality. Once words disappear, they start falling into the impersonal. And they are very much afraid of the impersonal.

The impersonal is your reality. And you are afraid of the reality and you are clinging to the illusions that words create.

YOU WERE MADE FOR WORK: A ROBE OF HONOR
AWAITS YOU. HOW IS IT THAT YOU ARE SATISFIED
WITH MERE RAGS?

People are satisfied with mere words; they are rags. Sanai says: It is unbelievable. How are you satisfied with mere rags? You were made to work your way through this darkness of existence. This is a task to be done, this is a way of growth. To be here on the earth simply means that God has given an opportunity to you to grow. This earth is a challenge. Accept the challenge, encounter life: don't escape.

A few people escape in words, a few people escape into monasteries, a few people escape into politics, a few people escape into money – these are all escapes. A few become learned people, a few become rich, a few become very powerful in the world, a few become very respectable, moral and virtuous. But the real work is not done.

What is the real work? Sufis call only one thing real work, and that is self-remembrance.

Gurdjieff learned the word 'work' from the Sufis. He used to call his teachings "the work." He also learned the word *zikr*, self-remembering, from the Sufis.

The work is remember oneself. The only work worth doing is to remember oneself.

> YOU WERE MADE FOR WORK: A ROBE OF HONOR
> AWAITS YOU. HOW IS IT THAT YOU ARE SATISFIED
> WITH MERE RAGS? HOW WILL YOU EVER HAVE
> RICHES IF YOU ARE IDLE SIXTY DAYS A MONTH?

This is a very strange expression, "sixty days a month." It contains a great insight. The man who remembers himself has sixty days in one month: thirty are his inner life, and thirty the outer life. He lives in a double way. His life has not only one dimension, the horizontal; his life has double dimensions, the vertical too is there.

Thirty days he lives outside through the senses in the world. Thirty days he lives within himself in silence in his interiormost core. He has sixty days: this is a beautiful expression. The really rich life cannot be only horizontal, it cannot be linear, because the line cannot have any depth and the line cannot have any height either. The real life has to be both horizontal *and* vertical. Then there is all that is needed.

You meet God outside, you meet God inside. You move

between the outer God and the inner God: that movement is real richness. Wherever you go you find God. You open your eyes and the tree is there, and God is green in it and God is gold in it and God is red in it. And you close your eyes: the pure consciousness, the silence – and God is silence there. God is in you and in the other. Life becomes multidimensional.

Once a man asked Emerson, "How old are you?" Emerson was nearabout sixty, but he said, "I am three hundred and sixty years old."

The person who had inquired was very much puzzled, he could not believe his own ears. Three hundred and sixty years? He thought he must have hears wrongly, so he said, "Pardon me, sir, can you repeat that again? How old are you?"

And Emerson said again, "Three hundred and sixty years." The man said, "You must be joking."

Emerson said, "No. Comparatively speaking, in sixty years I have lived six times more than other people live. In sixty years I have lived six times more, hence I count my age as three hundred and sixty years."

And there have been people, and there are people, who live so intensely that their single moment is equivalent to eternity.

> KNOWING WHAT YOU KNOW BE SERENE ALSO,
> LIKE A MOUNTAIN; AND DO NOT BE DISTRESSED
> BY MISFORTUNE. KNOWLEDGE WITHOUT SERENITY
> IS AN UNLIT CANDLE; TOGETHER THEY ARE
> HONEY-COMB; HONEY WITHOUT WAX IS A NOBLE
> THING; WAX WITHOUT HONEY IS ONLY FIT FOR
> BURNING.
> KNOWING WHAT YOU KNOW, BE SERENE ALSO...

The real test is in serenity. The man who is simply knowledgeable is not serene. That has to be used as a criterion. The knowledgeable man is not calm and quiet and serene. His heart is constantly in turmoil, his head is continuously in a kind of insanity. Deep down in him there is a constant traffic of thoughts. There is no serenity, no stillness.

Sitting by the side of such a man – a learned man, a pundit, a scholar – you will feel a kind of uneasiness arising in you. You will not be surrounded by his serenity, you will not have any taste of his grace; he has none. Sanai says:

KNOWING WHAT YOU KNOW BE SERENE ALSO...

Knowledge alone is not enough. In fact, knowledge without serenity is not true knowledge. The true knowledge is born out of serenity, silence and meditativeness. First one falls into deep silence inside, and out of that silence arises knowing. Then it is true knowing. It does not arise out of scriptures, it arises when you open the book of your own being.

...BE SERENE ALSO, LIKE A MOUNTAIN;
AND DO NOT BE DISTURBED BY MISFORTUNE.

The man of serenity is not disturbed by anything because he accepts. Sadness comes, he accepts it. Joy comes, he accepts it. He has no preference, he has no choice. He lives in a choiceless consciousness: whatsoever happens happens, whatsoever is is, and he is totally open to it. He drinks it, he absorbs it. He has no likes and dislikes, no preferences, no choices. He is not against sadness, he is not against anger, he is not against sex, he is not against love. He is neither against nor for, he is simply serene.

If you choose, immediately you are disturbed. Watch it: whenever you choose you will be disturbed. Choice brings disturbance, because choice means alternatives: to be this or to be that, to be or not to be. Choice means you are standing at a crossroad: now which road to follow? If you go to the right, who knows? It may just lead you into a cul-de-sac. Maybe the left was the right choice. Who knows? How to decide?

The moment you choose, you become disturbed. And you always choose against yourself, against a part of yourself. One part says, "Choose this," another part says, "Choose that." Now you have to decide, and in that decision you will be divided. The part that was saying, "Don't choose this," has been denied, has been rejected. That rejected, denied part will take revenge. Sooner or later it will say, "Now see what happened: now repent. I told you beforehand not to choose this, that this was wrong, but you didn't listen to me."

And the same would have happened if you had chosen the other. The man who chooses remains disturbed.

Serenity means a state of choicelessness. Just like a mirror, it simply reflects, with no choice. An ugly man comes, it reflects. A beautiful man comes, it reflects. It has no choice; there is no question of choice. Just reflecting.

Sadness comes, and the man of serenity says, "I am sadness. This moment, this is how I am. This moment, this is my reality." He does not compare either: "The last moment was better, I was joyous. Now I am sad." He never compares two moments, he never hankers for something else in the future. Whatsoever is, he is totally relaxed with it. This is serenity – and out of serenity comes real knowing.

> KNOWLEDGE WITHOUT SERENITY IS AN UNLIT
> CANDLE...

And what is the point of an unlit candle? There will be no light. That's how the knowledgeable people are: great knowledge, candles and candles and candles, but all unlit. They stink of wax but no light comes out of them.

> KNOWLEDGE WITHOUT SERENITY IS AN UNLIT
> CANDLE; TOGETHER THEY ARE HONEY-COMB...

Together they are beautiful.

HONEY WITHOUT WAX IS A NOBLE THING...

Even if there is only serenity, it's better. Without knowledge, serenity is better; it is still a noble thing.

...WAX WITHOUT HONEY IS ONLY FIT FOR
BURNING.

But knowledge without serenity is of no use, it is worthless.

LEAVE THIS ABODE OF BIRTH AND DECAY; LEAVE
THIS PIT, AND MAKE FOR YOUR DESTINED HOME.
THIS HEAP OF DUST IS A MIRAGE, WHERE FIRE
SEEMS LIKE WATER.

Here, you are deluded in many ways. Ignorance pretends to be knowledge, fire appears like water, poison is labeled as nectar. You are living in a very very delusory world. Unless you wake yourself up you will continue to move from one mirage to another mirage, from one dream to another dream.

LEAVE HIS ABODE...

This abode of illusions and mirages. Leave this abode of past and future, imagination and memory, of birth and decay. Leave this abode of time, of beginnings and ends.

LEAVE THIS PIT AND MAKE FOR YOUR DESTINED
HOME.

Where is the destined home? It is within you. It is what I call falling into your own source, relaxing into your own being.

Be the truth that you are, and you will be liberated: you will be liberated from all illusions, from all mirages. Each moment, be the truth that you are. This is the message of all the buddhas and all the Sufis: Each moment, be the truth that you are. Don't hanker for anything else, don't desire anything else. Don't try to become anything, just be what you are in the moment. Relaxed, serene, utterly at home: this is the destined home.

THIS HEAP OF DUST IS A MIRAGE, WHERE FIRE SEEMS LIKE WATER.

Beware. You are surrounded by many things which are not what they appear to be. Don't be deceived by appearances. And time is slipping by: each moment an opportunity is wasted. There is a Sufi saying: Don't be inattentive to the Beloved, not even for the blink of an eye; for perhaps in that moment she will look and you will have missed Her.

Sufis call God "the Beloved." They think of God as "she," as their woman, as their beloved. Don't be inattentive to the Beloved, not even for the blink of an eye...

No moment has to be missed, because who knows what moment the destined home may have arrived? Who knows in what moment she will look at you? And if you are inattentive and lost in your imaginations of the future — of how and what you would like to be — and you are lost in memories of the past, you will go on missing.

God can be contacted only in the present moment: this moment, now and here. And only now and here. And time is fast slipping by. Every moment you lose some tremendously valuable opportunity.

As the young bachelor sat having coffee with a friend's stunning wife, she announced, "I think I'd better warn you, my husband will be home in an hour." "But I haven't done anything wrong," responded the bachelor, somewhat surprised. "I know. I thought you'd want to know how much time you have."

There is not much time, you don't have much time. Don't postpone: this is the moment. Don't say, "Tomorrow" — tomorrow is a mirage. Be alert now, be awake now, this moment, and there is serenity and there is calmness. And suddenly one is relaxed, and the source is contacted and one has arrived home.

This is the home for which you have been searching for so many lives. But your very methodology of search has been wrong. You made it a goal. And it is not a goal, it is the source.

God is not where we are going, God is from where we are coming. God is not there, God is here. God is not then, God is now.

What I have been telling you this morning is of immense value. This is my message to my sannyasins, to my Sufis: Accept yourself in tremendous gratitude. Whatsoever is is, and it can't be otherwise. So don't fight with it.

No fact ever creates any psychological pain. It is the interpretation that brings pain to you. Pain is your creation, because it is your interpretation. Change the interpretation and the same fact becomes pleasant. Drop all interpretations and the fact is simply a fact, neither painful nor pleasant. Don't choose, don't have any preferences. Just be watchful, accepting and watchful, and you have the secret key in your hands.

This will create the first unity in you, the unity with yourself. And then the second happens of it sown accord; you need not worry about it. You do the first step, the second step is taken by God himself. You move half, he moves half.

.

4 A Pearl of Exceeding Beauty

The first question:

BUDDHA DID NOT HAVE A MASTER, JESUS DID NOT
HAVE A MASTER, YOU DID NOT HAVE A MASTER.
WHY DO WE NEED A MASTER?

Devamo, because you are not yet capable of allowing life to
be your master. Because you don't know how to listen, how to
learn. Because you are incapable of learning, that's why you
need a master.

The need arises out of your insensitivity, out of your unin-
telligence. If you are intelligent then life is enough. Then there
are sermons in the stones, and every leaf of a tree is a message,
and the river going to the ocean carries all the scriptures with
it. You need not go to the Vedas and to the Koran and to the
Bible, there is no need. The whole existence is every moment
singing the song of the divine.

But you are not able to listen to it, you are not yet capable
of opening yourself to it. Hence the need of a master. The
master is only a beginning. He will teach you how to listen, he
will teach you how to be open. He will give you love so that
you can warm up – you have become too cold. Once you are
warmed up a little, there is no need for a master, then the
whole of life is the master. The master simply becomes a
jumping-board.

You say: BUDDHA DID NOT HAVE A MASTER. That is wrong – Buddha had many masters. His last master was Alar Kalam, a very rare man.

You say: JESUS DID NOT HAVE A MASTER. You don't know. He was a disciple of a great master, John the Baptist; he was initiated by him. Buddha had many, Jesus had one, and I had millions. I have been learning from all possible sources – from men, from women, from trees, from mountains. I cannot show you a particular master, because there have been so many. I have been constantly learning and listening.

And you ask: "Why do we need a master?" Your very question shows the need. If you cannot answer this simple question you will need a master. Why do you ask me? Why can't you answer it yourself? Even this question has to be answered by somebody else: the need is there.

But why has this question arisen? the need is certainly there, otherwise why should you be here? The need is there, but the reluctance to surrender is also there. Although you have become a sannyasin, still, deep down you are not yet surrendered. Hence the question.

You would like not to be a disciple. It hurts the ego, it is humiliating. You would like to be the master yourself; that is ego-satisfying. The question has not arisen because you don't need a master; the need is there, the very question says the need is there, but somewhere deep down there is resistance. You don't like it; you don't like surrendering yourself, you don't like to be bowing in trust to somebody. That hurts, that is painful.

To be a disciple needs guts. To be a disciple means one is courageous enough to dissolve oneself. It is no ordinary matter. And unless you are capable of becoming a disciple, you will never become a master.

The very word 'disciple' is beautiful; it comes from a root which means 'learning'. The disciple is one who is courageous enough to accept the fact that "I don't know, so I am ready to learn. Then from wherever the light comes, I am open to it. I will not close my windows and my doors, I will allow the wind and the sun and the rain to come in. I am ready to go on this voyage into the unknown; it is uncharted territory."

A disciple simply means one who has decided to learn. It is a great commitment to learning. And it is natural that one should start from somewhere; from some point the journey has to start – from A, from B, from C.

Let me be the point from where the journey starts. The master is not the point where the journey ends, the master is the point from where you start the journey into the unknown. He will go with you only to the point where he feels now you can go alone. Then he will leave you of his own accord.

And that is the criterion of a true master. You will not need him to leave, he will leave you of his own accord. If you leave, it will be a wrong step. If the desire to leave arises in you, that simply means you have not yet learned, you have not yet known the master. When you know the master there is no question of leaving him, because there is nobody *found* whom you can leave. There has never been anybody, from the very beginning.

When you enter into the being of the master you will find utter emptiness – a presence, certainly, but not a person whom you can leave.

The disciple can never leave the master. First he cannot leave because he is not yet capable of walking on his own, of being on his own. Secondly, he cannot leave; even when he becomes capable of going on his own he cannot leave, because there is nobody to leave. Now he knows.

But the master leaves of his own accord. He starts dropping out of your existence, he starts disappearing more and more and more, because now you are ready to go on your own.

The mother is happy when the child can walk without her support. If the mother tries to go on supporting the child for-ever, then that mother does not love the child. Then that mother is pathological and neurotic. She is crippling the child, she will be a paralysis to the child.

So is the case with a master. If a master wants you to always remain dependent on him then he is not a true master, he is pseudo and phony. The master does not need you. If he needs you in some way, if he depends on you depending on him, that means he needs you. That means somewhere your dependence on him is fulfilling his ego. He feels good: "Look how many disciples I have got." He goes on counting his disciples: "I have so many disciples, I am a great master."

Certainly he will not allow you to leave. He will prevent you from leaving, because your going means one prop to his ego disappearing. He will be dependent on you. And the master who is dependent on you, how can he help you? He himself needs the help. he himself is in confusion, in darkness. He himself is not yet capable of being alone. He has not arrived home.

But the true master will always watch when to leave you. He will be always ready, whenever you are ready to be on your own, to leave you. He will not leave you before you are ready, that is true. And only *he* can know when you are ready; you cannot know it.

Just the other day, one sannyasin wrote me a letter saying that now he feels he is capable of being on his own, that now he can go on all alone. And he wants to drop out of sannyas. I said, "That's perfectly okay."

Now he wants to see me. I said, "Why?" He wrote a letter to get last instructions from me. Now, what kind of readiness is this? If you still need instructions from me, then what kind of readiness is this to be on your own?

When you are ready I will tell you that you are ready. And the paradox is, I will tell you, "Drop the sannyas!" and you will not drop it. How can you drop it? It is the sannyas that has brought you so far.

When Sariputta became an enlightened person in his own

right, Buddha told him, "Now there is no need to bow down to me. You are in the same exalted state as I am." but Sariputta continued to bow down just the same, with no difference. Just as on the first day he had come, years before, and touched Buddha's feet, he continued to touch them. And Buddha would say to him again and again, "Sariputta, now there is no need!" And he wouldn't listen.

One day Buddha asked him, "Why don't you listen to me?" Sariputta said, "Now I am a buddha in my own right. why should I listen to you? This is something tremendously beautiful. And how can I stop bowing to you and touching your feet? It is a sweet nostalgia, it is sweet memory. It is through these feet I have come to this point; it is sheer gratitude."

Buddha sent Sariputta away. He told him, "Now go. There are millions of people stumbling in darkness: help them." and Sariputta was crying and he said, "No, don't tell me to go anywhere."

And Buddha said, "Now you are a buddha in your own right, and it doesn't suit a buddha to cry. You are capable of going on your own."

And Sariputta said, "There are no conditions on a buddha; he can cry, he can laugh. There are no conditions on a buddha, his existence is unconditional."

But he had to go, the master was insistent. He went. But every day, wherever he was, he would bow down in the direction where Buddha was. Every morning, every evening, his disciples would ask, "To whom are you bowing down?"

He said, "Buddha must be there in the east. I have information that he must be in a certain town today, so I am bowing down in that direction where he is."

This is becoming a buddha in your own right. Now here you are, and you write to me saying, "I have arrived; now I can move on my own."

So I said, "Okay, move!" Now why should you need last

instructions from me? If you still need instructions then dropping the sannyas is not because you are ready but just because you are going back. For four months you were here; it is easy to be in orange here.

Now the sannyasin is going back to Germany; it will be difficult there. And there must have been a cunning strategy behind it. You must have planned it already, before you took sannyas, that for four months while you are here you will be a sannyasin. And when you are leaving you can always say, "Now I am ready to be on my own, so I can leave." Then why the need for last instructions?

When a disciple is ready I will tell you, "Now you can move on your own." You need not tell me; your telling me is pointless. You ask me, WHY DO WE NEED A MASTER?

There must be some pain inside. Just the idea that you are a disciple, that you have to be in somebody else's hands, totally surrendered, is against the ego.

And that's why you need a master. The master is a device so that you can drop your ego. The master is just a strategy, a situation. It will be very difficult to drop the ego on your own. Who will drop whom? How will you drop your ego on your own? It will be almost impossible.

The master is just a device: you can trust the master in deep love, and you can put the ego aside. Otherwise you don't have anything else but the ego – if you put that aside, you will fall into utter emptiness. And you will not be able to fall into that abysmal, bottomless emptiness. You will become very much afraid, you will again cling to anything that you can find around you. And the ego is the closest.

It will be impossible for you to go into nothingness unless somebody is there calling you forth – from your very nothingness, somebody calling you forth, "Come on! Don't be afraid."

Once you have learned that dropping the ego is not death, once you have learned and tasted that dropping the ego is real life, that real life begins only when the ego is dropped – when you have tasted that, there will be no need of the master. but it will not be so easy to leave the master.

How can you leave somebody who has been such a transformation to you? The very idea is stupid. And there is nobody to leave; nobody is clinging to you. In fact between the master and the disciple, the relationship is one-way. The master has no relationship with you.

Listen well: don't be shocked. The master has no relationship with you. It is only YOU who need a relationship; it is just in your mind that the master exists. Otherwise there is nobody there. One day when you know the truth, the master will have disappeared.

The disciple disappears when he surrenders to the master. And when he knows nothingness, the master disappears. There's nobody leaving and nobody to be left. In that utter purity is nirvana, is enlightenment.

But it is painful. Growth is painful, and the greatest pain comes when you have to drop your idea of the self.

A parable:

Said one oyster to a neighboring oyster, "I have a very great pain within me. It is heavy and round and I am in distress."

And the other oyster replied with haughty complacence, "Praise be to the heavens and to the sea, I have no pain within me. I am well and whole both within and without."

At that moment a crab was passing by and heard the two oysters, and he said to the one who was well and whole both within and without, "Yes, you are well and whole; but the pain that your neighbor bears is a pearl of exceeding beauty."

The disciple is in a deep pain, because the ego is to be dropped and it is not easy. The ego is not like a garment that you can put off easily. The ego is like your skin, it has to be peeled and it is painful.

You have lived with the ego for so many many lives. You have changed bodies many times, but the ego is the same. It has persisted as a continuous thing in you, it is very ancient. To drop it is not easy; it is arduous, it is great agony. But only out of this agony is ecstasy born – a pearl of exceeding beauty, a state of consciousness of utter benediction. But in the beginning you will feel, "I have a very great pain within me. It is heavy and round and I am in distress."

And those who don't know the pain of disciplehood will tell you, "Praise be to the heavens and to the sea, I have no pain within me. I am well and whole both within and without."

You can go and look around: there are millions of people who have no idea what it means to be a disciple, who have never tasted anything of disciplehood, who have never surrendered to anybody, who have never loved somebody so deeply that they are ready to die form him, who have never loved anybody so intimately that they disappear into that intimacy, that they melt into that intimacy.

They will tell you that you are a little bit abnormal: "There is no need to be a disciple, and there is no need to be a master. Look at us! We are whole, within and without. We don't need a master, so why should you need a master?"

And yes, they are whole within and without, and healthy. But their health is valueless and their wholeness is of a very low order, their wholeness is very mundane. And one who wants to attain to the sacred realm will have to pass through pain – the pain of losing the mundane, the pain of being nowhere, the pain of being in limbo, the pain of losing that which you know and yet not gaining that which you desire to know. When you are just in the middle, that's where the disciple is. He is dropping that which is known, perfectly known, and trying to enter into something of which he is absolutely unaware what exactly it is.

He is going into the unknown: dropping the secure for the insecure, dropping the safe for the unsafe, dropping the so-called sanity and becoming insane.

That's what the Sufis say: Unless you become mad for God,

you will not attain to him. Madness is a must.

The disciple is mad. He has fallen in love with a master, and love makes one mad. Now nobody is going to understand you; you will be utterly incapable of logically p roving to somebody what you are doing. And it is not that you don't know logic.

My sannyasins are from the most educated classes of the world. We have all kinds of people – artists, painters, professors, scientists, psychologists, therapists, doctors, engineers – all well educated. It is not that they don't know how to argue; they are very clever in arguing. But now something has happened which is beyond argument.

And talking about your master and about the love that has arisen in you, you will look almost foolish before anybody. It is painful. But only through this pain does growth happen. This is a growth pain, and a growth pain is far more valuable than the health which does not allow growth. To be abnormal and mad is far better if growth comes through it than to be normal and sane if no growth comes through it.

The whole point is growth: you should not remain what you are. You should not remain the seed, you should burst forth into thousands of flowers. But before that the seed has to die in the soil.

The master is just a climate, a soil, in which the disciple dies. Trusting, he falls into the soil and dies. There is no way of guaranteeing your future, what will happen. How can you guarantee a seed that "It is absolutely certain that a sprout will come when you are gone. There will be great foliage and greenery and red flowers, and there will be great joy when you have died." But the seed will say, "How can I be convinced about it? Because I will not be there to witness it. What guarantee is there? Who knows? I may simply die and nothing may happen."

What can be said to the seed? It is impossible to convince the seed. But the seed falls in love with a tree which has already grown – that which was hidden has become manifest.

The seed falls in love with the flowers and the fragrance of the tree, and the seed asks, "What is the way? How can I become like you?"

That's what the meaning of being a disciple is. You come close to a buddha and you see the flowers and the fragrance and you ask the Buddha, "How can I become like you?"

And Buddha says, "I died, that's how I became like this. You must also die."

And seeing the Buddha and the fragrance and the silence and the calmness, a trust arises, a love arises. And the seed risks: the seed dies by the side of the great tree. And one day there is a sprout. But there is no logical way to convince anybody, unless you are already convinced through your love.

So it is not a question of my convincing you to become disciples; there is no way to do it. It is by your being convinced through your own love that you become a disciple. And yes, it is painful, Devamo. But all growth is painful.

Go through this pain. Let this ego be gone completely, howsoever painful it is. It is better to be miserable in insecurity than to be miserable in security, because one who is miserable in security will not grow. And growth is the highest value there is. Man is potential God: the God has to be realized.

And much will have to be dropped. You will have to be unburdened of much, only then can you reach to that sunlit peak. The higher you go, the more will have to be dropped, because everything will become a weight on you and a hindrance on the journey. You can reach to the peak only when all that you were has been dropped on the way.

You will reach to the peak only as a nothingness, a nobody. And it is painful, I know it. And I'm trying to create a climate here, an energy-field, so that you can go through the pain as joyously as possible.

The second question:

BELOVED MASTER, TELL ME THE WAY FROM
SEXUALITY TO LOVE.

Amit Prem, sex is beautiful, sexuality ugly. And the differ-
ence has to be understood. Sex is a natural phenomenon;
sexuality is unnatural, abnormal and pathological. When sex
becomes cerebral, when sex enters into your head, it becomes
sexuality.

Now, the head is not the center for sex. That is getting into
a confusion, it is getting upside-down, it is getting deranged.
Sex is not the function of the head. But when sex enters in
through the head it becomes sexuality. Then you *think* about
sex, then you fantasize about sex. And the more you think, the
more you fantasize about it, the more you will get into trou-
ble. Then nothing real will ever satisfy you, because there is no
limitation on fantasy, and reality *is* limited.

For example, if you start thinking too much about sex you
can create beautiful women, women which exist only in your
fantasy; you will never find them anywhere in the world. Or
men: you will never come across them. No real woman or
man will ever satisfy you, because of the fantasy. No real man
or woman can fulfill your expectations of fantasy. Fantasy is
fantasy; it is a dream.

You can fantasize a woman who does not perspire, whose
body has no body smell. You can fantasize a woman who is al-
ways sweet and never bitter. You can fantasize a woman who is
always loving and warm and welcoming and never nags you
and is never angry, never throws pillows at you. You can fanta-
size a woman who never ages, who remains always stuck at
eighteen years of age – who is always fresh, always young,
always beautiful, never falls ill, never makes any demands on
you, never betrays you, never looks at any other man with
longing, with desire. You can fantasize to no limit, but you will
not find this woman anywhere. Now you have created a prob-
lem: you are no more naturally attuned to your sex.

Nature is perfectly capable of being fulfilled, but fantasy cannot be fulfilled. You may find your woman in girlie magazines, in pornographic books, but you will not find her in reality. And whosoever you do find in reality will fall short.

That is the problem the West is facing; it has fantasized too much about sex. The West has become sexual through fantasy, the East has become sexual through repression. Both have become sexual and both have lost the natural capacities of enjoying sex. Both have become pathological, through different routes. The West has become pathological by fantasizing sex to be the ultimate goal of life, and the East has become pathological by thinking that sex is the ultimate barrier between God and man.

Sex is neither. Neither is it the ultimate goal nor the ultimate barrier. Sex is a simple phenomenon like hunger or thirst; there is nothing more to it. It is not what the Eastern mind has been thinking about it. The Eastern mind is too afraid of sex. Out of fear, sex has moved into the head; through the door of fear it has entered into the head.

So the Eastern so-called saints are simply fantasizing about sex, because they have repressed it. And that which you repress goes on coming up again and again. It cannot be destroyed; nothing can ever be destroyed by repression. Repression makes sex pathological sexuality. This is one extreme.

The West has moved to another extreme. The other extreme is, fantasize about it. Sex is all, everything else is secondary, so have as much sex as you can. You cannot really have too much sex, there are limitations to the body. But you can fantasize as much as you want, there is no limitation to it.

So pornography exists, blue films exist, girlie magazines exist. And people are being fed on these illusory mirages. Then no real woman, no real man, will ever satisfy you.

These are both pathological states. Sexuality is pathological, whether you come to it through fear or greed does not matter. The East has become ill through fear, the West has become ill through greed. Greed and fear are two aspects of the same coin. So on the surface it looks very different, as if the Eat and the West are poles apart. They are not. Those who know, those who can see, they can see that it is the same foolishness, the same stupidity. They have arrived at the same stupidity from different doors, that is true, but they have entered into the same place. And both have to be awakened, and both have to be made more enlightened about sex.

Don't make much fuss about sex *either* way. That is the first fundamental. If you want sex to become love, the first fundamental is: accept sex as an absolutely natural phenomenon. Don't bring your metaphysics to it, don't bring your religion to it. It has nothing to do with religion or metaphysics, it is a simple fact of life. It is a way that life reproduces itself. It is as simple as the trees bringing flowers and fruits: you don't condemn the flowers. Flowers are sex energy; it is through the flowers that the tree is sending its seeds, its potentiality, to reproduce other trees.

When a peacock dances you don't condemn it. But the dance is sex; it is to attract the female. When the cuckoo calls you don't condemn it; it is sex. The cuckoo is simply declaring, "I am ready." The cuckoo is simply calling forth the woman. The sound, the beautiful sound, is just a seduction; it is courtship.

If you watch life you will be surprised. The whole of life is through sex. Life reproduces itself through sex, it is a natural phenomenon. Don't drag unnecessary rationalizations into it.

This is the first thing to be understood if you ever want any transformation of sex energy. The first thing is: don't deny it, don't reject it, don't repress it. Don't be too greedy about it, don't think that this is all – this is not. There is much more to life. And sex is beautiful, yet there is still much more to life. Sex is only the foundation, it is not the whole temple.

Repressed, it becomes sexuality. Fantasized, it becomes sexuality. One is an Eastern way of transforming sex into

pathology, the other is a Western way. But nobody, either in
the East or in the West, accepts that sex is a simple natural phe-
nomenon. Neither the saints nor the sinners, nobody accepts
sex to be a simple natural phenomenon. Both are obsessed
with it, hence I say both are not different. Sex accepted,
respected, lived, becomes love.

Just as I was saying to you the other day, when sadness is
there, accept it: it is you. Don't say, "I am sad." Say, "I am sad-
ness." Don't say, "I have sadness" – it is as if you are separate
and sadness is something that you have. Simply say, "I am sad-
ness." In that moment there is no division between you and
what you call sadness. In that moment you *are* sadness. The
next moment you may be peace, and still the next moment
you may be joy.

Life is change. Life knows only one thing as permanent,
and that is change. Only change is unchanging; everything else
changes except change. That means only change has eternity. It
is a continuum; you are not a fixed thing. And it is good that
you are not fixed, otherwise you would have been a thing, a
commodity in the marketplace. You are a no-thing. You are not
a fixed phenomenon; you are a constant opening, you are
change.

One moment there is sadness, and the river takes a turn.
Another moment there is joy, and the river takes still another
turn and there is peace. And it goes on and on. The moment
has to be accepted in its totality: it is you. When there is sex,
there is sex: it is you. Don't say, "I have a sexual desire." That is
a way of dividing yourself, that is a way of creating a split.

If you have a sexual desire then there are two possibilities. If
you are against it repress it: that is the Eastern way of becom-
ing mad, insane and pathological. The other way is, "I have the
sex desire: how to enhance it? How to make it more intense?
How to enjoy it to the optimum?" That is the way of greed,
the Western way. But the end is the same, the end-product is
the same: both become obsessed with it.

Just let it be, whatsoever it is. It is you. You don't have a sex desire; if you have a sex desire then something can be done to the sex desire. If you are it, nothing can be done about it, because there is nobody else to do anything: you *are* it.

This has to become the meditation of all my sannyasins: you are it, there is no division. Just see the beauty of it. When there is no division there is no conflict. When there is no division there is no fear, no greed. It is division that brings fear and greed. Greed and fear are your interpretations of the division, but the division is first and then come your interpretations.

The sex desire is there, you take it as something separate that is happening to you. It is like a thing in your hands: now you have to decide whether you want more or less of it, as if it is something of which you can have more or less. It is as it is; there is no more, no less.

Simply live it, be it, love it. This is your moment, this is the truth of the moment. And never compare, because one moment ago it was not there. So don't start comparing, because comparison again brings a split. Next moment it may be gone again. Don't compare. Life is change. That's what Buddha said: Life is change.

That's what Heraclitus said: You cannot step in the same river twice. Life, the river, is constantly moving.

Deep down you want life to be static. Why? Because with a static and dormant life you will be more safe, more secure. But life is not dormant, only death is dormant. Life is dynamic, flowing – the more flowing it is, the more alive you are. Life is not a stagnant pool, it is a river. It is the Ganges, coming from the Himalayas, going to the ocean, coming from the heights, going to the depths. And again from the ocean the Ganges will evaporate from the depths to the heights, and again the clouds will gather on the Himalayas and again the river will be born. It is a beautiful perfect circle.

That's how you move. Each moment has to be accepted as it is, with no condemnation, with no evaluation. And when you can accept sex as natural, it stops being cerebral. It drops from the head, it goes to the sex center where it belongs. If sex remains in the sex center it is beautiful. If it goes to the head it is ugly.

Eating is beautiful. You are hungry and you eat and it is needed; it is nourishment. But then there are two types of people. A few people eat too much: eating too much means the head has entered into it. When you are eating, the body is always sane. The body always says to you, "Stop now." It immediately gives you an indication, a signal: "It is enough, now stop! No more is needed, my needs are fulfilled."

But the head says, "It is so tasty, it is so delicious – have one plate more." It is the head, it is not the body. The body is recoiling, the body is saying, "No!" The body is always sane.

And this is one of the fundamentals I would like to tell you about. Down the ages, your so-called saints have been telling you that the body is your enemy. It is not; the body is always your friend. If there is some enemy it is the head, never the body. The body is always sane.

Watch it. I am not talking philosophy, I am simply stating a fact. See for yourself: if you are ill the body says, "Don't eat." But the head says, "If you don't eat you will become weak. So many vitamins are absolutely needed; you will become pale, you will not be strong." This is the head. The body is saying, "You are ill, and to eat will be unnecessarily burdening the system. The system needs rest; it is better not to eat."

And that's what animals do. No animal will eat when he is ill; he simply stops eating. That's what children do, no children will eat. But grown-ups will force them: they will say, "Eat, otherwise you will become ill, you will become more weak. You need it." They force them. You can see small children crying and their mothers forcing them: "Eat a little more." It is the head that creates the trouble.

And then there are people who will fast when there is no need for fasting. The body is hungry, but if you are a Jaina and the *paryushana*, your religious days, have come, you have to fast. The body is hungry and the body wants food, but you cannot eat because unfortunately you are a Jaina and the religious days are there and if you eat you will be thrown into hellfire.

It is the head interfering. The body says, "Eat," but unfortunately you are a Mohammedan and it is the month of *Ramadan* and you have to fast. Now this is the head interfering.

The head interferes in two ways: either it makes you indulgent or it makes you repressive. Again, one is the Eastern way, another is the Western way. Eat more than is needed: this is indulgence. Don't eat when the body needs food: this is fasting, this is repression.

It is always the head that interferes. It interferes in your food, it interferes in your sex, it interferes in your sleep, it goes on interfering in everything!

Remember the Zen master, the great Zen master, Bokuju. Somebody asked him, "What is your discipline?" He said, "No discipline at all. When I feel hungry I eat, and when I feel sleepy I sleep. And no other discipline." The man said, "But this is what we all do." And Bokuju said, "No. It is very rare to find a person who does it, because one who does it becomes a buddha. Only a buddha can do it truly."

You don't eat according to the needs of the body, you don't sleep according to the needs of the body. You go on imposing your head needs on the body. That interference makes everything pathological. That's how sex is disturbed and becomes sexuality. If sex is accepted, respected, lived, it becomes love.

Amit Prem, you ask: TELL ME THE WAY FROM SEXUALITY TO LOVE.

The way is: first sexuality has to come back to sex. Directly, there is no way, no route; from sexuality to love there is no route. There is simply no route, nothing can be done about it. From sexuality to love there is no route, because sexuality is in the head, and love is a heart phenomenon.

From sexuality come back to the sex center. From sex to

love there is a direct route; they are bridged. In fact nothing needs to be done. Just live your sex moments with utter joy, silence, peacefulness, with celebration. Live your sex moments meditatively, and meditation transforms sex into love.

Not only does sex become love: one day it becomes prayer, worship. It goes higher and higher. The highest form is prayer, the lowest form is sex. Between the two is love, love is the bridge. And sexuality is abnormal, it is pathological, it is ill. So whether you have chosen a path of being pathological like the Eastern people or like the Western people, it doesn't matter.

Accept your life a sit is, and let the acceptance be as total as possible. When you don't fight with yourself your energy starts falling into a subtle harmony. And that harmony brings you to love. And when the harmony becomes more and more refined, it brings you to prayer. And unless sex has become prayer, remember, the goal has not been achieved.

The third question:

WHY DO THE SUFIS SAY THAT MAN IS A MACHINE?

Man is a machine, that's why. Man as he is is utterly uncon-scious. He is nothing but his habits, the sum total of his habits. Man is a robot. Man is not yet man: unless consciousness en-ters into your being, you will remain a machine.

That's why the Sufis say man is a machine. It is from the Sufis that Gurdjieff introduced the idea to the West that man is a machine. It is very rarely that you are conscious. In your whole seventy years' life, if you live the ordinary so-called life – healthy and whole within and without, with no pain of growth, with no pain within you of a growing pearl of exceed-ing beauty – then you will not know even seven moments of awareness in your whole life.

And even if you know those seven moments or less, they will be only accidental. For example, you may know a moment of awareness if somebody suddenly comes and puts a revolver on your heart. In that moment, your thinking, your habitual thinking, stops. For a moment you become aware, because it is so dangerous, you cannot remain ordinarily asleep.

In some dangerous situation you become aware. Otherwise you remain fast asleep. You are perfectly skillful at doing your things mechanically.

Just stand by the side of the road and watch people, and you will be able to see that they are all walking in their sleep. All are sleep-walkers, somnambulists. And so are you.

Two bums were arrested and charged with a murder that had been committed in the neighborhood. The jury found them guilty and the judge sentenced them to hang by their necks until dead and God have mercy on their souls.

The two bore up pretty well until the morning of the day set for the execution arrived. As they were being prepared for the gallows, one turned to the other and said, "Dam' me if I ain't about off my nut. I can't get my thoughts together. Why, I don't even know what the day of the week is." "This is a Monday," said the other bum. "Monday? My Gawd! What a rotten way to start the week!"

Just watch yourself. Even to the very point of death, people go on repeating old habitual patterns. Now there is going to be no week; the morning has come when they are to be hanged. But just the old habit – somebody says it is Monday, and you say, "Monday? My God! What a rotten way to start the week!"

Man reacts. That's why the Sufis say man is a machine. Unless you start responding, unless you become responsible.... Reaction comes out of the past, responses comes out of the present moment. Response is spontaneous, reaction is just old habit.

Just watch yourself. Your woman says something to you:

then whatsoever you say, watch, ponder over it. Is it just a reaction? And you will be surprised: ninety-nine percent of your acts are not acts, because they are not responses, they are just mechanical. Just mechanical.

It has been happening again and again: you say the same thing and your woman reacts the same way, and then you react, and it ends in the same thing again and again. You know it, she knows it, everything is predictable. I have heard:

"Pop," said a boy of ten, "how do wars get started?"

"Well, son," began Pop, "let's say America quarreled with England..."

"America's not quarreling with England," interrupted Mother.

"Who said she was?" said Pop, visibly irritated. "I merely was giving the boy a hypothetical instance."

"Ridiculous!" snorted Mother. "You'll put all sorts of wrong ideas in his head."

"Ridiculous, nothing!" countered Pop. "If he listens to you he'll never have any ideas at all in his head."

Just as the dish-throwing stage approached, the son spoke up again. "Thanks Mom, thanks Pop. I'll never have to ask how wars get started again."

Just watch yourself. The things that you are doing, you have done so many times. The ways you react, you have been reacting always. In the same situation you always do the same thing. You are feeling nervous and you take out your cigarette and you start smoking. It is a reaction; whenever you have felt nervous you have done it.

You are a machine. It is just a built-in program in you now: you feel nervous, your hand goes into the pocket, the packet comes out. It is almost like a machine doing things. You take the cigarette out, you put the cigarette in your mouth, you light the cigarette, and this is all going on mechanically. This has been done millions of times, and you are doing it again.

And each time you do this it is strengthened; the machine

becomes more mechanical, the machine becomes more skill-ful. The more you do it, the less awareness is needed to do it.

This is why the Sufis say man functions as a machine. Unless you start destroying these mechanical habits.... Sufis have many methods to destroy them. For example, they teach many devices. They say: Do something just contrary to what you have always done.

Try it. You come home, you are afraid, you are as late as ever, and the wife will be there ready to quarrel with you. And you are planning how to answer, what to say – that there was too much work in the office, and this and that. And she knows all that you are planning, and she knows what you are going to say if she asks why you are late. And you know if you say that you are late because there was too much work she is not going to believe it either. She has never believed it. She may have already checked; she may have phoned the office, she may have already inquired where you are.

But, still, this is just a pattern. The Sufis say: Today go home and behave totally differently. The wife asks you, "Where have you been?" And you say, "I was with a woman making love." And then see what happens. She will be shocked! She will not know what to say, she will not even have any way to find words to express it. For a moment she will be completely lost, because no reaction, no old pattern, is applicable.

Or maybe, if she has become too much of a machine, she will say, "I don't believe you!" – just as she has never believed you. "You must be joking!" Every day you come home...

I have heard about a psychoanalyst who was telling his pa-tient – must have been giving him a Sufi device – "Today when you go home..." because the patient was complaining again and again. "I am always afraid of going home. My wife looks so miserable, so sad, always in despair, that my heart starts sinking. I want to escape from the home."

The psychologist said, "Maybe you are the cause of it. Do something: today take flowers and ice cream and sweets for the woman, and when she opens the door hug her, give her a good kiss. And then immediately start helping her: clean the table and the pots and the floor. Do something absolutely new that you have never done before."

The idea was appealing and the man tried it. He went home. The moment the wife opened the door and saw flowers and ice cream and sweets, and this beaming man who had never been laughing hugged her, she could not believe what was happening! She was in an utter shock, she could not believe her eyes: maybe this is somebody else! She had to look again.

And then when he kissed her and immediately just started cleaning the table and went to the sink and started washing the pots, the woman started crying. When he came out he said, "Why are you crying?" She said, "Have you gone mad? I always suspected one day or other you would go mad. Now it has happened. Why don't you go and see a psychiatrist?"

Sufis have such devices. They say: Act totally differently, and not only will others be surprised, *you* will be surprised. And just in small things. For example, when you are nervous you walk fast. Don't walk fast, go very slow and see. You will be surprised that it doesn't fit, that your whole mechanical mind immediately says, "What are you doing? You have never done this!" And if you walk slowly you will be surprised: nervousness disappears, because you have brought in something new.

These are the methods of Vipassana and Zazen. If you go deep into them the fundamentals are the same. When you are doing Vipassana walking, you have to walk more slowly than you have ever walked before, so slowly that it is absolutely new. The whole feeling is new, and the reactive mind cannot function. It cannot function because it has no program for it; it simply stops functioning.

That's why in Vipassana you feel so silent watching the breath. You have always breathed but you have never watched it; this is something new. When you sit silently and just watch you breath – coming in, going out, coming in, going out – the mind feels puzzled: what are you doing? Because you have never done it. It is so new that the mind cannot supply an immediate reaction to it. Hence it falls silent.

The fundamental is the same. Whether Sufi or Buddhist or Hindu or Mohammedan is not the question. If you go deep into meditation's fundamentals then the essential thing is one: how to de-automatize you.

Gurdjieff used to do very bizarre things to his disciples. Somebody would come who had always been a vegetarian, and he would say, "Eat meat." Now, it is the same fundamental – this man is just a little too much of himself, a little eccentric. He would say, "Eat meat." Now, watch a vegetarian eating meat. The whole body wants to throw it out and he wants to vomit, and the whole mind is puzzled and disturbed and he starts perspiring, because the mind has no way to cope with it.

That's what Gurdjieff wanted to see, how you would react to a new situation. To the man who had never taken any alcohol Gurdjieff would say, "Drink. Drink as much as you can."

And to the man who had been drinking alcohol Gurdjieff would say, "Stop for one month. Completely stop."

He wanted to create some situation which is so new for the mind that the mind simply falls silent; it has no answer for it, no ready-made answer for it. The mind functions in a parrot-like way.

That's why Zen masters will hit the disciple sometimes. That is again the same fundamental. Now, when you go to a master you don't expect a buddha to hit you, or do you? When you go to Buddha you go with expectations that he will be compassionate and loving, that he will shower love and put his hand on your head. And this buddha gives you a hit – takes his staff and hits you hard on the head. Now, it is so shocking: a buddha, hitting you? For a moment the mind stops; it has no idea what to do, it does not function.

And that nonfunctioning is the beginning. Sometimes a person has become enlightened just because the master did something absurd.

People have expectations, people live through expectations. They don't know that masters don't fit with any kind of expectations.

India was accustomed to Krishna and Rama and people like that. Then came Mahavira, he stood naked. You cannot think of Krishna standing naked; he was always wearing beautiful clothes, as beautiful as possible. He was one of the most beautiful persons ever; he used to wear ornaments made of gold and diamonds.

And then suddenly there is Mahavira. What did Mahavira mean by being naked? He shocked the whole country: he helped many people because of that shock.

Each master has to decide how to shock. Now, in India they have not known a man like me for centuries. So whatsoever I do, whatsoever I say, is a shock. The whole country goes into shock; a great shiver runs through the spine of the whole country. I really enjoy it, because they cannot think....

I have just received a letter saying, "We always thought that you were above politics. Then why have you started speaking on politics?" That's why, because I am above it. Who else can speak about it? Those who are in it, they cannot speak about it – they are partisans.

The man who is on the hilltop has a far better vision of the valley down below. The bird who is on the wing can see all that is happening on the earth; he has more perspective, more vision.

I can see in a better way, because I am no more part of the valley. I can see what is happening in the valley, I can see what is happening in New Delhi, because I am far above it. But the Indian mind has its accustomed expectations. A saint is not supposed to speak about politics. But a saint in fact never follows anybody's expectations.

I am not here to fulfill your expectations. If I fulfill your expectations I will never be able to transform you. I am here to destroy all your expectations, I am here to shock you. And in those shocking experiences your mind will stop. You will not be able to figure it out: and that is the point where something new enters you.

So once in a while I say something which Indians think should not be said. But who are you to decide what I should say and what I should not say? And naturally, when something goes against their expectations they immediately react according to their old conditionings.

Those who react according to their old conditionings miss the point. Those who don't react according to the old conditionings fall silent, get into a new space.

I am talking to my disciples: I am trying to hit them, this way and that. It is all deliberate. When I criticize Morarji Desai it is not so much about Morarji Desai. It is much more about the Morarji Desai in *you*, because everybody has the politician within them. Hitting Morarji Desai I have hit the Morarji Desai in you, the politician within you.

Everybody has the politician in them. The politician means the desire to dominate, the desire to be number one. The politician means ambition, the ambitious mind. And when I hit Morarji Desai, if you feel hit and you start thinking, "This man cannot be a really enlightened person, otherwise why should he be hitting Morarji Desai so hard?" you are simply rationalizing. You have nothing to do with Morarji Desai: you are saving your own Morarji Desai inside, you are trying to protect your own politician.

I have nothing to do with Morarji Desai. What can I have to do with poor Morarji Desai? But I have everything to do with the politician within you.

The Sufis say man is a machine because man only reacts according to the programs that have been fed to him. Start behaving responsively, and then you are not a machine. And when you are not a machine you are a man: then the man is born.

Watch, become alert, observe, and go on dropping all the reactive patterns in you. Each moment try to respond to the reality – not according to the ready-made idea in you but according to the reality as it is there outside. Respond to the reality! Respond with your total consciousness but not with your mind.

And then when you respond spontaneously and you don't react, action is born. Action is beautiful, reaction is ugly. Only a man of awareness acts, the man of unawareness *reacts*. Action liberates. Reaction goes on creating the same chains, goes on making them thicker and harder and stronger. Live a life of response and not of reaction.

The fourth question:

OSHO, I AM SO TERRIBLY UGLY, AND I HAVE
SUFFERED MUCH BECAUSE OF IT.
WHAT SHOULD I DO?

Become a politician! Just the other day, Subhuti sent me the report of a survey done in a London school of researchers, the London Polytechnic. The survey says that ugly and stupid-looking people have more poll appeal. They have researched into it, and this is a very strange conclusion – strange but true.

Ugly, stupid-looking, unintelligent people have poll appeal. why? Because they look so like the masses, the masses think they belong to them. The beautiful person, the intelligent-looking person, immediately is felt as belonging to the aristoc-racy. Naturally – he is not of the masses, he belongs to the leisured class. The masses feel him as the enemy.

Now, you ask: I AM SO TERRIBLY UGLY...

Use it, this is a great opportunity: become a politician. And particularly in India, you can see all kinds of ugly people. It is very rare to find a politician who is intelligent-looking, beautiful, handsome, who has some grace and charm. No – the uglier you are, the more is the possibility of your becoming the representative of the masses, because the masses will feel some affinity with you, a deep affinity and accord. You belong to them, they belong to you. You are one of them.

Maybe that is one of the causes of why Indira Gandhi lost the last elections. She has a subtle beauty and grace. She was the only politician in India who looked graceful and intelligent; she has been replaced by very ugly people. But this may be the psychological reason: she is aristocratic.

And the revolt that has happened in India may be a proof for this survey being done in the London Polytechnic.

Her father was a beautiful man, one of the most beautiful men in the world. He dominated Indian politics; then she came into power. She is aristocratic. And, slowly slowly, the masses started feeling as if the country is still not ruled by them, by their people. Now they have chosen very dull, placid people, old and rotten. And they have chosen them for a certain reason: they fit perfectly well with the masses, they are exactly like the masses. Now they are not going to help this country, because a country can be helped only by intelligent people.

But remember always: in the world, the more socialism has been talked about, the more all kinds of aristocratic people have lost their grip on world affairs. They could have helped. Remember, there are many kinds of aristocracies. It is not only a question of riches and birth, the person who has a higher IQ belongs to an aristocracy of intelligence. And if the idea spreads that everybody is equal, when in truth nobody is equal.... There are people who have very low IQs and there are people who have high IQs and they are not equal, they are as far apart as people can be.

There are ugly people and there are beautiful people: these

again are aristocracies. And if the idea spreads...which it *has*; it has gone into the world. Marx created one of the greatest myths, the myth of equality. People are not equal. But once the idea has spread then there is great jealousy. Whoever is above you has to be pulled own, he has to be made equal, because all are equal. And if they are not, they have to be made equal.

The world is, by and by, slowly slowly, becoming dominated by the lower intelligence. It is happening all over the world. And the lower intelligence cannot solve the problems. The lower intelligence is incapable of solving the problems, the problems are too big. It needs intelligence to solve them, it needs great intelligence to solve them; the problems are very complicated. It is not a question of equality. The world will have to listen to the intelligent people, the world will have to listen to the people who have vision, who can create a future.

But whenever somebody wants to create a new future, it goes against the habits of the masses, their old traditions, their old superstitions. So whosoever is ready and willing to accept those superstitions and traditions will easily become the dominant politician, will become powerful.

That's how it has happened in India, that's how it is happening all over the world. The people who can easily accommodate themselves to the superstitious masses and who *look* like the masses, they will have more power. That is very dangerous, but that seems to be happening more and more and the world is coming closer and closer to a catastrophe. It can be avoided only if intelligent people are listened to. If people who have some grace, who have some silence in them, who have tasted something of the no-mind, if they are heard the world can be saved, humanity can be saved. Otherwise it cannot be saved. This is really a difficult problem. How to tackle it? Because they will not be heard; the masses will feel that they are against them.

For example, I cannot be listened to in this country. what I am saying can open doors of great riches to this country. What

I am saying can transform all its miseries and problems into opportunities. But what I am saying goes against the superstitions, what I am saying goes against the traditions. If they listen to me they will have to go against their superstitions, which is difficult. If they listen to their traditions and their superstitions they will follow Morarji Desai and people like that. But they cannot solve the problems.

That's where Indira got into trouble, she tried to solve the problems. She *dared* to do something drastic to change the situation of this country. But then it was too much against the people and their tradition and their superstitions. It was too much against their old mind: they rebelled against her.

You ask me: I AM SO TERRIBLY UGLY AND I HAVE SUFFERED MUCH BECAUSE OF THAT. WHAT SHOULD I DO?

What I have been saying, I was just joking – please don't become a politician! There are ugly people, so many ugly people, enough; you need not worry about them. You ask me: WHAT SHOULD I DO?

Ugliness has nothing to do with your body. Neither has beauty much to do with the body. The beauty or the ugliness of the body is very superficial; the real thing comes from within. If you can become beautiful within, you will become luminous. It has happened many times: even an ugly person, when he becomes meditative, starts looking beautiful.

This I have watched continuously, hear in and year out. When people come here they have totally different faces. When they start meditating, when they start dancing, when they start singing, their faces relax. Their tensions drop. Their misery, which had become part of their face, slowly slowly wars off. They become relaxed like children. Their faces start gleaming with a new inner joy, they become luminous.

Physical beauty and ugliness is not very important. The real thing is the inner. I can teach you how to be beautiful from within, and that is real beauty. Once it is there, your physical form won't matter much. Your eyes will start shining with joy; your face will have a gleam, a glory. The form will become immaterial. When something starts flowing from within you, some grace, then the outer form is just put aside. Comparatively it loses all significance: don't be worried about it.

And whatsoever I have been saying was just a joke. Don't become a politician, because if you become a politician you will become more ugly. It works both ways: ugly people become politicians, and politicians become more ugly. It will be impossible for you not to become more ugly, because the whole world of politics is one of continuous quarrel, continuous violence, continuous competition. It will make you more tense, it will make you more graceless, it will make you more and more insipid and dull. Because only dullards can succeed in the world of politics.

I would suggest to the researchers of the London Polytechnic that this is only half the story: please work to find the other half too. This is the half which finds that political success is more possible for ugly and unintelligent-looking people. The other half is that those who become politicians become more and more ugly, more and more unintelligent-looking. They have to, because whatsoever makes you successful, you have to practice it more – naturally, obviously. whatsoever helps you to succeed will become your very style of life. That is the other half of the story, that politicians become ugly.

Meditate, love, dance, sing, celebrate here with me, and the ugliness will disappear. Bring something higher into yourself, and the lower will be forgotten, because it is all comparative, it is all relative. If you can bring something higher into yourself.... It is as if there is a small candle burning in the room: bring a bigger light into the room and the small candle simply loses all significance.

Bring the beauty of the within, which is easier. With the other beauty I cannot help much; I am not a plastic surgeon. You can find some plastic surgeon who can help you, but that will not help in any way. You may have a little longer nose, better shaped, but that will not help anything much. If you remain the same inside, your outer beauty will simply show your inner ugliness; it will become a contrast. Bring some inner beauty.

That's what we are doing here. Sannyas is the science of bringing inner beauty, inner beatitude, inner benediction. Let God shower on you, and the body is completely forgotten. The body becomes compost and your whole life becomes a garden and great flowers, golden flowers, bloom in you.

5 The Fire Test

Life exists through duality. The very process of life depends on polar opposites. Life is like a river: for the river to exist, two banks are needed. The river cannot exist without two banks to support it, just as the bird cannot fly without two wings and you cannot walk without two legs.

Life needs duality. Everywhere you will find it, till the ultimate arrives. The ultimate, the absolute, or call it God, transcends duality. But then life disappears. Then you become invisible. Then you have no form, no name; then you have gone beyond. That is nirvana.

These two things have to be understood: life cannot exist without polar opposites. Life is a dialectical process – between man and woman, between darkness and light, between life and death, between good and bad. Life cannot exist without this duality; manifestation is not possible without duality.

Hence, another vision becomes possible to be understood: if duality disappears, life as you know it disappears. Life in time and space disappears. Then another door opens. You move to another plane: the plane of the invisible, the plane of the mysterious, the plane where there is no form, no name. All remains, but unmanifest. That is called nirvana, moksha: the ultimate state of samadhi where all disappears.

If duality is the way of life, then nonduality is the way of religion – because religion is nothing but an art of transcending the manifested form and going into the unmanifest, going to the original source from where we come and for which we long. Because we belong there. Wherever we are we cannot feel at home; something remains unfulfilled. We go on missing the original source, because only in the source is rest.

Today's sutras are of immense value. Meditate over each word:

THE PURE MAN UNITES TWO IN ONE;
THE LOVER UNITES THREE IN ONE.

The gnostic tradition says there are two paths to transcend duality, to transcend multiplicity, to transcend this constant conflict between life and death. The first path is called by the gnostics *via purgativa:* 'through purity'. And the second path is called *via unitiva:* 'through unity'. The first is the path of meditation, the second the path of love. The first is Zen, the second is Sufism.

On the path of meditation, one has to eliminate, one has to empty oneself totally. On the path of love, just the reverse process has to be followed: one has to become more and more full. One has to become so full that one starts overflowing.

On the path of meditation, one has to become so empty that nothing remains, one is just a pure nothingness. That's why Buddha says that there is no soul. He says in the ultimate experience, nothing is found; only nothing is found. It is utter emptiness, state of no-self: *anatta*. Hence he has called it nirvana. Nirvana means "putting out a candle" – the ego just disappears as if you have put out a candle. Nothing remains.

Only when nothing remains is there purity. If something is there, that is impurity. When on the mirror there is nothing then the mirror is pure: no reflection, no dust, no content in the consciousness. Nothing remains to be known – then one is pure. This is *via purgativa*: go on eliminating.

The Upanishads say, "*neti-neti*: this is not That, that too is not That, neither this nor that." Go on denying, go on negating, go on eliminating, until nothing remains. And when you have arrived at that utter emptiness, that is the goal. Then all is peace, all is silence. One has moved beyond duality, beyond multiplicity.

In this state, the observer becomes the observed. There is no distinction between the observer and the observed. Hence J. Krishnamurti's famous statement, "The observer is the observed": it is the very essence of meditation. Then there are not two – neither the knower nor the known, no subject, no object. Only one is there. But you cannot even call it one, because there is nobody to call it one. One is there, but utterly quiet and calm. One is there, but there is nobody to declare it. One is there, but as if all is absent, not present.

This is what Hakim Sanai says:

THE PURE MAN UNITES TWO IN ONE...

The observer and the observed. "The pure man" means the man of meditation. "The pure man" means one who has been trying the path of *via purgativa* – who has been simply emptying himself of all that is foreign and who goes on eliminating all that is not his essential self. And then nothing is left in the hand.

That's what Zen people say, that man is like an onion: you go on peeling, layer upon layer, go on peeling, and finally nothing is left. But that's what the search is. When the hands are empty, nothing is left, you have arrived. Now there can be no misery, because there is nobody to be miserable. Now there can be no pain, because there is nobody to feel pain. Now there is neither knowledge nor ignorance, because there is no knower. Now there is neither bondage nor liberation, because there is nobody to be bound or to be liberated. All is gone, all has disappeared. You have fallen back into the source.

The manifest is there no more; you have become unmanifest. In this state you are neither man nor woman, in this state you are neither happy nor unhappy, because those are all parts of the dual world: happy/unhappy, man/woman, beautiful/ugly, good/bad. That is all gone. You are neither good nor bad. There is no Devil now, and no God – that is part of duality, the same duality. And in duality there is always tension, in duality there is always conflict. In duality there is always the other.

And the Zen people will agree with Jean-Paul Sartre when he says, "The other is hell." The Zen people will also say, "Yes, the other is hell, the other has to disappear. But the other can disappear only if you also disappear." "I" and "thou" exist as two aspects of the same coin. If "thou" disappears "I" disappears, if "I" disappears "thou" disappears. They cannot exist separately; they are part of one phenomenon. So there is neither "I" nor "thou."

That's why Buddha would not say anything about the soul or God. His is the purest path of meditation. And this has been a very confusing thing to others who don't understand the path of purity. Buddha called it *visuddha marga*. That has exactly the same meaning as *via purgativa*: the path of purity.

Christians, Hindus and Mohammedans cannot understand what Buddha is trying to say. No God, no soul – then what is religion? And Buddha says this state of no God and no soul is religion. Christians or Mohammedans or Hindus cannot conceive of what kind of religion he is talking about, because they think of religion as something centered on the idea of God. Without God how can there be religion?

But there is a religion, Jainism, which is without God. Jainas agree so far with Buddha, that there is no God. But when Buddha says there is no soul, even Jainas don't agree. They say, "Without a soul how can there be a religion?" Christians, Hindus and Mohammedans say, "Without God and the soul there can be no religion; those two are essential." And Buddha says, "Unless those two are dropped, you don't enter into the world of religion. Those two are the barriers."

Jainas say, "God can be dropped, it is an unnecessary

hypothesis. Just purify yourself, that's all. There is no need for God, there is no need for prayers, just meditation will do. You go on purifying." They agree with Buddha halfway. And they also agree with Hindus and Mohammedans and Christians halfway.

That's why in India although Buddhism and Jainism were born together, Hindus destroyed Buddhism completely. They did not destroy Jainism, they allowed it to exist side by side with them. Because Jainism seems to be agreeing at least to one basic ingredient: the soul. Buddha goes too far in Hindu eyes, in at he denies both.

But he has a point there: if God is not, then the soul cannot be. "I" and "thou" can only be part of a pair. They exist as a couple, they cannot be divorced. What will the word 'I' mean if there is no "thou"? It won't mean anything. It will be meaningless; the meaning is given only through the other. What will light mean if there is no darkness? And what will life mean if there is no death?

Just see the duality of language. All language is dual; the meaning comes from the opposite word. It looks very strange that the meaning should come to a word from the opposite word. Light has meaning only because of darkness, love has meaning only because of hate, compassion has meaning only because of anger, and the saint has meaning only because of the sinner. The monastery is meaningful because of the marketplace. This is strange, but this is how it is. Words depend on their opposites.

If you look in the dictionary of the philosophers and inquire, "What is matter?" you will find the answer, "Not mind." And if you inquire, "What is mind?" you will find the answer, "Not matter." This is very absurd. You define matter by saying, "Not mind" and you define mind by saying, "Not matter." And it seems you don't know what matter is or what mind is. Nobody knows.

Language depends on duality, as the whole of life depends

on duality. Language arises out of life experiences; it is utterly rooted in life experiences. That's why truth is inexpressible.

And Lao Tzu is right when he says, "The moment you utter the truth it becomes a lie. Say it, and you have falsified it. The Tao that can be said is not the true Tao. The truth that can be expressed is no longer truth, the God that can be formulated and defined is no longer God." What he is saying is that language is rooted in duality, and truth is transcendental to duality – nothing can be said about it.

That's why Buddha does not say anything about truth, not even yes or no. He will not even nod his head, this way or that. If you ask about truth he remains like a stone statue. No response comes from him – no response, negative or positive, as if he has not heard what you have asked. He *has* heard it, but to say anything will be wrong. *Anything* will be wrong. Even to say that nothing can be said about it will be wrong, because you have already said something. "Nothing can be said about truth" is already a statement which defines it, an expression which gives it meaning.

Buddha is the most misunderstood man in the world. And the reason? – he has chosen the path of the negative, the path of emptying oneself, the path of elimination. He is the purest form of meditation, where two become one. And when two become one, nothing can be said. He cannot even dance, because that will be a statement. He cannot even sing, because that will be a statement. He cannot even give you an indirect indication, not even a gesture. He is utterly quiet. He is just pure silence. If you have the eyes to see, you will be able to see. If you have the heart to understand, you will understand. But he is utterly unavailable to the world of language and communication.

Hakim Sanai says:

> THE PURE MAN UNITES TWO IN ONE;
> THE LOVER UNITES THREE IN ONE.

He says: But what about the lover? His unity is far richer, because he unites three in one: the lover, the beloved, and love. His unity is a kind of trinity. That is the second path – the path of the devotee, the *bhakta*, the Sufi, the lover. And Sanai says it is far richer than the path of purity. Because of the unity of three, it had richness and it is far more juicy. And because it is a path of love, it does not negate, it affirms.

The path of the meditator says *neti-neti*: neither this nor that. The path of love says *iti iti*: this too, this too. It accepts, it affirms. it welcomes, it is positive. It does not empty one; rather, it fills one with the Beloved. It invites God, it becomes a host to God. And there arises a unity which is not a unity of the disappearance of the observer into the observed or the observed into the observer. It is not a unity of disappearance: it is an orgasmic unity. It is like when two lovers move to the height of their passion – when they dissolve into each other but they *are*, and far more so than they have ever been.

Have you observed it? If somebody takes your hand very lovingly in his hand and presses it with warmth and love and caring, suddenly your hand becomes alive. It pulsates with new joy. Just a moment before, you may not have even been aware of your hand. Now the hand is alive, more alive than any other part of your body. The hand stands out; it becomes warmer and warmer. It feels the joy of the other in greeting you, it feels the love of the other pouring into you; it starts responding. It vibrates, it pulsates, it streams.

The psychologists say that a child who has not been hugged by the parents remains somehow dead. His body never comes alive. The child needs to be hugged. The child needs to be hugged again and again, caressed and kissed. Otherwise the child will never know the life pulsating in his body. He will remain literally cold, because he will never know warmth pouring into him. And when warmth is not pouring into him, he cannot respond with his own warmth. His warmth has to be challenged, provoked, seduced.

But our world has become more and more non-loving, non-caressing, non-hugging. People keep apart, people live at a distance. Even if they are standing side by side in a train, touching each other's body, still they keep themselves distant and aloof. That touch has to remain cold, because if the touch becomes warm the other may feel offended. You have transgressed, you have entered into his territory – and how dare you! The bodies may be touching, but the souls should not touch. The bodies may be touching, but they should touch as corpses touch; they should not become warm, they should not respond.

This has created a very encapsulated man who lives in a kind of grave, who lives in a cold world, dark and cold.

When somebody hugs you and the hug is not just an empty motion, an empty gesture, when the hug is real and authentic and he pours his love into you, your love energy rises to the occasion. Your body becomes alive, you feel a totally different kind of life. You start moving towards the optimum. Otherwise, people live at the minimum. They live a dull life, their life has no sharpness – it can't have without love.

I am saying observe your body when you are lovingly holding somebody – what happens? The part of the body that is in touch with the other's love and is feeling the other's love becomes more alive. Love gives a life that nothing else can give.

The meditator is cold. It is no accident that Buddha is the first man of whom marble statues were made. He is the first, and the marble fits with him perfectly. He is cold as marble, and of course as silent as marble. But he is more a statue than a man.

You cannot make a statue of a Sufi, because the statue will not express his dance, the statue will not express his song, the statue will not express his love, his prayer, his gratitude. His ecstatic madness will not be expressed by the statue. Statues can be made only of a meditator. The meditator is a statue – cold, silent, empty. Emptiness has a purity, that is true, but something is missing in it. Richness is missing in it, life is missing in it, orgasmic joy is missing in it.

And that is what happens to the people who move through the path of *via unitiva*: their path is of orgasmic unity. Just as two lovers embrace each other, penetrate each other – not only physically but spiritually too – become dissolved and a kind of unity arises... Two individuals become one. And when these two individuals become one, in fact there are three things becoming one: the lover, the beloved and the love.

Love is a very solid phenomenon to the lovers. In fact the lover and the beloved are nothing compared to the reality of love. The love is far more real than their existence separate from each other. So when lovers meet, three things meet.

To symbolize this, in India we have created a beautiful sacred place, Preyag, where three rivers are said to meet. Two are visible, the third is invisible. One is the Ganges, very visible; another is Yamuna, very visible, and the third is Saraswati – nobody can see it. It is there, but it just has to be believed in; it is invisible.

To the scientific mind it looks absurd. How can there be an invisible river? Nobody has ever seen it, but Hindus go on saying that there is a meeting of three rivers: two are of this world, and the third is of the other. Two belong to the earth and the third belongs to the beyond.

This is really a metaphor of love. When two lovers meet, three things meet, three energies meet: two are of this earth, one is of the beyond. Two are visible, you can see the lover and the beloved – but you will not be able to see love, which is far more valuable than both. In fact it is because of the third that the two are meeting, it is in the third that the two are dissolving. And when the two dissolve, the third also dissolves – but again, it is a totally different phenomenon.

Bahauddin is totally different from Buddha, Hakim Sanai is totally different from Sosan. And the difference is: Buddha will be utterly empty, Bahauddin will be utterly full. Buddha will be cool and cold, aloof, detached and silent. Bahauddin will be dancing in tremendous ecstasy. Buddha will be just peace. Bahauddin will be bliss also – peace will be secondary, bliss will be primary. In Buddha, peace will be primary, bliss will be secondary. In Buddha, peace will be visible, bliss will remain invisible. In Bahauddin, bliss will be there dancing – very visible, tangible, you can almost touch it – but peace will remain hidden, peace will be just a shadow. You can only infer it; you can guess, but you cannot touch it.

In Sosan you will find purity but emptiness. And in Sanai you will find fulfillment, utter fulfillment, overflowing. These are two ways to meet the beyond: either disappear completely like Buddha, or become total like a Sufi or a *bhakta*.

THE PURE MAN UNITES TWO IN ONE;
THE LOVER UNITES THREE IN ONE.

That's why Sanai calls his path "the path of the garden." The path of the meditator is a kind of desert. The desert has its own beauty: if you have been in the desert in the night, it has a coolness you will never find anywhere else, and it has an immense silence, a huge enormous silence, and it has infinity. It has a taste of its own. Under the starry sky, of you have been in a desert alone, you will never find that aloneness anywhere else.

No other place on the earth is as full of solitude as a desert. And there is no variety, so you cannot be distracted. It is the same for miles and miles – as far as you can see up to the horizon it is the same. There is nothing to see; if you have seen one desert you have seen all. It is the same: the same scene goes on stretching farther and farther away. There is no distraction.

That's why many meditators have moved to the desert. Down the ages, many people have moved to the desert. The attraction has been the silence and the beauty of a non-distracting situation. Nothing distracts, nothing moves, all is utterly quiet. Death can only be as quiet as the desert. It has a beauty of its own – but it lacks in richness and variety.

The garden has variety: many trees, much green foliage, many flowers, many colors, birds singing, streams flowing by, the sound of running water and the wind passing through the pines. And there are a thousand and one things happening together. The garden is full, the desert is empty.

The inner being of a meditator becomes like a desert, and the inner being of a lover becomes like a garden. Hence, Sanai has called these sutras *The Hadiqa*: the Garden.

Still, it depends on you. One may like the desert more than the garden, then that is his path. Nothing is wrong in it, one should go on that path. One has to look within oneself and see one's potential, one's possibilities, one's leanings.

It is possible the desert may be a garden to you or the garden may be a desert to you, because one man's food is another man's poison. It is Sanai who says the lover's world is far richer – it is a lover talking about his world, remember it.

BUT I AM FRIGHTENED LEST YOUR IGNORANCE
AND STUPIDITY LEAVE YOU STRANDED ON THE
BRIDGE.

Sanai says: But remember one thing... Each and every master has said it, because the problem is there on both the paths. The problem is, one can be stranded on the bridge. The meditator may become so addicted to meditation that he may be stranded on the bridge. The lover may become too much addicted to love, then he will be stranded on the bridge. Love is a bridge, meditation is a bridge. And you have to go beyond the bridge.

In the ultimate state, the meditator has to drop his meditation and the lover has to forget all about his love. Otherwise you will just be close to the door but you will not be able to enter into the temple. The method has to be forgotten.

Buddha said that each method is like a raft, like a boat: use it to go to the other shore, but then leave it there and forget all about it and go on your way. There is no need to carry the raft on your head. If you carry the raft on your head you are just stupid.

But this is what is happening: millions of people become too addicted to their method. And the method *can* be addictive because it gives such beautiful experiences. The last barrier is the method, the last barrier is the bridge.

Just see the point – it is very paradoxical. The bridge takes you to the other shore: certainly it is a help, and you should be grateful to it, and you should be thankful to it. But it can become a problem. You may fall in love with the bridge and you may make your house on the bridge. And if you start living on the bridge, you are neither of this shore nor of that shore; you are in a kind of limbo. And many so-called religious practitioners live in a kind of limbo – they are neither of this world nor of that. They have become addicted to the bridge.

And the bridge *is* beautiful! Hence the fear of Sanai. Sanai says: I am afraid...

I AM FRIGHTENED LEST YOUR IGNORANCE AND
STUPIDITY LEAVE YOU STRANDED ON THE BRIDGE.

Every disciple has to be told this in the beginning: "One day the method that has helped you so far has to be dropped. When its work is finished, don't carry it, not even for a single moment longer. When your illness is gone, you have to drop the medicine. If you continue the medicine then *it* will become your illness."

All methods are methods, all means are means. And if you want to reach the end you will have to drop all means and all methods. That is the only way to enter into the ultimate. The lover will have to forget all about love, and the meditator will have to forget all about meditation. Yes, there comes a moment when the meditator does not meditate, because he has become meditation himself; now meditation is not a separate activity. And there comes a moment when the lover does not love, because he is love himself. There is nobody else separate from love, love has become his being – he has forgotten all about it. A great Indian Sufi, Kabir, says: Since the day when I met with my Lord, there has been no end to the sport of our love... I see with eyes open and smile, and behold his beauty everywhere. I utter his name, and whatever I see, it reminds me of him; whatever I do, it becomes his worship...Wherever I go, I move round him, all I achieve is his service: when I lie down, I lie prostrate at his feet...Whether I rise or sit down, I can never forget him; for the rhythm of his music beats in my ears.

Slowly slowly, gradually, *all* that you do becomes your prayer, your worship. All that you are becomes your meditation. Kabir says: I see with eyes open and smile, and behold his beauty everywhere. I utter his name, and whatever I see, it reminds me of him; whatever I do, it becomes his worship... Wherever I go, I move round him, all I achieve is his service.

Each act of the devotee or the meditator becomes suffused with his meditation or love. Slowly slowly, there is no doer left. Just as trees are blooming unselfconsciously, the meditator is in meditation unselfconsciously and the lover is in love unselfconsciously. But man's stupidity can create trouble.

The Sufi master, Najmaini, dismissed a student with these words: "Your fidelity has been tested. I find it so unshakable that you must go."

The student said, "Go I shall, but I cannot understand how fidelity can be a ground for dismissal."

Najmaini said, "For three years we have tested your fidelity. Your fidelity to useless knowledge and superficial judgments is complete. That's why you must go."

Fidelity to the useless is stupidity. Fidelity is not always good, not unconditionally good. Fidelity to the useless is a dangerous thing. And there are people who are very faithful to their stupidity, who are very faithful to their prejudices, who believe tremendously in their ignorance, who are very much attached to all that they have gathered. It is useless. It may even be harmful, it may be poisonous. But whatsoever people have, they cling to it; they cannot let it go.

So what to say about beautiful experiences, spiritual experiences? People are even addicted to their misery, they cannot even drop their misery. They go on suffering but they cannot drop it, they cannot detach themselves from their misery. so what to say about ecstatic experiences of meditation and love? The danger *is* there.

If one can become so attached to pain, one can easily become attached to those pleasant, utterly pleasant experiences that happen on the path of meditation and love. One can become stranded on the bridge: remember it! No method is so valuable that you have to cling to it. Use it, but use it wisely. Use it when it is helpful, use it when it helps your growth. Stop using it the moment you see that now you have used it enough and it is no longer helping your growth. Then it has to be dropped.

A master is needed for many things. This is also one of the needs, a very essential need of the disciple – being told in the right moment, "Now stop, it is enough. You have used this method, it has been of great help to you, but carrying it any more will become detrimental."

People live with such tremendous stupidity that if you watch their life you will be surprised. How do they manage? How can they go on befooling themselves? I have heard:

Two Irish Catholic laborers were repairing the underground cables in the street opposite a well-known house of prostitution. While they had the advantage of seeing the street, they could not be observed. Along came a rabbi who carefully looked in all directions to make sure he was not being observed and quickly ducked into the house. Pat turned to Mike: "Look at that dirty no-good Jew going into that evil house!"

A few moments later they saw the Methodist minister look carefully about him before he too entered this house. Again Pat turned to Mike: "Look at that heathen bastard sneaking into the evil house."

And about one hour later who should appear on the scene but the parish priest who also looked carefully in both directions before entering the house. Pat turned to Mike: "Poor Father O'Toole, I wonder who happens to be sick at that place?"

Now it is different. Now it is your own priest, the whole interpretation has changed. This is stupidity. Not being able to see one's prejudices, clingings, attachments and addictions, is stupidity. And man is really very stupid.

The EST people illustrate it with a little parable. They use the parable telling that if you release a rat into a cage which has many rooms and in room number seven you always put a little piece of cheese, the rat will go around, he will search in all the rooms and will find the cheese in room number seven. Once, twice, thrice, you do it, then the rat immediately goes to room number seven. He knows where the cheese is.

When he becomes accustomed to going to room number seven you change it: you put the cheese in room number three. He will rush to room number seven, will look around, will not find it, will be a little puzzled, will run around the house and start searching in other directions. Once or twice he will go into room number seven, again hoping. But sooner or later he will find the cheese in room number three, and he will stop going into room number seven.

Not so with man. He will continue going to room number seven his whole life! Even if cheese is no more found there, that is not the point. His fidelity, his devotion, to room number seven, his consistency: how can he change?

The Christian goes to the church, whether the cheese is available there or not. The Hindu goes to the Hindu temple – the cheese disappeared thousands of years ago. The Buddhist goes on worshipping the Buddha – yes, there was cheese, but twenty-five centuries have passed since then. Now the cheese is here!

Man is like that. Man is the most stupid animal on the earth. No other animal is so stupid; all animals are clever in that way, intelligent in that way. You cannot expect the rat to go on and on for ever and ever, whether the cheese is there or not. At least he is alert – if the cheese is not there, finished! Why go on reciting the Koran if you don't find any cheese there? But because your fathers were reciting it...and they were also not finding the cheese, but they were reciting it because *their* fathers were reciting it.

Now look: not only will you go to room number seven, your children will also go, and your children's children, and it will continue. This is stupidity!

A wandering dervish ran to where a Sufi master sat deep in contemplation, and said, "Quick! We must do something. A monkey has just picked up a knife." "Don't worry," said the master. "so long as it was not a *man*." When the dervish saw the monkey again he found, sure enough, that it had thrown the knife away.

Animals have a very intrinsic intelligence of their own. No animal is as stupid as man is. And the reason is because no animal lives through the head. Animals live through their experience, you live through your head. You make a ready-made program for your life and you go on following the blueprint. And if you don't follow it you feel guilty. If you don't go to the church you will feel guilty.

Many people come to me and they say, "We pray, we meditate." And I ask them, "Have you been growing through it?" They say, "Nothing is happening. But if we don't pray then we feel guilty."

Do you think the rat will feel guilty because this time he has not gone to room number seven? What does he care about room number seven? All that he cares about is cheese.

You go on praying – you start feeling guilty because your father told you to pray, your mother told you to pray, and if you don't pray you feel as if you are betraying your father and mother.

You are betraying your own intelligence! And that is the only betrayal to be worried about. Never betray your intelligence. Remain alert that you don't betray your intelligence, otherwise you will be stranded somewhere or other – on the bridge. Because the bridge is immensely beautiful: you have not known anything like it. If you start moving into the world of meditation you will come across beautiful psychedelic experiences, so utterly mysterious that you are bound to be caught by them.

For example, one day you find great energy rising in your spine and it feels so cooling. Suddenly you feel transported to another world. You feel so alive, tingling with life, and as the energy moves higher and higher in the spine you are moving higher and higher. You are no more here on the earth, you have moved somewhere else. And it is so beautiful, so gratifying, so pleasant, that a thousand sexual orgasms are nothing. Just a single penetration of the energy through the spine to the head, and a thousand sexual orgasms are nothing. Then you will sit every day and wait for it and pray for it and work for it. You will try somehow to help the energy to move.

Do you know how Indian yogis started standing on their heads? Because of this experience. Mm? It is a natural inference that it will be easier for the energy to move towards the head if you are standing on your head. Naturally – gravitation will work, it will pull up your energy. When you are sitting upright the energy finds it difficult to go up, because it has to be pumped all the way up, pulled all the way up, against gravitation. so stupid people devised the idea: Why not stand on your head? Then it will be simply pouring without any effort.

And sometimes it happens, standing on your head it goes easier. But you are caught, stranded. And the experience is so beautiful, so otherworldly, so superb, and so independent – now you are not dependent on a woman or on a man. You are utterly independent, you are free, and enjoying all that no love affair can ever give to you. You are stranded.

That's how people become addicted to drugs. These are inner drugs; these are also part of your body chemistry. There is nothing spiritual in kundalini, it is as physiological as your blood. It is really the electricity of your body, gathering at the base of the spine. When really too much of it is there it starts rising upwards in the spine and the very movement of the electricity makes you stoned. But this is no different really – whether you take LSD or you try some method of yoga posture to create that inner drug, it is the same! It can happen through fasting. It can happen through certain exercises of breathing, because when you exercise in a certain way it changes your body chemistry; certain glands are pressed and it changes your inner chemistry. When you breathe in a certain method, with a certain process, more oxygen goes in, more carbon dioxide goes out, and the balance changes inside you.

And I am not saying not to enjoy these things – just remember that these are beautiful experiences but you should not be stranded. The bridge is immensely psychedelic, and as you reach more and more close to the other shore, experiences will become more and more ecstatic and outlandish. Beware – because the more ecstatic they are, the more is the possibility for you to think, "I have arrived."

HE IS THE PROVIDER OF BOTH FAITH
AND WORLDLY GOODS;
HE IS NONE OTHER THAN THE DISPOSER
OF OUR LIVES.
HE IS NO TYRANT: FOR EVERYTHING HE TAKES,
HE GIVES BACK SEVENTY-FOLD;
AND IF HE CLOSES ONE DOOR
HE OPENS TEN OTHERS TO YOU.

Sanai says: Remember when these spiritual experiences, so-called spiritual experiences, start happening, remember that you are not the doer of them; it is again his gift. Then you will not become addicted. If you think, "I am the doer, and I have become a *siddha* and I have achieved, and now I am capable of creating these experiences," then you are caught, your ego has come back in from the back door. It used to feel strengthened by having more money, by having a bigger house, by having a beautiful woman, this and that. Now, the same ego is enjoying another trip of spiritual experiences.

Sanai says: If you become egoistic in any way about your experiences that happen on the way, you will become addicted and be stranded on the bridge. Then what has to be done? Remember:

> HE IS THE PROVIDER OF BOTH FAITH
> AND WORLDLY GOODS;
> HE IS NONE OTHER THAN THE DISPOSER
> OF OUR LIVES.
> HE IS NO TYRANT: FOR EVERYTHING HE TAKES,
> HE GIVES BACK SEVENTY-FOLD;
>
> IF HE CLOSES ONE DOOR HE OPENS
> TEN OTHERS TO YOU.

Remember that all comes from him. This is possible only on the path of love. On the path of meditation you are left alone. There is more danger of ego arising on the path of meditation than on the path of love, because you are utterly alone. There is no God. You cannot surrender yourself to anything, you cannot use God to protect you from yourself. But on the path of love, that beautiful help is available.

Remember: HE IS NO TYRANT. why? Because there is another thing of which you need to be reminded: when these beautiful experiences happen, simultaneously many painful experiences will also happen – because you are being up-rooted from your identity, old identity, and there will be pain.

Whenever you move into the new reality there will be great bliss, and whenever you are uprooted from the old there will be great pain. There will be nights and days, there will be pain and pleasure moments. don't take those pleasure moments as you creation: surrender them to God. He is the provider of all; he is the giver of life itself.

And then pain comes and agony comes and you are in a great chaos and confusion, a dark night of the soul, don't be worried. Remember: HE IS NO TYRANT. How can he be? He is the source of your life. He is your mother, your father.

> ...FOR EVERYTHING HE TAKES,
> HE GIVES BACK SEVENTY-FOLD...

Remember it. Yes, it happens exactly like that. If you have to suffer a little bit, remember, seventy-fold will be given to you. Whatsoever is taken away, much more will be given to you – because that which is taken away from you is illusory, and that which is going to happen to you is going to be far more real.

And at each step this will be so, at each step you will become richer and richer. But you will have to be ready for one thing: you will have to pass through many fires. Each experience of passing through the fire is a new growth experience. Passing through the fire will be pain, utter pain, but the moment you are out of it you will see the point that it *had* to be gone through. Now you will be on a higher plane, and far more superior joys will become available to you.

It is by passing through fire that one becomes pure gold. Remember: HE IS NO TYRANT. That will help you. He is not a sadist, he does not enjoy torturing you. If you feel the torture, that is your interpretation. He is simply making more and more joys available to you, but you have to drop your toys.

And dropping your old toys is painful. The pain is created by your attachment to the toys. We believe immensely in our toys. And we *know* they are toys and still we believe in them, our foolishness is such. We know that money is a toy and it will be taken away when death comes – all will be taken away. But still we go on gathering things, and hoping meanwhile that "This happens to everybody but this is not going to happen to me. I am special, I am an exception."

Nobody is an exception: all will be taken away from you. But we go on playing, we go on believing in our fantasies, we go on projecting.

A French mouse and an elephant go to the magistrate and ask for a special license to be married right away. The magistrate shakes his head and says it is impossible, because elephants and mice just don't mix. And the little mouse looks up with tears in her eyes and says, "But please, monsieur Magistrate, we've got to."

People go on believing in absurd things. Now the little mouse thinks she is pregnant: "We've got to; now there is no way of avoiding it!"

Look at your own absurdities. Look at your own life, at what you go on doing. It is so ridiculous, the way people live, the way people waste their lives. And when these toys are taken away – and they *have* to be taken away, otherwise you will never become mature – there will be pain. On the path of love, God is available to you.

> HE IS NO TYRANT: FOR EVERYTHING HE TAKES,
> HE GIVES BACK SEVENTY-FOLD;
> AND IF HE CLOSES ONE DOOR
> HE OPENS TEN OTHERS TO YOU.

But the trouble is with the human mind. The human mind becomes focused on certain things. For example, if you have become accustomed to going through one door, you create a kind of tunnel vision: you cannot see any other doors. You only see that door, you become oblivious of other doors. And when that one door closes you are in a panic, because of your tunnel vision.

The man who is searching for God has to learn how to drop tunnel vision, how to remain alert and available to all possibilities.

If one door closes, ten doors are immediately opened for you. This is not a philosophical statement, this is simply a fact. But you only look through your past. You are so obsessed by the past that you cannot see that other doors are opening. You cannot even believe that there are other doors. You know only one door, you have become familiar with it. You can go out and in from that one door mechanically, with no awareness – there is no need; you have become habituated to it.

Now it closes, and there is great pain and great fear and great agony. The agony is not happening because the door is closed, the agony is happening because you have tunnel vision. You cannot see anywhere else, you only have a focused vision. Let your eyes be a little wider.

And remember, Sanai says, that he never closes a door unless he has already opened ten for you. So just look around and you will find them.

And this is my experience too, working with thousands of meditators. It comes every day: whenever one door closes... and old doors *have* to be closed, otherwise how are you going to grow and move upwards? If you always go on moving through the same door then there is no transformation possible. Doors will have to be closed so that you are forced to move from a new angle, into a new dimension.

The master tries in every way to close your old doors. And that's why there is fear of the master too. And that's why people keep at a distance – they keep a certain distance so they can escape. If things become too much, unbearable, they can always escape.

And it hurts whenever a door is closed. You ask for growth, but whenever a door is closed, it hurts. You become angry, you are in a rage. And you don't understand simple arithmetic: if you desire growth you will have to be always ready to move through new visions, new territories, new planes. And the old is safe and the old is secure and convenient – that I know and every master knows. But if you remain with the old, *you* remain the old and you remain dead.

Life is with the new. Each moment has to be a death and a resurrection. Die to the past each moment!

And that is where the disciple is tested: that is the first test. When a door is closed, the disciple believes ten others must have been opened. He forgets about the closed door and he starts looking around for the doors that must have been opened. This is trust. Trust life, trust God, trust existence.

HE TREASURES YOU MORE
THAN YOU DO YOURSELF.

Remember: God created you. You cannot be unnecessary, you cannot be accidental. And God has created you as so unique, so individual, that there is no other "you" like you. You are the only one! He has never created a person like you before, and will never create another person exactly like you. See how much respect he has paid to you.

God is not like an assembly line that Ford cars go on coming out of – the same Ford cars, millions of Ford cars, all alike. God is a creator, not an assembly line. Each individual has been made not according to a model, not according to a certain fixed pattern – each individual has been paid *individual* attention. He has painted you individually, he has cut you in a certain way, given you a certain shape, a certain being. You are unique, you are original, you are not a copy.

HE TREASURES YOU MORE...

And certainly you are his creation – if you are lost, it is his loss.

HE TREASURES YOU MORE THAN YOU DO
YOURSELF.

And that's a very obvious fact. People don't love themselves, they don't respect themselves. On the contrary, they condemn themselves. You are all self-condemners. That's what you have been brought by the priests, again and again, everywhere in the world: you have been conditioned to condemn yourself. And you go on condemning yourself. You don't think yourself of any worth. And this is one of the barriers, greatest barriers.

Love yourself, respect yourself, and you will be giving respect to God – because to respect the painting is to respect the painter, and to love the poetry is to love the poet. And you are the poetry and you are the painting. You are the music created by him. You are the visible proof that God is; the creation is the visible proof that the creator is. Love the creation, relish it, celebrate it: this is the only way to celebrate God. And you are the closest creation.

The man who condemns himself cannot love anybody else either. And the man who condemns himself condemns the whole existence. The world is full of these condemners, they have poisoned everybody. And the first thing that a master has to do with the disciple is to take all this poison out of his being. The greatest problem is to make you respectful of yourself, to make you aware that you are precious, that you are incomparable, that you have a great potential in you, that buddhas are hidden in you, that you are seeds of buddhas.

RISE, HAVE DONE WITH FAIRY-TALES;
LEAVE YOUR BASE PASSIONS,
AND COME TO ME.

Sanai says, as every master has always said: Come to me! But you will have to leave a few things, only then can you come to the master. If you cannot leave those few things you will remain with the priests and you will never find the master. And the priests are the enemies of all the masters.

The priest is never the master, and the master is never the priest; they don't belong to the same dimension. The priest has nothing to do with God. The priest has made a business out of God: he is exploiting the hypothesis of God. The priest is so ugly that he cannot leave even the idea of God unexploited.

According to one story, when God created the world and saw that it was good, Satan joined him in his appreciation and exclaimed, as he gazed from one wonder to another, "It is good! It is good! Let us make it an institution!"

Now, that is the priest. The priest makes everything a business, the priest makes everything an institution. Every insight of the great buddhas is finally reduced to an institution, to a church. The priest is in the service of Satan.

RISE, HAVE DONE WITH FAIRY-TALES...

And it is the priest who keeps feeding you on fairy-tales. He talks about God and he talks about heaven and hell and the angels and the rewards that the virtuous one will be given and the punishments that the sinners will have to suffer. These are all fairy-tales.

The priest goes on feeding you on fairy-tales. And because you remain attached to fairy-tales you remain stupid, you never mature. Beware: the priest is a salesman in the service of Satan. And the priest's whole work consists in decorating fairy-tales. He goes on inventing more and more fairy-tales. He is not concerned about truth, in fact he is very much afraid of truth.

So whenever there is a man like Buddha the priest is against him. When there is a man like Jesus the priest is against him.

Immediately the priest becomes alert, there is danger – because these people like Buddha and Jesus are against fairy-tales. They will destroy all the childish nonsense that goes on in the name of religion. And the priest lives on it, and down the ages he has become really skillful. The priest is the greatest salesman in the world.

A man came into a grocery store and asked for five cents' worth of salt. The proprietor asked, "What kind of salt do you want?"

"What kind of salt do I want? I want salt, plain and simple. How many kinds of salt are there?"

"Ha ha!" chuckled the store owner. "What you don't know about salt! You come with me." And he took him downstairs and showed him a cellar that contained no less than forty or fifty barrels of salt. The customer was amazed. "All these are different salts?" he asked.

"Yes, they're all different. We have salt for all kinds of prices and uses."

"My goodness, you are a specialist. I suppose, if you have all these barrels of different kinds of salt, you must sell one hell of a lot of salt. You must really know how to sell salt!"

"Oh," said the other, "me – I'm not so good at selling salt, but the guy who sold it all to me, boy, can he sell salt!"

The priest is continuously inventing fairy-tales. And he invents them for all kinds of people, for all sorts of minds. That's why there are three hundred religions on the earth – that means three hundred kinds of fairy-tales, available in all sizes, available at all prices, available according to everybody's need. Otherwise, what is the need for three hundred religions on the earth? There are not three hundred sciences on the earth. Science is one, because the scientific approach is one and the fundamental of science is one.

Religion will be one – if priests disappear and only Buddhas and Bahauddins and Sanais and Sosans are there, there will be only one religion. There will be a kind of religiousness in the world, not any religion in fact – a kind of religiousness.

You will have to drop your fairy-tales – Christian, Hindu, Mohammedan.

RISE, HAVE DONE WITH FAIRY-TALES; LEAVE YOUR BASE PASSIONS, AND COME TO ME.

There are base passions: money, power, sexuality, greed, anger, possessiveness, and so on and so forth. And man lives only in those base passions. Nothing is wrong in them, they are the foundation of the temple of life. But if there is only the foundation and no temple, then the foundation is utterly useless. It is useful in the context of the temple; if the whole temple is built then the foundation is useful. But if the temple is not built ever and you go on building only the foundation for ever and ever, it is utterly futile, pointless, a wastage of life and energy.

Sigmund Freud remained concerned with the base passions. That is his inadequacy. And because of that, psychoanalysis has not yet been able to become a temple. It is only a foundation, a bare naked foundation. It is not yet a house where you can live.

He wrote once to a friend:"I have always confined myself to the ground floor and basement of the edifice called man."

Aldous Huxley once said he should have said the base-ment-basement.

Man has a basement, that is true, but he also has an attic. Man is unconsciousness, true, but man also has the potential for super-consciousness. And unless you start searching for the super-conscious you will remain in the basement, or even the basement-basement. You will remain crawling on the earth – and you have the capacity to fly. You can become a butterfly, and you are not opening your wings because your attachment to the earth is too much. That attachment has to be trans-formed. You have to start looking at the stars.

That's what Sufis call *adab*: to be in the presence of the master. Hindus call it *satsang*. To be in the presence of the master means to look at the stars, to become aware of the attic, that something higher is possible in you. Be thrilled that you are not finished as you are, that you can have wings, that you an fly as high as you desire, that even the sky is not the limit.

RISE, HAVE DONE WITH FAIRY-TALES; LEAVE YOUR
BASE PASSIONS, AND COME TO ME.

And there are two kinds of people in the world. The worldly people remain the basement, they remain concerned with the base passions. And the so-called otherworldly, the religious, they become concerned with fairly-tales. And both are lost.

The real seeker will drop two things. First he will drop fairy-tales – that's why Sanai mentions first:

RISE, HAVE DONE WITH FAIRY-TALES...

The first thing is to drop fairy-tales, the inventions of the priests.

And then the second thing is: watch your base passions, because in your base passions a great energy is hidden – if released, it will become the bridge which will join the earth and the sky.

...AND COME TO ME.
YOU HAVE TO REALIZE THAT IT IS HIS GUIDANCE
THAT KEEPS YOU ON THE PATH AND NOT YOUR
OWN STRENGTH.

But again Sanai reminds you that on the path of love this has to be remembered continuously, don't forget it even for a single moment.

YOU HAVE TO REALIZE THAT IT IS HIS GUIDANCE...

Always remember that if you start moving towards God it is he who has chosen you. Don't for a moment think, "Look! I am a great seeker of God. I am no ordinary man, I am not worldly, I am not like these worldly creatures. I am a spiritual man. I search for God, I don't seek and search for money or power." You have fallen again; again you have fallen into the basement. The ego is back.

Never for a single moment think that it is you who is searching for God. On the contrary, on the path of love, remember it must be he who has called you – otherwise how could you have searched for him? It must be he who has chosen you, it must be he who is pulling you. It must be he who is in some unknown, mysterious way taking you farther away to some unknown existence. It is he who has taken possession of you.

YOU HAVE TO REALIZE THAT IT IS HIS GUIDANCE
THAT KEEPS YOU ON THE PATH...

And never for a single moment think, "It is because of my strength that I am on the path." No. If you think it is because of your strength that you are on the path, you have already gone astray. You have already become an egoist: you have created the separation between you and God.

"It is he who keeps me on the path. It is he who keeps reminding me not to go astray."

Plato used a beautiful word for truth. The word is *alethia*: it means non-forgetting, no-forgetting. It means remembering, it means constant remembering.

Truth is a constant remembering. Truth is not forgetting for a single moment that "God is: only God is. He has given me life, he has given me the desire to search for truth, he has chosen me to search for him. He must have called me in some mysterious way – otherwise how could I have moved in his direction?"

The lover keeps on reminding himself, "It is the Beloved who is functioning like a magnet – I am being pulled, I am being drawn. It is not my work, it is his grace."

And if you can remember this, that it is his grace, the ego will not arise. And, slowly slowly, the ego will be dropped. And when the ego is dropped you have arrived. Then the three are one: then the lover and the beloved and the love are one. You have entered into the Garden – *The Hadiqa*.

6 The Bridge of Love and Laughter

The first question:

BELOVED MASTER,
WHAT IS CREATIVITY?

Deva Mohan, action is not creativity, inaction also is not creativity. Creativity is a very paradoxical state of consciousness and being: it is action through inaction, it is what Lao Tzu calls *wei-wu-wei*. It is allowing something to happen through you. It is not a doing, it is an allowing. It is becoming a passage so the whole can flow through you. It is becoming a hollow bamboo, just a hollow bamboo.

And then immediately something starts happening, because hidden behind man is god. Just give him a little way, a little passage, to come through you. That is creativity: allowing God to happen is creativity.

Creativity is a religious state. That's why I say that a poet is far closer to God than a theologian, a dancer even closer. The philosopher is the farthest away, because the more you think, the greater the wall you create between you and the whole. The more you think, the more you are. The ego is nothing but all the thoughts accumulated in the past. When you are not, God is. That is creativity.

Creativity simply means you are in a total relaxation. It does not mean inaction, it means relaxation, because out of relaxation much action will be born. But that will not be your doing, you will be just a vehicle. A song will start coming through you – you are not the creator of it, it comes from the beyond. It always comes from the beyond. When you create it, it is just ordinary, mundane. When it comes through you it has superb beauty, it brings something of the unknown in it.

When the great poet Coleridge died he left thousands of poems incomplete. Many times in his life he was asked, "Why don't you complete these poems" – because a few poems were missing only one line or two lines. "Why don't you complete them?"

And he would say, "I cannot. I have tried, but when I complete them something goes amiss, something goes wrong. My line never falls in tune with that which has come through me. It remains a stumbling block, it becomes a rock, it hinders the flow. So I have to wait. Whosoever has been flowing through me, whenever he again starts flowing and completes the poem it will be completed, not before it."

He completed only a few poems. But those are of superb beauty, of great mystic splendor. That has always been so: the poet disappears, then there is creativity. Then he is possessed. Yes, that is the word, he is possessed. To be possessed by God is creativity.

Simone de Beauvoir has said, "Life is occupied both in perpetuating itself and in surpassing itself; if all it does is maintain itself, then living is only not dying."

And the man who is not creative is only not dying, that's all. His life has no depth. His life is not yet life but just a preface; the book of life has not yet started. He is born, true, but he is not alive.

When you become creative, when you allow creativity to happen through you, when you start singing a song that is not your own – that you cannot sign and you cannot say, "It is my own," on which you cannot put your signature – then life take wings, it upsurges.

In creativity is the surpassing. Otherwise, at the most we can go on perpetuating ourselves. You create a child – it is not creativity. You will die and the child will be here to perpetuate life. But to perpetuate is not enough unless you start surpassing yourself. And surpassing happens only when something of the beyond comes in contact with you.

That is the point of transcendence – surpassing. And in surpassing, the miracle happens: you are not, and yet for the first time you are.

The essence of wisdom is to act in harmony with nature. That is the message of all the great mystics – Lao Tzu, Buddha, Bahauddin, Sosan, Sanai – to act in harmony with nature. Animals act unconsciously in harmony with nature. Man has to act consciously in harmony with nature, because man has consciousness. Man can choose not to act in harmony, hence the great responsibility.

Man has responsibility. Only man has responsibility, that is his grandeur. No other animal is responsible – he simply acts in harmony, there is no way of going astray. The animal cannot go astray; he is not yet able to go astray, there is no consciousness yet. He functions as you function in deep sleep.

In deep sleep you also fall in harmony with nature. That's why deep sleep is so rejuvenating, so relaxing. Just a few minutes of deep sleep, and you are fresh and young again and all the dust that you had gathered and all weariness and boredom disappears. You have contacted the source.

But this is an animal way to contact the source; sleep is an animal way to contact the source. Animals are horizontal, man is vertical. When you want to go into sleep you have to fall into a horizontal position. Only in a horizontal position can you fall asleep; you cannot fall asleep standing, it will be very difficult. You have to go back again, millions of years back, just like an animal. You are horizontal, parallel to the earth, suddenly you start losing consciousness, suddenly you are no longer responsible.

It is because of this factor that Sigmund Freud chose the couch for the patient. It is not for the comfort of the patient, it is a strategy. Once the patient is horizontal he starts being irresponsible. And unless he feels utterly free to say things he will not say unconscious things. If he remains responsible and vertical he will be continuously judging whether to say a thing or not. He will be censoring.

When he is lying horizontal on the couch – and the psychoanalyst is hidden behind, you cannot see him – suddenly he is again like an animal. He has no responsibility. He starts babbling things which he would never have said to anybody, to a stranger. He starts saying things which are deep in his unconscious; those unconscious things start surfacing. It is a strategy, a Freudian strategy, to make the patient utterly helpless like a child or like an animal.

Once you don't feel responsible you become natural. And psychotherapy has been of great help; it relaxes you. All that you have repressed surfaces, and after surfacing it evaporates. After going through psychoanalysis you become less burdened, you become more natural, you are more in harmony with nature and with yourself. That is the meaning of being healthy.

But this is going back, this is regression. This is what I was talking about the other day: going to the basement. There is another way to surpass, and that is going to the attic – not the way of Sigmund Freud but the way of Buddha. You can surpass yourself by being in contact consciously with nature.

And that is the essence of wisdom – to be in harmony with nature, with the natural rhythm of the universe. And whenever you are in harmony with the natural rhythm of the universe you are a poet, you are a painter, you are a musician. you are a dancer.

Try it. Some time sitting by the side of a tree, fall in tune consciously. Become one with nature; let boundaries dissolve. Become the tree, become the grass, become the wind – and suddenly you will see, something that has never happened to you before is happening. Your eyes are becoming psychedelic: trees are greener than they have ever been, and roses are rosier, and everything seems to be luminous. And suddenly you want to sing a song, not knowing from where it comes. Your feet are ready to dance; you can feel the dance murmuring inside your veins, you can hear the sound of music within and without.

This is the state of creativity. This can be called the basic quality: being in harmony with nature, being in tune with life, with the universe.

Lao Tzu has given it a beautiful name, *wei-wu-wei*: action through inaction. You can call it "creative quietude" – a process that combines within a single individual two seeming incompatibles: supreme activity and supreme relaxation.

That's the paradox of creativity. If you see a painter painting, certainly he is active, utterly active, madly active – he is all action. Or if you see a dander dancing, he is all action. But still, deep down there is no actor, no doer; there is only silence. Hence I called creativity the state of paradox. All beautiful states are paradoxical. The higher you go, the deeper you go into the paradox of reality.

Supreme action with supreme relaxation: on the surface great action is happening, in the depth nothing is happening, or *only* nothing is happening. Creative quietude is the supreme action – the precious suppleness, simplicity, spontaneity and freedom that flows from us, or rather through us, when our private egos and conscious efforts yield to a power not their own. Yielding to a power not of your own, surrendering to a power that is beyond you, is creativity. Meditation is creativity. And when the ego disappears, the wound in you disappears; you are healed, you are whole. The ego is your disease. And when the ego disappears you are no more dormant, you start flowing. You start flowing with the immense flow of existence.

Norbert Weiner has said, "We are not stuff that abides, but patterns that perpetuate themselves; whirlpools of water in an ever-flowing river."

Then you are not an ego but an event or a process of events. Then you are a process, not a thing. Consciousness is not a thing, it is a process; and we have made it a thing. The moment you call it "I" it becomes a thing – defined, bounded, dormant, stagnant. And you start dying.

The ego is your death. And the death of the ego is the beginning of your real life. And real life is creativity.

You need not go to any school to learn creativity. All that you need is to go withinwards and help the ego dissolve. Don't support it, don't go on strengthening and nourishing it. And whenever the ego is not, all is truth, all is beautiful. And then whatsoever happens is good.

And I am not saying that you all will become Picassos or Shakespeares, I am not saying that. A few of you will become painters, a few of you will become singers, a few of you will become musicians, a few of you dancers – but that is not the point. Each of you will become creative in his own way. You may be a cook, but then there will be creativity. Or you may be just a cleaner, but then there will be creativity. There will be no boredom.

You will become inventive in small things. Even in cleaning there will be a kind of worship, a prayer. So whatsoever you do then will have the taste of creativity. And we don't need many painters – if all turn out to be painters, life will become very difficult. We don't need many poets; we need gardeners too, we need farmers too, and we need all kinds of people. But each person can be creative. If he is meditative and egoless then God starts flowing through him. According to his capacities, according to his potential, God starts taking forms.

And then all is good. You need not become famous. A really creative person does not care a bit about becoming famous; there is no need. He is so tremendously fulfilled in whatsoever he is doing, he is so content with whatsoever he is and wherever he is, that there is no question of desire. When you are creative, desires disappear. When you are creative, ambitions disappear. When you are creative, you are already that which you always wanted to be.

The second question:

I ALWAYS THOUGHT THAT YOU WERE AGAINST
POLITICIANS, SO I WAS VERY MUCH SURPRISED TO
KNOW THAT YOU HAVE BLESSED INDIRA GANDHI.
BELOVED MASTER, WOULD YOU LIKE TO SAY
SOMETHING ABOUT IT?

I am against the political mind. The political mind means the cunning mind, the political mind means the murderous, violent mind. The political mind means the mind that is only interested in dominating others, that is only interested in being in such a position where millions of people's lives are in his hands, this way or that. The politician's mind is the mind of the perfect egoist.

I am certainly against the political mind. I would like a world which does not go round and round the political mind. I would like a world which has the religious quality, not the political quality. At least I would like the political quality of the mind to recede into the background. At the center should be the creative mind. Politics is destructive.

But this cannot happen right now. For millions of years politics has been in the center, so this cannot happen right now. A great meditative energy has to be released first. If millions of people become meditators then, slowly slowly, the structure of the energy on this earth will change – will start moving from the political mind to the religious mind. I am against the political mind, but I know that this cannot happen right now. It may take thousands of years. The beginning has to happen right now, the seed has to be sown right now. But the fruits will come only later on. You can become a

non-political person right now, and your life will have a flow-
ering. But as far as the whole earth is concerned, it is going to
take time. What are we going to do meanwhile?

I have blessed Indira Gandhi because to me she seems to be
the least political amongst the Indian politicians. It will again
look strange to you, because whatsoever has been said about
her, spread about her, rumored about her, is just the opposite.
But my own observation is this, that she has the least political
mind. And why do I say so? These are the reasons.

First: had she been really a politician and only a politician
she would not have tried to do anything that goes against the
Indian tradition. The politician never goes against the tradi-
tion; he always follows his own followers. That's a mutual
arrangement. Particularly in a democratic system, the politician
cannot afford to go against the traditions because after five
years the elections will be there. If you go against people's tra-
ditions – whether they are right or wrong is not the point – if
you go against their traditions they will take revenge.

So the real politicians only *talk* about change, but they
never try to change anything. They only talk. The talk is okay,
it hurts nobody; even the masses enjoy the talk. Talk about rev-
olution, but don't try to do it – because when you try to do it
then many of the traditions and superstitions of the masses will
have to be destroyed. Then those people will be angry, and in a
democratic set-up their anger can be dangerous.

Indira Gandhi tried to *do* something, sincerely tried to do
something. In fact that's what created trouble for her. She was
trying to help the poor, against the rich. She angered the rich,
the people who are powerful; she angered the vested interest.
No politician would afford it, no politician *can* afford it. Talk-
ing about great things is allowed, nobody is worried about
what you say – just don't try to do anything. Go on creating
beautiful ideals, but never practice them.

She annoyed the rich people of this country because she
was doing something for the poor. And she annoyed the poor

because whatsoever she did went against their traditions. For example, she imposed birth control: the Indian masses cannot tolerate it. For thousands of years they have thought that it is God who gives children, and who are you to prevent it? It is a gift from God – that has been their idea. Now the gift is becoming very dangerous. The gift is becoming so dangerous that it is almost suicidal.

No politician would have tried that. Let the country go to its death – who bothers?

Since Morarji Desai came into power, all the programs for birth control have been put aside. And that is the only hope for this country. If this country is to survive, the only hope is to reduce the population. Already there are too many people. Seventy-five percent of the people are living below human standards, fifty percent of the people are almost starving. Within twenty-five years, by the end of this century, the whole country will be starving.

But that is not the point. The politician thinks only of *his* power *now*. He will be here as prime minister for five or ten years at the most. Who cares what happens later on? Why should he risk he power and position?

Indira risked it. Hence I call her the least political person Indian politics.

Secondly: she started succeeding in her programs. That is dangerous; you should not succeed. If the man in power fails, all other politicians are happy – because the man in power is failing and that is their chance. If the man in power succeeds then there is no chance for them to ever come into power. And she was the first Indian prime minister who was succeeding in bringing a certain order into the country, in creating some disciple out of chaos. She was succeeding in raising people's standard of living, she was succeeding in helping people to be more productive and less destructive. She was succeeding in many many ways.

But that angers other politicians: now what is *their* chance?

Other politicians live only on the failure of those who are in power. One should not be successful; there is nothing more dangerous than to succeed.

This is strange, but this is a fact in the history of man. If somebody succeeds, his own success is going to boomerang upon him. If she had failed, there would have been no trouble. Then the politicians who were against her would have remained divided, and if they had been divided there would have been no danger for her. But she started succeeding, and their chances to come into power started becoming less and less.

They all joined together. They *had* to – it was a question of life and death for them. Now there was no question of ideologies.

A strange phenomenon has happened in India, very strange. Morarji Desai is a follower of Mahatma Gandhi, and is in power through the help of those who murdered Mahatma Gandhi. Strange bedfellows! But when it is a question of life and death who cares about ideologies? Ideologies are good as playthings, toys.

All the Indian politicians of different attitudes, approaches, and diametrically opposite ideologies, gathered together and became one force against Indira Gandhi. Why? How did it happen?

She was succeeding. Politicians only pretend; they never really do anything. But she was sincere, she really tried to do something for this country. That's why this country can never forgive her.

Thirdly: Indian bureaucracy is the worst in the world. No work ever happens, files just go on moving from one table to another table for years and years.

I knew a man who fought a single case in the courts his whole life – for almost fifty years. All the judges died, whosoever tried his case; all the lawyers died for and against. And finally he himself died, but the case was unfinished. Not only the judges and lawyers died, even the government changed: in

'47 India became independent. The case was started by the British government. Even the government died, another government came into power, but the case continued. If you want to do something in this country with such a bureaucracy it is impossible. You have to force this bureaucracy to do things.

The bureaucracy was angry. It was really the bureaucracy who deceived Indira Gandhi. She was given false reports. She was given false reports that her position was perfectly okay, she could allow an election, she was going to win. She depended on the reports of the bureaucracy, and those reports were false. The bureaucracy was absolutely against her. Nobody had ever forced them to do anything, and she was forcing them to do things.

Since Morarji has come, the bureaucracy is perfectly happy. Again things are moving at such a slow pace that nothing ever moves. Morarji himself is a bureaucrat, he started his life as a deputy collector. He knows how the bureaucracy functions; he does not interfere. If you are just there to be in power – that is the mind of a politician – you don't interfere, you don't make so many enemies.

The rich people are against Indira because she tried to bring the poor people up a little higher from their mire. The poor people were angry because she imposed birth control on them forcibly – and it can be imposed only forcibly; otherwise it is not possible. The bureaucracy was against her because she forced the bureaucracy to *do* things, to implement things, and *fast*. The whole country was angry. Had she been a politician, this would not have happened.

Fourth: she imposed an Emergency. She was straightforward. Had she been a politician she would have done everything that is done through an Emergency, without imposing the Emergency. That's what is being done now – everything is being done just as it was done in the Emergency, but without declaring it. The cunning politician always works indirectly, not directly. He is not straightforward.

Morarji Desai said in one of his interviews to the BBC – it was asked by the BBC men, and it was particularly and deliberately asked for you and the work that is happening here: "Will you allow us freedom to make films in your country?" He said, "I will allow it, unless it is dangerous to our defense.

Now, how are my sannyasins dangerous to the defense of this country? Doing Dynamic and Kundalini and dancing and singing, how can they be dangerous? And if there is something that Morarji thinks is dangerous he can simply tell the BBC people and all the other TV agencies that have asked to film the ashram, "Make your film, but your film will have to go through the censor board." So simple! If you feel that something is going to be against your country, you can cut it.

But this is a cunning political mind: talk about freedom – just *talk* about freedom, that's all – and go on creating more and more bondage for people.

Indira was straightforward, she declared Emergency. she was honest. The Emergency was needed: this country can only be changed if things are to be taken very seriously, as if the country is at war. Unless things are taken in that proportion and with that intensity, as if the country is at a war, nothing is going to happen.

And the war IS there. The war is with the population explosion. It is far more dangerous than a war with Pakistan or China, because China cannot destroy you, neither can Pakistan destroy you. Maybe China can take few miles of land – but the population explosion is the real enemy. The children that are going to come will destroy you.

Things are in a dangerous situation. It is a greater crisis than India has ever faced in the past; it knows no way to tackle it. Things have to be taken seriously.

That was the effort behind imposing Emergency. But imposing Emergency in a democratic country is dangerous. It can be done only by a non-political mind. It can be done only by one who really wants to change the situation, whatsoever the cost. She risked her power, her prime ministership, to change the course of the history of this country.

This Emergency angered the journalists and other media people. And no politician would ever like to anger the journalists, because much depends on them, too much depends on them. It can be safely said that fifty percent of Indira's fall was made possible by the Indian journalists. They were getting angrier and angrier. They were not allowed to gossip, they were not allowed to make rumors, they were not allowed what they call "freedom of the press." So when Emergency was removed, they took great revenge. It is how the human mind functions. A politician would have been alert about it.

Fifth: her son, Sanjay Gandhi, entered politics. A real politician, a cunning politician, would have allowed him to enter only from the back door. Otherwise, others become jealous. She allowed him to enter from the front door, and the whole country became jealous.

There is no reason to prevent anybody from entering politics. Even though the person happens to be the son of the prime minister, he has as much right to enter into politics as anybody else. And Sanjay Gandhi has a certain potential. There was nothing wrong in it, but to allow him through the front door is a nonpolitical thing. She functioned more as a mother and a human being than as a cunning politician.

Her own father never allowed her through the front door; he was more cautious. Again and again, he was asked. "Who after you?" He never mentioned Indira Gandhi – never. Once to a friend he said, "I cannot tell you the name of the person who will succeed me, because if I tell you the name then there is no possibility for the poor person to succeed me. Just by mentioning it I will anger all the other people who are competitors, and they will join together against him."

There is every possibility he meant "her" not "him." He was a more seasoned politician than Indira Gandhi; he knew the ways of politics.

Indira Gandhi herself came through the back door. But she is more a mother than a politician: she allowed Sanjay Gandhi to enter through the front door. That was dangerous; that became one of the most important causes of her fall. And it was *more* dangerous because Sanjay has potential. Sooner or later, he is going to become a prime minister; he has the potential and the guts. It cannot be prevented. But Indira was functioning very nonpolitically.

Morarji Desai is more cunning, His son is also there, but always behind a screen. And these who are even more interested in power, they go even further. The chief minister of Haryana, Devi Dayal, has disowned his son and saved his seat – saved his power and disowned his son. This is how a politician functions.

Indira Gandhi risked her power and tried to save her son. That is not the way of a politician – maybe the way of a mother, of a human being.

Sixth: she mad the greatest error that a politician can commit, a very fundamental error and very obvious: Indira Gandhi forced all the political parties into jail together. That is so absurd! Even a man like me, who has nothing to do with politics, can see that it is absolutely absurd. If you put all your enemies into jail together, you are forcing them to be united against you.

She should have studied Machiavelli a little more. It is so simple; a politician would never do that. Keep at least half the enemies out of prison, and half the enemies in prison. Keep them fighting, keep them separate, because that is the only way to rule: to divide. This is utterly stupid – putting all your enemies together in jail you have almost imposed unity on them; they cannot avoid it. Now you are the enemy of all of them.

They became friendly. And they saw the point that if they could become friendly and if they could get together, then Indira would be gone. This they had not seen for thirty ears; for thirty years they had remained divided. Suddenly Indira brought them together and they became aware that "It is so simple: if we join together then Indira is gone." The Congress Party had ruled for thirty years because the enemies were divided. Indira functioned as a non-politician.

And seventh: after emergency, immediately after emergency and after a great effort to impose birth control on the people – when rich people, poor people, and the journalists and everybody was annoyed and angry – immediately after emergency declaring a general election: that is again incomprehensible.

If she had asked me, I would have told her, "Wait at least for one year. Remove the Emergency, wait for one year." That one year would have done. The steam of the journalists would have been released, people would have forgotten the imposition – people's memories are very short – and in one year the enemies, all the political enemies, would have again fallen into their old habits, would have started quarreling with one another again.

Immediately giving a general election to the country was utterly unpolitical. That's how she got defeated.

Because of these errors, I say she is the least political of all the Indian politicians. Hence I have blessed her. I have blessed her, and I bless her again.

The third question:

WHAT DO YOU SAY ABOUT SEX EDUCATION FOR SMALL CHILDREN?

Truth is truth, and nobody should be debarred from it. Just because children are small, do they have to be fed on lies? Is truth only for grown-ups? Does that mean truth is dangerous for the delicate consciousness of the child?

Truth is never dangerous, untruth is dangerous. And if you tell an untruth to the grown-up he may be able to defend himself; it can be forgiven. But never tell an untruth to the child, because he is so helpless, so indefensible. He depends so much on you, he trusts so much in you – don't betray him. This is betraying! Telling any lie means you have betrayed the child.

And finally you will be in trouble. Sooner or later, the child will discover that you have been telling lies. That very day, all trust in you will disappear.

If young people start rebelling against the parents, the responsibility is not theirs, the responsibility is of the parents. They have been telling so many lies; and now, by and by, the children start discovering that they were *all* lies. And if you have been telling so many lies, even the truth that you have told them becomes suspicious. And one thing is certain, they lose trust in you. You have betrayed them, you have deceived them: you become ugly in their consciousness. Their impression of you is no good any more. In fact they will never be able to trust anybody.

That's the problem I am facing every day. When you come and become sannyasins, the problem that you have with your parents starts being imposed on me. You cannot trust me either; in a subtle way I become your father-figure. And because your parents have deceived you, who knows? I am a stranger – if even your parents deceive you, if even parents cannot be relied upon, then how can you rely upon me?

You will never be able to trust the woman you love, the man you love. You will never be able to trust the master you surrender to. You will never in your life again be able to regain your trust. And for what has your trust been destroyed? For such foolish things.

What is wrong? Sex is a simple fact: tell it the way it is. And children are very very perceptive – even if you don't tell them they will discover it on their own. They are very curious people.

Carl was assigned to write a composition entitled, "Where

I came from." When he returned home from school, he entered the kitchen where his mother was preparing dinner. "Where did I come from, Mama?" he asked. "The stork brought you." "And where did Daddy come from?" "The stork brought him, too." "And what about Grandpa?" "Why, the stork brought him too, darling."

Carl very carefully made notes on what Mama had told him, and the next day he handed in the following composition:"According to my calculations, there hasn't been a natural birth in my family for the past three generations."

Children are very perceptive; they go on watching, they go on seeing what foolishness you are telling them.And how long can you deceive them? Life is there, and life is sexual.And they are watching life: they will see animals making love, they will see birds making love.

And you may go on believing that they have never seen you making love – you can go on believing it, but children know that their parents make love. In the beginning they may think they are fighting or something, but sooner or later they discover that something is going on behind their backs.

Why create these suspicions and doubts? Why not be true? Truth is always good, truth is always divine. Let them know things as they are.

I know a friend who was determined to have it out with his older boy and spent several hours painstakingly explaining sexual physiology to him.At the conclusion, feeling utterly exhausted and knowing that he did not want to go through it again with his younger son, he said,"And Billy, now that I've explained it to you, can I count on you passing it on to Bobby?" "Okay Dad," said young William.

His elder son went out in search of his younger brother at once. "Bobby," he said when he found him,"I just had a long lecture from Dad and he wants me to pass on what he told me to you." "Go ahead," said Bobby.

"Well, you know what you and I were doing with those

girls behind the barn last month? Dad wants me to tell you that the birds and the bees do it too!"

Don't be foolish, let things be as they are. Truth can never be the enemy, sexual or otherwise. Befriend truth.

And children are very understanding, they immediately accept the fact. They have no prejudices, they have no notion of right and wrong. If you tell them the truth they understand it is so and they forget all about it. And it will create a great trust in you: you never deceived them.

Sex education is one of the fundamental causes of the rift between the generations. They day the child discovers that his parents have been deceiving him, he loses all roots in trust. That is the most devastating shock you can give to that delicate system.

Go on telling the truth as it is, and don't try to philosophize about it and don't go on round and round. Tell it the way it is.

Why is there so much fear about it in you? Because your parents did not tell *you*. So you feel a little shaky, nervous, afraid, as if you are moving in some dangerous territory.

Be very simple, direct. And whenever a child inquires about anything, if you know about it, tell it. If you don't know about it, say that you don't know. There are two wrongs that you can do. One is saying something which is not so – that is one danger. Another is saying something which you don't know.

For example, the child asks, "Who created the world?" and you say, "God." Again you are leading him into some mischief. You don't know; you are pretending that you know. Soon the child will discover that you know nothing, your God is bogus.

And the problem is not that *your* God is proven bogus, the problem is that now the whole concept of God is proved bogus. You have destroyed a great possibility of inquiring into God. You should have said, "I don't know. I am trying to know; I am as ignorant as you are. If I find out before you do,

I will tell you, if you find out before I do, please tell me."

And your son will respect you for ever for this sincerity of heart, for this equality, that you never pretended, that you never tried to show, "I know, and you don't know," that you were never egoistic.

Saying to the child that God created the world, without knowing it, is nothing but an ego trip. You are enjoying yourself at the cost of the child's ignorance. But how long can you enjoy this knowledge?

Never tell the child that which you yourself are incapable of doing. Don't tell the child, "Be truthful, always be truthful" – because once he catches you red-handed being untruthful, you have destroyed something immensely valuable. And there is nothing more precious than trust.

And how long can you hide the fact? One day somebody knocks on the door and you say to the child, "Tell him that Daddy is not at home." And now the child knows that to talk about truth is one thing, but it is not meant to be followed and practiced. You have created a duality in him of saying something, pretending something, and being something else quite the contrary of it. You have created the split.

And if you know something – if the child asks about sex or how children come into the world, and you know – then simply tell it as it is. Make it as simple as possible, because the child is not asking about the physiology or about the chemistry or about the inner mechanism of sex. He is not asking about all that nonsense; that is not his interest. Don't start telling him about physiology, because in the name of sex education what they do in schools is only teach physiology. And the child is simply bored; he is not interested.

He simply wants the truth: how children come, from where they come. Just tell it. And never try to give him more information than he needs and asks form, because that will be too early. That too is happening, particularly in the West where the idea has become prevalent that children have to be given sex education. So parents are in a hurry: even if the child has not inquired, they go on pouring out the knowledge that they have acquired from books. Children feel simply bored.

Unless the inquiry has arisen in the child there is no need to say anything. When the inquiry has arisen there is no need to *hide* anything.

And it is not a question of age at all, so don't ask about small children. Whom do you call small? What age limit? Is seven years old small? Or is nine years old small? It is not a question of age; whenever the child inquires he is ready to be given the information. He may be four, he may be five, he may be seven. The more intelligent a child is, the earlier he will inquire, that much is certain. The stupid, the mediocre, may not inquire so early; he may inquire when he is twelve or fourteen. But the intelligent child is bound to inquire early, because life is such a mystery that from the very beginning the child becomes aware that something is happening. All around, life is happening, life is perpetuating itself.

He sees the eggs of the birds in the garden, and then one day the eggs are broken and the birds come out. He goes on seeing his mother's belly growing bigger and bigger, and he certainly becomes curious. What is happening? Is his mother ill or something?

And then one day she comes from the hospital with a child. And from where has the child come? It has been brought by the stork. And he sees the belly is not big anymore. Now he is puzzled: what happened to the belly?

Don't create unnecessary puzzles for children. Life is puzzling enough as it is. Life is so mysterious, the inquiry is bound to be there. But remember, the more intelligent a child is, the sooner he is going to inquire. So if your child inquires early, don't think that he seems to be dirty from the very beginning. He is not dirty, he is intelligent. If anybody is dirty, *you* are dirty. He is simply intelligent.

Tell him things as they are, and tell him the way he can

understand. Don't philosophize, don't go indirectly round and round, go directly to the point. Make it as clear as two plus two is four.

And you will be surprised: once the fact has been told the child goes away and starts playing. He is not really interested anymore; he never brings the question up again. If you falsify things he will bring up the question again and again – from this side, from that side, any excuse and he will bring up the question – because he wants to know the fact, and unless the fact is given he is not going to be satisfied. Only facts satisfy. Falsifications can postpone but they cannot satisfy.

The fourth question:

BELOVED MASTER, WHY DO I CONTINUE TO TAKE
MYSELF AND LIFE IN GENERAL SO SERIOUSLY?

Tada, everybody takes life seriously because everybody is so empty. By being serious you hide your emptiness, by being serious you pretend. By being serious you are just escaping from the loneliness that is there inside you, the nothingness that is inside you.

You cannot laugh, you cannot be at ease, because whenever you are at ease you become aware of the emptiness within. You have to be serious. Serious, you remain clinging to the surface. Relaxed, you start diving deep into your being – and there is fear.

People are serious for a certain reason. The reason is, they don't want to face themselves. And seriousness gives a certain dignity also; it is ego-fulfilling. If you are serious everybody thinks you must be important.

Seriousness has a connotation of importance. Important people are very serious – you don't see saints laughing. Christians say Jesus never laughed. They can't be right. I know Jesus far better, they must be wrong. But they indicate a certain attitude: how can Jesus laugh? He must be serious, utterly serious.

And all the Christian paintings about Jesus are ugly and false, because the face is made so serious. And the painters were doing something great; they were thinking it *had* to be serious because Jesus is the savior, and how can the savior laugh and tell jokes? You don't expect a savior of the world to tell jokes; he has to be serious. He has a great burden, he is carrying the greatest burden: the burden of the whole earth, of the whole of humanity, of the original sin of man, and other unoriginal sins too. Millions of people and their sins, and he is carrying the burden of all: he is the savior.

Christians cannot believe Krishna can dance and sing and play the flute, because of their idea. Krishna seems to be very nonserious. How can you play the flute when so many people are suffering from so many sins? Everybody is bound for hell, and you are playing the flute? Is this the time to play the flute? And you are dancing – and with so many girlfriends!

This seems to be very irresponsible. A savior dancing with girlfriends under the full-moon night, and the whole world in such a misery! Krishna should open a hospital or at least a primary school to educate people. He should do some missionary work. What is he doing under the full moon when the whole earth is drowning deeper and deeper into sin? He looks frivolous. Jesus is serious.

Tada, you ask me: WHY DO I CONTINUE TO TAKE MYSELF AND LIFE IN GENERAL SO SERIOUSLY?

It gives gratification to your ego that you are a serious person, that you are not ordinary, you are special. That you are not like people who go to the movies and laugh and talk nonsense and gossip. You are a serious person: you only meditate, you only read the Bible or the Koran. You only remain with great high things, you are not interested in the mundane.

Seriousness supports the ego, seriousness is the climate in

which the ego can thrive. Nonseriousness is the death of the ego. I teach you nonseriousness.

And because of this seriousness you make mountains out of molehills. Just small things, and you make mountains. Somebody smokes cigarettes and he is very serious, as if by smoking cigarettes he is going to hell. He thins he is committing a great sin.

Don't be so stupid. Just by taking smoke in and out you cannot commit any sin. It may show that you are stupid but it doesn't show that you are a sinner. And I don't think that people are sent to hell for stupidity. Otherwise, the whole earth would have been in hell. Why are people here? All the stupid people are here in the world!

But you make mountains. You cannot bear small things, you have to be with big things.

They tell the story of the lady who went to confession and told the priest a long story about her sexual activities and as a result, for penance, the priest told her to go into the next room, say twelve Hail Marys and wash her sins away by washing her hands in the holy water which was contained in a basin on the table.

As she was busy in the next room saying her Hail Marys and washing her hands in the basin of holy water, in walked another young lady who took one look at the scene and exclaimed, "Please take your damn hands out of that water! Don't you realize I have to gargle with it!"

You think you are committing great sins? There are other people who are far more serious. You must remember one thing: even in hell you will not be the first, you will be standing in a long long queue. Wherever you are, you will be standing in a long long queue. Forget all about being the first, even in hell.

George Bernard Shaw once said... Somebody asked, "Where would you like to go, to heaven or to hell?" He said, "Wherever I go, I would like to be the first. I am even ready to go to hell, but I want to be the first. And if I have to be the second in heaven, I don't care for heaven at all."

The ego wants to be the first everywhere. The ego wants to be the greatest saint; if it is not possible then the greatest sinner – but the greatest.

Why can't you be ordinary? To be ordinary is immensely beautiful, and to be just human is divine.

Forget ideals and goals, those ideals and goals keep you neurotic. And people go on changing their goals. First they used to have paradise as the goal, saintliness or God-realization or enlightenment. They change: now they have to attain total orgasm. Now no smaller orgasm will do – total orgasm.

And what is total orgasm anyway? And how are you going to know that this is total orgasm? Is there any way to measure it? So you will remain in misery; the total orgasm will never be achieved.

Now there are people who are continuously hankering for peak experiences, they want a peak experience every moment. They go nuts. If one moment is passed without a peak experience then life is lost. Then one moment is wasted: where is the peak experience? They want to remain on the peak continuously, twenty-four hours.

These things keep people insane. Life should be lived more sanely. And what do I mean when I say life should be lived more sanely? One should be able to accept the ordinariness of it. There is tremendous joy out of ordinariness – and that joy is not something like a peak experience, it is more diffused. It is not a peak, because peaks exist only with the valleys. If you want a peak experience then you will have to fall again and again into the valley.

You will have to repeat the myth of Sisyphus. He takes the rock to the peak and by the time it reaches the peak, the peak is so small and the rock is so big that it rolls back down the other side. He has to rush back into the valley, then he again starts the journey, again hankers for the peak experience. And

by the time he reaches to the peak, just reaching, just reaching
– and finished! Flat, back to the valley.

And that's what happens to you. Each peak experience is
momentary; it is the repetition of the myth of Sisyphus.

Forget all about it. Rather live a more ordinary life. That
is the life of a Zen disciple, that is the life of a Sufi disciple –
ordinary.

I have heard: An American inquirer came to Dacca, to
Bangladesh. He had heard about a great Sufi master. He was in
a hurry to meet the master: he inquired from many people, but
nobody had heard of him. At the airport he went from one
person to another: nobody had heard of him. He became sus-
picious, and he became very depressed. He had come from so
far, and he had heard so much about the Sufi master who lives
in Dacca, Bangladesh – and nobody even knows his name!

But as a last try, he asked a taxi driver. And the taxi driver
said, "Sit in the taxi and I will take you to him." He could not
believe it, so suddenly – because nobody knew about the mas-
ter. He had asked but nobody knew.

The taxi driver said, "Don't be worried, I know him. In fact
I am him."

And that's how it turned out to be. He was the Sufi master,
but he was working as a taxi driver – just an ordinary life.

Sufis function that way. Somebody is a weaver, somebody
may be a potter, somebody may be making carpets.

Do you know what Gurdjieff used to do in the West? His
business was carpet selling. He was a carpet salesman, that was
his business. If you had seen him you would have never recog-
nized that a great master was there.

That's how the Sufis have existed, down the ages. They
don't stand out, there is no need.

It is always the ego that hankers for the peak, and it is
the ego that does not allow you to live in constant joy. And
constant joy is not a peak, remember. In fact it is more like
peace than like bliss, more like peace. Bliss is there, but like a

fragrance; you cannot catch hold of it. It is there, but very indirect, very subtle, very delicate. It is not a peak, certainly. It is very plan and simple.

Tada, you are serious because you are afraid to know your ordinariness. And that is the truth, and truth is never ordinary. Once you have accepted the ordinariness, in your very ordinariness arises an extraordinariness. Your ordinariness becomes luminous, radiant. Then each moment is a gift, and each moment bring sits own joy, its own peace, its own beatitude.

But never hanker after peaks. The idea of the peak is an ego projection. And don't become serious and don't make mountains out of molehills; there is nothing to be serious about.

Laugh a little, live a little and be playful, and you will know what life is. It comes in laughter, non in seriousness. A serious person is a closed person, a serious person is an unavailable person. A serious person exists with all the windows and doors closed. A serious person is encapsulated in himself; he never makes any bridges with people. He closes doors, he never makes any bridges.

Laugh, because laughter is a bridge. Love, because love is a bridge. Enjoy small things, because life consists of small things and enjoying small things is a bridge.

That's why Zen people have made even tea drinking a meditation. Just tea drinking, who thinks of it as something religious? But it can be transformed; it depends on your attitude. You can drink tea so meditatively: sip it meditatively, taste it, smell the flavor. Listen first to the samovar, the song of the samovar, the dance of the vapor inside, and the subtle fragrance that starts arising. Live it, be with it, make it a prayerful moment, and then just ordinary tea is transported into something divine. And if this can be done with tea, this can be done with everything else.

To live religiously does not mean to live seriously, it means to live meditatively. And meditation has nothing to do with seriousness. Meditation is playfulness.

That's why my insistence here is more and more on dancing, on singing. I have put Vipassana and zazen in the background, because they can create seriousness in you, and you are already serious and it is dangerous. First your seriousness has to be destroyed, only then will you be able to enjoy Vipassana without becoming serious.

First you have to dance, so in dance your armor drops. First you have to shout in joy, and sing, so your life becomes more vital. First you have to cathart, so all that you have repressed is thrown out and your body is purified of toxins and poisons, and your psyche also is purified from repressed traumas and wounds.

When this has happened and you have become able to laugh and you have become able to love, then Vipassana. Now Vipassana will not drive you serious, will not drive you in any way into some ego trip. Now you can sit silently; now sitting silently is not serious.

That is the special quality that I am trying to create here in Vipassana – it does not exist anywhere in the world. My whole effort here is to bring Tantra to the twentieth century and make it neo-Tantra, to bring Tao to the twentieth century and make it neo-Tao, to bring Zen to the twentieth century and make it neo-Zen, and so on and so forth: neo-Sufis and neo-yoga...

Centuries divide you from these beautiful things; those centuries have to be dropped. And those centuries can only be dropped if *you* drop what has been done to you in those centuries. You have become too serious. Modern man is very serious; it has never been so before. And this seriousness is creating a distance from God, from the whole.

Tada, go into your seriousness and see what you are hiding behind it. You are alone, you are empty, and you are not capable of facing it. It has to be faced, because emptiness is not bad, emptiness is immensely beautiful. If you escape from it, then it becomes ugly. If you go into it, it becomes silence and quietude. And if you disappear into it, it becomes creativity.

And aloneness is beautiful. It is only the person who is alone who becomes capable of love. Those who cannot be alone, they cannot be in love at all, because their love remains a kind of need.

Love can be of two types. One is when you say to somebody, "I need you, I really love you." This is ugly love, because it is based in need. You say, "I need you": you want to use the other. You are not yet able to be alone; you want to be together with somebody, you want to cling to the other. The other keeps you occupied – without each other you become afraid of your own aloneness.

And this is what people say, and lovers enjoy it very much. When somebody says to you, "I need you, I really love you," you feel you are entering into something beautiful. You are not; you are entering into something destructive. This is the wrong kind of love.

And this is the love that exists in the world. Everybody is afraid of his loneliness and clings to the outer, uses the other as a means, someone to cling to. And when you use the other, the other is reduced to a thing. He is no longer a person, he becomes a husband or a wife. Freedom is lost. You cannot allow the other to be free, because if you allow freedom then you will have to face your loneliness. And that you don't want to do.

So you cling. You hold the other, you possess the other. Even if it means being possessed by the other, you are ready to lose your freedom. You become mutual slaves, mutual imprisonments to each other.

Love-as-need creates what the other day I was calling "tunnel vision." You become focused on one person and you are afraid that if the other person leaves you, you will not be able to live at all. The very idea of the other leaving you gives you immediate thoughts of committing suicide. Your life will not have meaning.

This is tunnel vision. One is willing to admit only a narrow range of sensations; all else is regarded as insignificant. And when such expectations fail, then one feels life is not worth living. And they always fail, because nobody can really be possessed. How can you possess a presence, a person? He is not a thing, you can never be the master. The other will go on asserting his freedom, the other will go on sabotaging your efforts to possess him. The other is trying to possess you, and you are trying to possess the other. Nobody wants to be possessed, and everybody wants to be the possessor. Now, this is doomed to fail.

Sooner or later, you will start feeling life has no meaning. This kind of love is pathological, and this is the only kind that exists and is available in the world. It drives people neurotic and psychotic. It should be changed into love which is not a need but a state. Then one can love life in more richness. Then one can love and yet allow the other freedom. Then love is nonpossessive.

But that love is possible only when you have learned how to live with your aloneness. When you can be alone and perfectly happy and you don't miss the other at all, only then can you love. But now a totally different kind of love arrives – even to think of it will shock you.

Then the lover says, "I don't need you, I love you." It will be almost incomprehensible, a lover saying to somebody, "I don't need you, I love you." It will look contradictory, because you have always heard, "I need you, I love you very much" – you are acquainted with that approach.

But this is *true* love, the other is destructive. It destroys both the people, it destroys all the possibilities of growing. This is true love, this is creative love, when you can say, "I don't need you, I simply love you."

Just meditate over it. Repeat it silently within yourself: "I don't need you, I love you" – and a totally different dimension opens up. Now there is no need to possess, now there is no need to reduce the other to a thing, now there is no need to destroy his or her freedom, now there is no need to allow the other to destroy your freedom. Now love can exist with freedom.

When love exists with freedom it has tremendous beauty; it has something of the ultimate in it. But now it is pure sharing. Now it is a luxury, it is no more a need.

I teach you love-as-luxury, not love-as-need. It is just an overflowing. You have so much that you cannot bear it any more, you have to give it to somebody. And from where are you getting so much? It comes if you learn how to live in your aloneness. If you learn how to live in your aloneness, enjoy it and celebrate it, if you learn how to be empty without any desire to fill yourself up, to stuff yourself with anything — food, love, money, power — when you are not in any way interested in stuffing your emptiness, then suddenly emptiness changes its color, its quality is transformed. You relax into it.

Then you don't feel, "I am empty." You feel, "I am emptiness — and if I am emptiness, I am emptiness." And the purity of emptiness is tremendous. In emptiness not even a particle of dust can collect. Emptiness cannot be polluted by anything, its purity is total and absolute. That emptiness is always virgin. Out of that emptiness, living in that emptiness, great joy and great peace arise and well up.

This is what I call creativity. It can become a song, it can become a painting, it can become a dance, it can become love, it can become all kinds of things. But one thing is similar: it overflows. This overflowing love is a state, a luxury, a sharing for the sheer joy of sharing. This love is celebration.

And, Tada, you have been avoiding your aloneness, you have been avoiding your emptiness. If you go on avoiding it you will never come to know this love, this creative love. And this is the greatest experience there is. You are avoiding your own great possibility and potential.

Don't be serious, please. Drop it. It is not going to give you anything except more and more misery.

Meditate on these words of Kahlil Gibran:

> Sing and dance together and be joyous
> But let each of you be alone
> Even as the strings of a lute are alone
> Though they quiver with the same music.
> Stand together, yet not too near together,
> For the pillars of the temple stand apart,
> And the oak tree and the cypress
> Grow not in each other's shadow.

Be alone: that is meditation. And in aloneness wells up love: that is creation. Then love can do miracles.

But the person who remains serious remains unavailable to his own sources, his own juice; he remains unavailable to his own soil and roots. The person who is serious goes on moving round and round outside his being.

Drop your seriousness. Laugh a little, love a little, and you will know what God is.

7 Cooked and Burnt

The Sufi is not an escapist, that is not his climate. He is utterly against escapism. He believes in celebrating the world, celebrating existence, celebrating life. It is the very fundamental of Sufism that the creator can be reached only through the creation. You need not renounce his creation to get to him; in fact if you renounce his creation you will never get to him. Renouncing his creation, indirectly you have renounced the creator himself.

But renunciation still happens. It is not that the Sufi renounces the world, but that he attains to God – and the moment God is attained, the world disappears. Then there is nothing to renounce: then only God is.

The Sufi does not escape from the world, but a moment comes when the world disappears and dissolves. The Sufi lives in the world and he finds that there is no world, only God is.

The Sufi is not an ascetic. He does not believe in inflicting pain on himself, he is not pathological. The Sufi lives life in an utterly normal way, with no perversions, with no obsessions. Although, slowly slowly, the quality of his life goes on changing, it is not that he tries to change it. His whole effort consists in remembering God, not in changing himself.

Let it sink deep in you; if you miss this point you will miss the whole point of Sufism. The Sufi concentrates on only one thing, remembrance of God – *zikr*. As that remembrance deepens, his obsession with the world lessens. As he comes closer and closer to the ultimate reality, the ordinary reality is no longer attractive; it starts receding back. Because when you find the real gold, how can you go on carrying the unreal gold? When you have found the real diamonds you will automatically drop the stones, colored stones, that you have been carrying all along.

The escapist says, "Renounce your colored stones so that you can get to the real diamonds." The Sufi says just the contrary: he says, "Get to the real diamonds, and that which is not real will drop out of your life of its own accord."

To know the real is enough, the unreal is renounced in that very knowing. And because the unreal is renounced in that very knowing, it leaves no scars and wounds on you. The ascetic suffers from great wounds. He is not ripe yet, otherwise the fruit would have fallen without leaving any scar on the body of the tree. If the fruit is unripe and you pluck it, it hurts the tree, it hurts the fruit; both will remain wounded.

Have you not seen the beauty of a ripe fruit fallen of its own accord? Silently, spontaneously. The tree may not even become aware that the fruit has disappeared, the fruit may not become aware that the tree is no more there.

Sufism is the simplest way possible. The Sufi lives a simple life. But the simplicity is not cultivated, because a cultivated simplicity is no longer simplicity; it is already complex. When you cultivate something, there is motivation, there is desire, there is longing; you are hankering for something. By cultivating something, you are trying to become something. Becoming is desire. And how can desire be simple? So cultivation is never simple. A practiced sannyas, a practiced simplicity, can never have beauty. In the first place it is not simplicity at all.

You can go and see so many saints in this country, or in other countries: their simplicity is cultivated, calculated, motivated. They are desirous of God, they are greedy for God, hence they are ready to pay the price.

The Sufi says: God is available, it is already available. All that you need is an uncomplicated mind, all that you need is a state of no-motivation. All that you need is to fall into the silence of this moment, no trying to achieve something tomorrow. And what is your afterlife? It is the prolonged shadow of the tomorrow. So those who are thinking to attain to heaven or to nirvana after death are very greedy people. They are not religious at all.

Sufism does not believe in any fairy-tales of the other world, of heaven and hell. And it is not that heaven does not exist, but that is not the concern of the Sufi. The Sufi lives totally in the moment. His simplicity comes out of his understanding, not out of cultivation; he does not practice it. Seeing life, he becomes aware of the austerity of a roseflower, how simple it is, and the beauty of its austerity. He becomes austere like a roseflower: it is not poor, the roseflower is simple and rich. What more richness can there be? The roseflower is simple and in utter luxury – what more luxury can there be?

The Sufi lives in the moment, blooms in the moment like a roseflower, simple yet rich. The poverty is not imposed; he is poor in spirit. And what does it mean to be poor in spirit? It simply means there is no ego, that's all; not that he is attached to poverty. Beware of that. There are people who are attached to wealth and there are people who are attached to poverty. But it is the same attachment. I have heard:

The story is told of a dervish who went to visit a great Sufi master. Seeing his affluence, the dervish thought to himself, "How can Sufism and such prosperity go hand in hand?" After staying a few days with the master, he decided to leave. The master said, "Let me accompany you on your journey!"

After they had gone a short distance, the dervish noticed that he had forgotten his *kashkul*, the begging-bowl. So he asked the master for permission to return and get it.

The master replied, "I departed from all my possessions, but you can't even leave behind your begging-bowl. Thus, we must part company from here."

The Sufi is not attached to wealth or to poverty; he is simply not attached to anything. And when you are not attached to anything, you need not renounce. Renunciation is the other side of attachment. Those who understand the foolishness of attachment don't renounce. They live in the world but yet they are not of the world.

To willfully insist upon being in poverty is still an attachment: remember it. And to willfully insist upon *anything* is again an ego trip.

The Sufi lives simply, the Sufi lives without any will of his own. If it happens to be a palace, he is happy; if it happens to be a hut, he is happy. If it happens to be that he is a king, it is okay; if it happens to be that he is a beggar, that too is perfectly okay. He has no preference. He simply lives in the moment, whatsoever God makes available to him. He does not change anything.

This has to be understood, because for centuries religions have been teaching you renunciation. For centuries religions have lived with a great inclination towards escapism. The Sufi has a totally different approach, far healthier, far more whole, far more human, far more natural. Because whenever you escape from something it is out of fear, and out of fear there is never any transformation.

When something drops of its own accord – not that you drop it, but simply that it has become nonessential, unimportant – then there is freedom.

Freedom is never out of fear, freedom is out of great awareness. The Sufi lives in the world, mindful of God. He lives in the world, but he remembers God. He moves in the marketplace, but his heart is throbbing with a certain remembrance. The *zikr* continues. He does not become forgetful in the world; that is his work.

Escape or no escape, if you are forgetful you will miss God anywhere you are, in e marketplace or in the monastery. If you are not forgetful, if you are mindful, alert and aware, then God is everywhere – as much here as anywhere else, as much now as then. There is no question of going anywhere; one can simply relax here and fall into a kind of watchful silence. And then life is simple and uncluttered.

Yes, that is what simplicity is: not a cultivated character but a life which is uncluttered by the nonessential, by the unimportant, by the mundane, by the trivial.

And again let me repeat that the Sufi does not believe in any fairy-tales, so there is no question of being motivated. He does not believe in the tomorrows. All that he knows of time is now, all that he knows of space is here.

These sounds of the birds are divine for him. There is no other God separate from this existence. The dancer is in the dance, so he has no idea of a personal God sitting somewhere above the clouds. His God is an impersonal presence.

Feel it now, this very moment. The presence is here, as it is everywhere else. All that is needed is your falling into a kind of attunement, your falling inwards into a kind of at-one-ment. Then the cawing of the crows and the cuckoo calling from far away...and all is silent. In that silence you start becoming aware of the impersonal presence that surrounds you.

A young bank clerk stole five thousand pounds from the bank and was unable to reimburse it when caught. In despair he went up to the cliff with the intention of committing suicide. As he was about to jump he was tapped on his left shoulder, and upon turning around he spied an especially ugly lady who claimed to be his fairy godmother, and granted him three wishes.

His first wish was to replace the five thousand pounds, which was granted. His second wish was to be the owner of a large mansion, and his third, the owner of a Rolls Royce. All these were granted to him by his fairy godmother.

Feeling very pleased with himself, he turned back to make his way home to get the five thousand pounds, the mansion and the Rolls Royce. His fairy godmother stopped him and requested that he, too, grant her a single wish. He was only too happy to oblige, whereupon she asked him to make love to her.

He was repelled by her, but obliged because of the wishes she had granted him. He made love to her in a great hurry and pulled his trousers up and was about to leave when she stopped him yet again. This time she asked, "How old are you, young man?"

His reply was, "I am thirty-five years of age – but why do you ask?" She said, 'You still believe in fairy godmothers?"

The person who believes in a personal God is still immature. There is nothing like that. That personal God is nothing but your idea of a father, projected and magnified. You are childish. When you pray, if you think you are praying to a personal God you are simply being stupid. There is nobody listening to your prayer. And yet God is. But God is not a person, God is an impersonal presence.

God is this whole, the totality of all that is. Hence prayer can only be a silence. You cannot address God – prayer can only be an utter silence.

If you are silent now, it is a prayerful moment. This is what prayer is all about. When everything stops: no thought moves in your head, your breathing slows down, a moment comes when there is almost no breath. In that state of silence you are connected, you are plugged into reality. You are more separate; you are one. That oneness is prayer.

Now the sutras.

A RUBY, THERE, IS JUST A PIECE OF STONE...

Where? What does Hakim Sanai mean by "there?" the silence that I was talking about. When you are utterly silent, in prayer, in samadhi...

A RUBY, THERE, IS JUST A PIECE OF STONE...

Your whole way of looking at things changes. When there are desires clamoring in your mind, even an ordinary stone can look like a ruby. You can project your desire on an ordinary stone; you can create an illusion that it is very precious.

Otherwise, when you are not possessed by desires, what is a ruby? An ordinary stone. All diamonds are nothing but ordinary stones. Just think of one day the third world war happens and the whole of humanity disappears from the earth, will there be any difference between a stone and a diamond? Will there be any difference at all between the great Kohinoor and the pebble by the side of the road? There will be none.

That means the difference is created by man, is projected by man. It is a manufactured difference. It is something in man's mind: if man disappears then there will be no rubies and no pebbles, they all will be the same. Then the Kohinoor cannot demand a special privilege.

It happened once, a Zen master used to live in a forest, and the king of the country came to pay a visit to him. And he had brought many presents, among them a beautiful robe studded with diamonds – very valuable, the most valuable robe that the king had. He presented the velvet robe.

The master accepted it, but then immediately gave it back and said, "Please take it back."

The king felt offended. He said, "This is a present from me. Will you not oblige me by accepting it? I will feel very rejected."

The master said, "It is not a question of my obliging you. If you insist, I can keep it here. But I must tell you one thing: I live here all alone, there are no human beings. So who will appreciate this robe? I live here with deer and peacocks, and sometimes the lion comes, and all those animals will laugh at me. Don't make me a laughingstock, please take it back. They will all laugh; they will think that now in this old age I have become foolish.

"I have all my companions, birds and beasts, and they won't

understand these diamonds and their value. Please take it back, please oblige me by taking it back. This is perfectly good where human stupidity prevails, but here it is meaningless."

It is man who has created the distinctions and categories, otherwise all is one. But there is no need for the third world war to happen to understand this. The moment you drop your mind, you will immediately be able to see. The mind dropped, the world is transformed – because the mind has created a certain kind of world. Once you are no more a mind, that whole world disappears. It was a dream. And then you are awake, and then you see things as they are in themselves.

A German philosopher, Immanuel Kant, used to say, "You cannot see things as they are in themselves."

Philosophically he is right. If you work through the mind you cannot see things as they are, because the mind will always be there to distort, to improve, to change, to project, to color this way or that, with all its prejudices. The mind will be there. The mind won't allow you to see things as they are in themselves, because whatsoever reaches to you will go through the mind. In that way, Immanuel Kant is right. I have heard:

An Englishman and an Irishman went to the captain of a ship bound for America and asked permission to work their passage over. The captain consented, let the Englishman go on board, but told the Irishman he must bring references. The Irishman went ashore and got them, but the discrimination angered him and he was determined to get even.

One day, when the two were aiding in washing down the deck, the Englishman went to the railing, roped bucket in hand, and let the bucket down into the water. He was just leaning over to pull it up when a great wave came aboard, caught him up and pulled him overboard.

The Irishman stopped scrubbing and went to the railing. He peered into the water. No sign of the Englishman.

Righteously indignant, the Irishman took himself up to the captain's cabin.

"Captain, perhaps yez remember, whin I shipped aboard this vessel ye asked me for references an' let thot Englishman come on without thim?"

"Of course I remember. You aren't complaining at this late date, are you?"

"Complainin',Captain? Not the likes of me. I'm jist here to tell you thot your trust was betrayed. You know, Captain, thim English..."

"Whatever do you mean, 'betrayed'?"

"Sure, an' that Englishman's gone off wid your pail!"

If you are carrying a certain prejudice in your mind, you will see only through the prejudice. And the mind is nothing but prejudices and prejudices. The mind means your whole past, and anything that enters you will have to go through your whole past. It will be distorted, it will be colored, it will be changed so much by the time it reaches you that you will not be able to know what in reality is the case.

Immanuel Kant is right, but philosophically only. He is not aware of the world of meditation, he is not aware of the Sufis and the Zen people and the Taoists. Otherwise there is a way to know things as they are in themselves: just put the mind aside. Look with empty eyes and then there is no interference with reality.

And suddenly you will see the pearl is no more a pearl, the ruby is no more a ruby, the diamond is no more a diamond. Then all distinctions, differences, evaluations and judgments have disappeared. Then suddenly things are there without any labels and names and categories.

A RUBY, THERE, IS JUST A PIECE OF STONE:
AND SPIRITUAL EXCELLENCE THE HEIGHT
OF FOLLY.

And those who have tasted something of meditation, the world is no more significant to them. They don't renounce it, it is simply no more significant – not even worth renouncing. It has no value at all.

When you renounce the world you are giving it value. You are saying, "It is so valuable that if I don't renounce it I will be caught in it." When you escape from the world you are afraid of the world. Otherwise why escape? Your very escape shows that you are obsessed by things, that you are too attached and afraid that if you live here you will be drowned by things. This simply shows your impotence. The escapist simply shows his cowardice and impotence.

The Sufis say: Don't be worried, attain to meditation. Attain to that uncultivated silence. Relax into your being, just be, and then see. And there is nothing to renounce. There is nothing to indulge in and there is nothing to renounce; both those polarities have disappeared.

A RUBY, THERE, IS JUST A PIECE OF STONE:
AND SPIRITUAL EXCELLENCE THE HEIGHT
OF FOLLY.

And not only worldly things disappear, your so-called otherworldly experiences also become stupid. All claims become foolish.

This is the criterion of a real Sufi: he will not claim any excellence, he will not claim any spiritual experience. He will live very ordinarily, he will live without claim. How can he claim anything? Because deep inside he has come to know that there is nobody to claim anything, it is all emptiness. He has come to see the state of *fana*: he has dissolved. Who is there to claim? He cannot claim worldly power and prestige, he cannot claim spiritual excellence.

Sanai says: That is the height of folly. why? Because one who claims, "I have riches of the world" can be forgiven – he is a fool but he can be forgiven. But the person who claims spiritual riches, he cannot be forgiven. This is the height of folly; you are still carrying the same categories of the world, you are still bragging about yourself. The really spiritual person simply becomes anonymous.

A strange story is told of a Zen master that when he attained to samadhi, birds started coming to him – birds which never used to come to him before. They would sit on his shoulders, on his head, they would play in his lap, they would sit around him, as if he was also a bird.

Great fame spread. His disciples started claiming, "See, this is a real master. This is what a real master should be. There is no other master like our master; he has attained to such heights of samadhi that birds no longer fear him. He has attained to such love and compassion that even birds understand it."

Then one day a very strange thing happened: the birds stopped coming, they disappeared. For days the disciples waited, but the birds were not coming anymore. They were puzzled. They asked the master and he said, "Now something really has happened. The birds were coming because there was some claim inside me that 'I have attained.' Now even that claim has disappeared, so the birds also have forgotten all about me.

"Now I am anonymous. Now even the birds know that I am anonymous, I am a nobody. they used to come because I was still somebody. Now they don't come; now the ultimate has happened. Now they don't come because they don't see anybody here – it is just absence."

This is *fana*. This is what Sufis call dissolution. In this state you cannot *claim* – spiritual excellence or anything. Remember always, any spiritual claim becomes a barrier.

SILENCE IS PRAISE...

And now there is not even any prayer. Words won't do; all your prayers are nothing but words. Now silence is praise, just to be silent is enough.

...HAVE DONE WITH SPEECH;
YOUR CHATTER WILL ONLY BRING YOU
HARM AND SORROW – HAVE DONE!

If you really want to be in a state of prayer, have done with words. You have been taught as Christians, as Hindus, as Mohammedans, how to pray, what words to use, what is proper prayer. All prayers are false. The real prayer has nothing to do with words and formalities, the real prayer is neither Hindu nor Mohammedan nor Christian.

How can silence be Hindu or Mohammedan? Silence is silence. Words can be Hindu and words can be Mohammedan, hence words create conflict, hence words create violence in the world. It is not that people are fighting for realities – they are fighting for words.

Thousands of wars have been fought, not for any real thing, but just for mere words. One believes in the Koran and one believes in the Gita: it is enough to kill millions of people. And both are words; neither the Koran nor the Gita is a reality.

Have you seen people killing each other for a roseflower or for the moon or for the sun? These are realities. but they can kill even in the name of the moon: if somebody claims, "The moon is our God," then he has imposed a word 'God' on the moon. And then somebody says, "You are a fool. The moon is not the real God, the real God is the sun." And the fight starts and the quarreling starts.

Words have been the cause of all wars – religious wars, political wars. Ideology is the root cause of all violence. And now there are people who try to bring peace to the world, and again they create another ideology.

For example, the followers of Mahatma Gandhi think that his ideology will bring peace to the world. You have not learned a single lesson from history. No ideology can ever bring peace to the world; all ideologies bring wars to the world in their wake.

Do you think Mohammed knowingly gave an ideology to the world to bring war? The name that he gave to his religion is "Islam": Islam means peace. But the ideology didn't bring peace, it brought thousands of wars.

Jesus is the man of peace. Who else can claim more peaceful attitudes towards life than Jesus? But Christianity, the ideology that was created around Jesus, has been a calamity.

All ideologies are bound to bring war, even ideologies based on peace and for peace. Then how can peace come? Peace can come only if man understands the stupidity of all ideologies and drops them. If man simply starts living without any ideology, there will be peace. Otherwise there cannot be any peace.

And remember, you can make an ideology out of it also: "This is our ideology, that we will not believe in any ideology." Then war will come again. Then those who won't believe in it and won't agree with you will start fighting with you.

I am not telling you that you have to make *this* an ideology, that no ideology is needed. I am simply saying try to understand what has happened through ideologies, words, theories, philosophies. Just see the point; and seeing it, let it drop.

Don't make a new ideology against ideologies. Just seeing the point, drop it, let it drop, be finished with it.

HAVE DONE!

Sanai is right. He says: Have done, and then live without ideology. Live without any theories of *how* to live. Live without any ideals, live without any shoulds and oughts.

Every fact sooner or later becomes an ought, and then it becomes dangerous. Every truth sooner or later becomes an ideology, and then it is harmful and poisonous.

Can't man live without any ideology? I don't see that there is any problem. If birds and animals and trees can live without ideology, man can live without ideology. Have you seen any

Catholic tree or any communist peacock? If the whole existence can live without ideology, why not man?

And the moment a man lives without ideology he is prayerful. Then his whole life is prayer, then he is religious. The man who has an ideology is political; all ideologies are political.

The religious person lives without any ideology. He simply lives, responding to reality moment to moment – not through words, not through disciplines, not through certain attitudes and conclusions, no. He simply responds to whatsoever is the case and whatsoever is right in the moment, not according to some idea.

Certainly a religious person will have to be very alert so that he can respond. The man who has a certain ideology need not be alert, he can remain asleep. He has a certain ideology; if any situation arises he has a ready-made answer for it. What need has he to be aware? That's why people are living in sleep, there is no *need* to be alert. You have been given ready-made answers for everything.

If you have to search for the answer each moment on your own, how can you live in sleep? The reality goes on creating challenges, and if you don't have any ready-made answers you will have to be alert and watchful.

The moment one drops words and ideologies, suddenly one becomes very very aware. And that awareness is prayer. Silence is always full of awareness, and the chattering mind is always unconscious.

> BELIEF AND UNBELIEF BOTH HAVE THEIR ORIGIN
> IN YOUR HYPOCRITE'S HEART...

See the revolutionary statement in these words:

> BELIEF AND UNBELIEF BOTH HAVE THEIR ORIGIN
> IN YOUR HYPOCRITE'S HEART...

From where comes belief? And from where unbelief? They are not different, they come from the same source; the hypocrite's heart.

You can see the hypocrites in the temples, mosques and churches. You can see them in so many shapes and so many sizes with so many different kinds of words, but it is the same source: hypocrisy.

Why is hypocrisy the source of belief and unbelief? A man says "I believe in God" without knowing anything about God. Without have ever experienced God, without having ever tasted God, he says, "I believe in God." From where is this belief coming? It is hypocrisy. He is pretending; he is deceiving others, he is deceiving himself.

If you have not known on your own, how can you believe in God? But your father has told you, your mother has told you, you have been taught by the priest, by the state. They go on giving you beliefs. If you are born in a Catholic country the Catholic belief will be given to you, if you are born in a communist country the communist belief will be given to you.

Before the child becomes aware, he is already conditioned, already poisoned. And then his whole life he will repeat the belief that has been put into him, and because of this belief he will remain a hypocrite.

The man who says, "There is no God" – has he known? Has he inquired? Has he explored the whole existence and *found* that there is no God? No, he has not explored it, this again is out of hypocrisy.

So remember: belief and unbelief, howsoever contradictory they look, the theist and the atheist, howsoever antagonistic they look, are the same. They come from the same source. Without knowing anything, without experiencing anything on their own, they go on believing, they go on declaring.

That's what hypocrisy is all about: to say something that you don't know, to utter something that is not your own authentic experience. To live in borrowed knowledge is hypocrisy. Deep down you are something, on the surface you pretend something else. This is hypocrisy.

And Sanai's statement is tremendously revolutionary, because he puts the believer and the unbeliever in the same category.

The religious person is neither a believer nor an unbeliever, because he is not a hypocrite. He will say only that which he knows, he will not utter a single word that he does not know. If he does not know, he will say that he does not know.

Socrates is a religious man, because he says, "I know only one thing, that I don't know anything." This is religiousness. This is sincerity of the heart, this is simplicity, this is humbleness.

...THE WAY IS ONLY LONG BECAUSE
YOU DELAY TO START ON IT...

And the way is only long because you delay to start on it. Otherwise it is not a long way. Between you and God there is only one step to be taken, just one step. But people go on postponing – and they can postpone because they have beliefs; beliefs help them to postpone.

The so-called religious man knows that God is there; without knowing, he knows that God is there. "So what is the hurry? Tomorrow, or the day after tomorrow, I will go and have a dip in the Ganges. Or I will go to Kaaba and pray there. Or at the last moment when I am dying I will remember him. He is there, so why be worried and why be in a hurry?" It can be postponed. Because of belief, there is no need to explore, inquire, investigate.

And for the one who says, "There is no God," there is no question of investigation either. If there is no God, what is the point of investigating and inquiring? Both are finished with inquiry.

And the man who is not in constant inquiry, he will go on missing — although the distance is not very long, the distance is of just a single step. And what is that step? From hypocrisy to sincerity: that is the single step.

Drop all that you don't know but you go on pretending to know. Let all borrowed knowledge disappear and just be true to one thing, to your own experience. Only that which is your own experience is going to help, and everything else is a hindrance.

Just see the point. Sanai is really making tremendously significant statements.

...ONE SINGLE STEP WOULD BRING YOU TO HIM...

From hypocrisy to sincerity. And this is not a long long journey, you can do it right now this very moment. You already know what is your experience and what is not your experience, don't you? Everybody knows. The believer knows, "I believe, but I don't know." The unbeliever knows, "I don't believe, but I don't know — maybe God is." The believer goes on doubting: "Maybe he is not."

You are perfectly aware about borrowed knowledge. But why do you cling to it? Because it gives you a good decoration for the ego. It gratifies your ego; you can pretend that you are knowledgeable. You can walk upright, you can tell people, "I know, and you don't know." You can go on carrying that holier-than-thou face. You can enjoy this trip, because you can recite the Gita like a parrot and because you know the Koran like a computer. This is not knowing. Have done with all this! And one single step is enough...

WOULD BRING YOU TO HIM:
BECOME A SALVE, AND YOU WILL BE A KING.

The moment you move from hypocrisy to sincerity,

suddenly your whole ego will disappear – because it is hypocrisy that helps your ego to remain there. If you drop all that is borrowed, you have taken away all the props of the ego: your ego will fall flat.

And in the fall of the ego is the beginning of a real life. When the ego falls you are in a state of surrender, you become a slave. Remember, this word 'slave' has a tremendously different connotation in the East than it has in the West. The West knows only one kind of slave: one who has been forced. That's why in any Western language the word 'slave' is ugly.

One day I gave sannyas to a young man and I gave him the name Devadasyo: divine slave. Immediately I could see on his face that he was feeling offended. "Slave?" Although he didn't say anything to me that moment, next day he wrote a letter saying, "Beloved Master, I have inquired into it. If instead of 'slave' the word can simply mean 'servant' it will be more appreciated – not 'slave' but just 'servant'. Can I make it mean just 'servant'? I have inquired into it and people said yes, both meanings are possible."

So much fear of the word 'slave' – because it only has a one-dimensional meaning in the West: when the slavery is imposed on somebody.

And similar is the case with the word 'surrender'. In the West it does not have a beautiful connotation. In the East 'slave' has two meanings. One, that you know, is forced slavery, which is ugly. Another is, willfully accepted slavery, which is beautiful – voluntarily accepted. Seeing that "I am only a part and not separate from the whole, so how can I be a master?" one surrenders.

This is a totally different meaning of surrender. It is utterly blissful. It is not that you are forced to surrender; if you are forced then it is not surrender. It is when you do it on your own, seeing that you are just a part, a wave in the ocean, and the wave surrenders to the ocean because "I am not separate, so why go on pretending that I am separate? The ocean is the master, the total is the master, and I am just a wave in the ocean. I am surrendered: let the ocean have its say."

That's what Jesus says on the cross:"Let thy kingdom come, let thy will be done." That is surrender, that is becoming a slave. In that moment Jesus dropped the last remaining shadow of his ego.

...BECOME A SLAVE, AND YOU WILL BE A KING.

And this is the miracle, that when you become a slave you become the king. Why? And how?

When you surrender to the ocean as a wave, you become the ocean. Separate from the ocean you are just a wave, continuously fighting and afraid of death. Separate from the ocean you are just a worry, an anguish, and nothing else.

One with the ocean, there is no question of death. The wave will disappear but you will remain in the ocean for ever and for ever. Now there is no worry, and now there is no goal either. Wherever the ocean is going is right; that is the only place to go. Now there is no private destiny, so no worry.

And even disappearance is no more disappearance, because you have already seen the point that you are not separate. When you are, you are in the ocean; when you are not, you are in the ocean. And the ocean remains. Only waves come and go; the wave was only a form. Forms come and go but the substance remains.

When the wave becomes one with the ocean — or *remem - bers* that it is one with the ocean, becomes aware of the oneness — it is no more a slave, it is the king. It has attained to the deathless, to the eternal.

THE DUMB FIND TONGUES, WHEN THE SCENT OF LIFE REACHES THEM FROM HIS SOUL.

And when this happens, even those who have been dumb

find tongues. Even those who have not said a single word before, whose life was only of prayer, whose life was only of silence, suddenly start singing. Their silence becomes a song.

The moment the slave disappears and the king arrives, the wave disappears and the ocean takes over, there is great creativity. Your life is no more ordinary and mundane. Now it has the flavor of the divine, of the sacred.

THE DUMB FIND TONGUES...

Those who have never spoken anything, they start saying things which are unbelievable, things which are incredible, words which are radiant, pregnant. Their gestures have a power now: if they touch you they will transform you by their touch, if they look in your eyes you will never be the same man again.

...WHEN THE SCENT OF LIFE REACHES THEM
FROM HIS SOUL.

The great Sufi master, Jalaluddin Rumi, wrote these three lines as his own epitaph: Not more than three words, My whole life is condensed in these three words: I was raw, now I am cooked and burnt. This is the death that brings resurrection. I was raw, now I am cooked and burnt.

Jalaluddin, the greatest Sufi, says, "These three words contain my whole life."

If you are separate, you are raw. If you join together with existence, you are cooked. And if you disappear absolutely, without leaving even a shadow of the ego, you are burnt.

Patanjali has called this state *nirbeej samadhi*: seedless samadhi, when the seed is burnt. Now there will be no more misery, no more coming and going, no more constant change of form. Now you will abide in the eternal as eternal. Jalaluddin also says: Listen to the reed. It is complaining. It tells of separation, saying, "Ever since they tore me from the reed bed, My lament has moved man and woman to tears. Everyone who is left far from his source Wishes back to the time of union.

"Listen to the reed...everyone who is left far from his source wishes back to the time of union." We are all searching for our source. We are all like reeds searching for the reed bed from which we have been torn.

Jalaluddin had a special love for the reed flute. "Do not ask why God created the flute" goes a folk song. "He wanted the people to understand Rumi." Otherwise how would people have understood Rumi? That's why he created the flute.

When a man attains to the ultimate he becomes a flute. A song is born: a song that goes on and on. Buddha sang it for forty-two years – day in and day out, year in and year out, for forty-two years he continued a song. Mahavira did the same, and so did Mohammed and Bahauddin and Jalaluddin. And it is this song that we are listening to and going into right now: Hakim Sanai.

From where comes this song? It comes out of silence. It is condensed silence, it comes from your absolute emptiness. You become just a passage to God, a hollow bamboo, a flute, and God starts singing through you.

All the great scriptures of the world are songs of the divine. But you will understand them only if you have understood silence. Not by going into the scriptures will you understand them, but by going into your own silence. When you are in the same state as Krishna, you will be able to understand the Bhagavadgita. 'Bhagavadgita' means the divine song, the celestial song. But how can you understand the song if you have not even understood silence, from where it comes? It consists of silence, it is condensed silence.

You will not be able to understand the Koran unless you attain to that state of *fana* where the Koran descended into Mohammed. Only then will you be able to understand the

Koran. And the beauty is that if you understand the silence of your being, you will be able to understand simultaneously all the great scriptures of the world, and you will not find any contradictions in them. But right now if you start reading the Koran and the bible and the Gita, you will be very much puzzled and confused. You will find contradictions and contradictions and nothing else.

What to say about contradictions between the Gita and the Koran? If you read the Gita itself you will find thousands of contradictions in it. It is not a question of comparing it with the Koran; just go on reading the Gita with a critical eye, and you will be puzzled – Krishna goes on contradicting himself. You will not be able to understand at all. Understanding arises only out of meditation.

And when you have attained to meditation, even your words will have the sweetness of the Koran and the Gita – even *your* words. You who have always been dumb will suddenly start speaking, which will not only surprise others, it will surprise you too, because you will not be able to understand from where they are coming. They come from the beyond: you are just a receptacle.

> THE DUMB FIND TONGUES, WHEN THE SCENT
> OF LIFE REACHES THEM FROM HIS SOUL.
> LISTEN TRULY – AND DON'T BE FOOLED
> – THIS IS NOT FOR FOOLS...

And when in silence something starts speaking to you, listen truly – don't be fooled! What does Sanai mean by "listen truly?" Don't bring your old mind in, don't start interpreting it, otherwise you will have missed. Just listen to whatsoever happens. Forget that you have to interpret it, forget the very idea that you have to understand it, forget absolutely about bringing your intellect into it.

Just listen as you listen to the sounds of the birds, or the sound of running water, or the wind passing through the pines: how do you listen? Do you try to decipher the meaning? How do you listen to somebody playing the guitar? You don't bring your intellect in, you listen from the heart. You only listen, for no other purpose; just listening is so tremendously joyful. You start swaying with the music, you feel like dancing with the music.

This is the right way of listening, when the infinite starts passing through you, when those sources from the beyond start pouring into you.

Please beware, don't be a fool. If you bring your mind in, you have disturbed the whole process. Then you will learn something which has not been told, and you will tell about something which you have not heard.

So the greatest preparation is silence: the silence of a no-mind. And only when the silence is absolutely ripe will you be able to listen.

The music is still going on, but you are not able to listen because you are not tuned to silence. It is not that one day suddenly, twenty-five centuries ago, underneath a bodhi tree, God spoke to Buddha. Or that fourteen centuries ago, suddenly on the mountains, God poured himself into Mohammed. No, it is not so: he is pouring every moment.

And when I say this to you, I am saying it as an eye-witness. He is pouring every moment. He cannot stop pouring, he is helpless, that is his way of being. The Koran is being poured into you every moment, the Gita is just showering all around you. But you are not tuned. You are like a pot put upside-down: it goes on raining but the pot remains empty.

It is as if the sun has risen but you are sitting with closed eyes. Open your eyes any moment, and for you it may appear that the sun has just risen because you have opened your eyes. It is not so: the sun has always been there.

God cannot be absent for a single moment, because if he is absent the whole world will collapse.

LISTEN TRULY — AND DON'T BE FOOLED
— THIS IS NOT FOR FOOLS...

And who are the fools? You will be surprised: the pundits, the scholars, the learned people. They are the fools, because they are so full of knowledge that they will not be able to listen. Even if God starts pouring into them, they will correct him. They will *have* to correct him; it is impossible for them not to interfere. If somebody is a follower of the Gita and God speaks through him, he will make God fit with his Gita. That is what proves him a fool.

God always speaks in a new way. He is always original and fresh: he need not repeat the old. He has spoken once that way as the Gita, now he will never speak the same way again. He has spoken once as a buddha in the Dhammapada, now he will never speak the same way again.

And this is what man goes on expecting. I receive thousands of letters, and the basic thing in those thousands of letters is: why don't I behave like a buddha? But why should I behave like a buddha? They have a fixed expectation. If they see that I am saying anything which goes differently from Buddha, they are immediately alert and alarmed. They are afraid something has gone wrong.

But do you know? Buddha spoke in *his* way — he was not repeating Krishna, not at all. And people must have been reaching him too, saying, "Why don't you speak like Krishna?" And Krishna spoke in his own way, and he was not repeating Rama either. And people must have been reaching him too: "why don't you speak like Rama? Why don't you live like Rama?"

These are the fools. And these are learned fools. They know much about scriptures, but they know nothing about life. Life is always new. When a roseflower comes on the rosebush it is not a repetition of any roseflower that has preceded it. It is unique, incomparable.

And that's how it happens every time God pours himself

through somebody. He is always unique. He never fits with his own past expressions. He always goes on transcending his own past, he goes on surpassing himself. He is never confined and contained by the past, because he is not dead.

If God speaks to you like he spoke through Krishna, that means that in these five thousand years he has not grown up at all. Then these five thousand years he had been dead. Then there is no need of him – a His Master's Voice record will do.

Remember it. If you feel something in you that fits with the bible, that fits with the Gita, that fits with anything else, beware: it may be your mind which is playing tricks on you. God never fits with anything, he is always unique. The song is always new.

> LISTEN TRULY – AND DON'T BE FOOLED
> – THIS IS NOT FOR FOOLS:
> ALL THESE DIFFERENT SHADES
> BECOME ONE COLOR IN THE JAR OF UNITY...

And if you have listened well, you will be surprised:

> ...ALL THESE DIFFERENT SHADES BECOME ONE
> COLOR...

The Koran and the Gita and the Bible and the Dhamma-pada and the Tao Te Ching – suddenly all become one color. All the shades dissolve into one color. The whole spectrum of seven colors disappears and all become one color, white. Hence the color white has always been a symbol for unity, for oneness, for purity.

> ...THE ROPE BECOMES SLENDER WHEN REDUCED
> TO A SINGLE STRAND.

This is the mystic union: *unio mystica*. When you have

dissolved yourself with the whole, then all differences disap-
pear. Then everything is separate and yet not separate, different
and yet not different. Then the songs are different but the
melody is the same. This is unity in multiplicity, and this is
the richness of life. All songs are different but the melody is the
same.

YOUR INTELLECT IS JUST A HOTCHPOTCH OF GUESSWORK AND THOUGHT, LIMPING OVER THE FACE OF THE EARTH...

Beware: your intellect is the root cause of your going astray.
It is all a hotchpotch of guesswork and thought.

The intellect can never give you truth. It can at the most
guess and infer – but truth is not an inference and it is not
guesswork. It is not a question of guessing: either you know or
you don't know.

And how can you guess about the unknown? You may
guess about the known, but you cannot guess about the un-
known. "The unknown" simply means that you have no idea
about it, no idea at all. How are you going to guess about it?
How are you going to think about the unknown? Only the
known can be thought about. So thinking is a repetitive
process, it goes on moving in a circle. It never leads you to
new truths, it never leads you to discoveries.

And this is not only so in religion, it is so everywhere, even
in science. All the great discoveries of science have not been
made by the process of thinking; all the great discoveries of
science have happened through no-mind. And now scientists
are becoming aware of the phenomenon.

For example, Madame Curie discovered something – for
three years she had been working hard on a problem; she had
tried all possible clues but the problem remained. One evening
she was utterly tired and finished, and she thought, "Now it is
enough. Enough is enough!"

In the same way, it happened to Buddha one night. For six years he had tried and tried to know who he is, and had failed and failed again and again. And there is a limit. That evening he decided, "It is finished. There seems to be no way, all is futile." He dropped the whole idea, went to sleep, and by the morning he was enlightened.

Because in that night's sleep something surfaced. There was no effort now; he had made every effort and he was done with it. That night he was relaxed, totally relaxed. Not even a single dream disturbed him, because when all desires are dropped, dreams disappear. Dreams are the shadows of your desires.

That whole night was just a peaceful prayer. A meditation that he had not been able to attain through effort, happened in that moment. It always happens when your efforts have failed, when you have reached the optimum of your efforts. Remember, it can't happen just now. If you go there – and the tree is still there in Bodhgaya: you can go and lie down underneath the tree the whole night – nothing will happen. You will simply dream about your girlfriend or boyfriend, and you will have nightmares. Your night will be *your* night, it will not be Buddha's night. You have not yet done anything to attain to that.

The attainment is paradoxical. First one has to do all that one can do, and then one has to drop that doing. Then it comes, then it comes rushing.

The same happened to Madame Curie. Of course, their worlds are totally different. Buddha was searching for "Who am I?" Madame Curie was searching for a mathematical conclusion to a certain problem; she was a mathematician, a scientist.

That night she was tired, finished; there seemed to be no hope, she was hopeless. She dropped the idea. "Wasted were those three years," she decided, "and now no more. From tomorrow morning I shall start some new project."

Now there was a gap. Tomorrow morning she would start a

new project, and the old project was gone. And this night, these eight or ten or twelve hours were in a gap. And in the night it happened. Silently something penetrated into her consciousness from the deeper layers. From intuition to intellect, something penetrated.

In her sleep she walked to her table, wrote the answer – in sleep – went back, fell asleep again. In the morning she found the answer scribbled in her own hand. She could not even remember immediately that she had done it. Then slowly slowly she remember that yes, there had been a dream. In a dream she had seen that she was going to the table and writing something. Now she knew it was not a dream, it had really happened and the answer was there. And for three years she had tried and the answer had remained elusive.

What happened? It is the same phenomenon. Intellect cannot reach to the unknown, the unknown is available to intuition. Intellect can work only in the world of the known – so it is good, but it has limitations.

> YOUR INTELLECT IS JUST A HOTCHPOTCH OF
> GUESSWORK AND THOUGHT, LIMPING OVER THE
> FACE OF THE EARTH; WHEREVER THEY ARE,
> HE IS NOT...

And whenever thoughts are there, whenever your intellect is there, God is not. Your intellect does not allow him entry, it keeps you occupied. He comes, he comes again and again, he knocks on the door, but he never finds you unoccupied, available, vulnerable. You are constantly engaged with your intellect; he has to go back.

> ...THEY ARE CONTAINED WITHIN HIS CREATION.

Your thoughts, your mind, your intellect, are contained within his creation. How can the part know the whole? Can your hand know your totality? Can a hair of your head know your totality? It is impossible.

And the intellect is a very small phenomenon in this immense existence. What is your intellect? And it is trying to do the impossible, it is trying to grasp the whole. The whole effort is futile.

Once you have understood it, that the whole effort is futile, you relax. And then the miracle happens; that which cannot be grabbed becomes available. But you cannot grab it. On the contrary, when you are silent it possesses you, it grabs you.

> MAN AND HIS REASON ARE JUST THE LATEST
> RIPENING PLANTS IN HIS GARDEN.
> WHATEVER YOU ASSERT ABOUT HIS NATURE,
> YOU ARE BOUND TO BE OUT OF YOUR DEPTH,
> LIKE A BLIND MAN TRYING TO DESCRIBE THE
> APPEARANCE OF HIS OWN MOTHER.

It is like a blind man trying to describe something that he has never seen. Although he has come from the mother, he has lived in the mother's womb for nine months, he still cannot describe the mother because he has no eyes.

We have lived in God, we *are* living in God. He is our womb: from eternity to eternity we never leave his womb. Still we cannot describe him, we still don't have the eyes which can see him.

Hence the symbol of the third eye. These two eyes can see his world, these two eyes can see the without. These two eyes can see the duality of day and night, summer and winter, life and death, man and woman, positive/negative, yin/yang – all kinds of dualities these two eyes can see. 'Two' means the dual.

The third eye means one single eye. That one single eye is still hidden in you, nonfunctioning. It is a metaphor, remember. It is not that there is some third eye as a fact – it is a metaphor, and of tremendous value, of great significance. It signifies *one*. Only one can know the one; two will always know the two.

Behind these two eyes there is one eye. The two go outwards, the one goes inwards. Unless that eye arises in you, you will not be able to know God. Belief is of no help, it is hypocrisy. Disbelief is of no help, it is hypocrisy again.

Don't be a theist and don't be an atheist, be an inquirer. Move with great passion into this inquiry about God. Don't say he is, don't say he is not. How can we say anything without knowing and seeing?

Go into this existence – and the beginning has to be from your very inner core. That one eye is created by meditation, by silence.

WHILE REASON IS STILL TRACKING DOWN THE
SECRET, YOU END YOUR QUEST ON THE OPEN
FIELD OF LOVE.

Such a beautiful statement. And you will be surprised one day: your two eyes were searching and searching and were not finding it, and suddenly one day the third eye has opened and you have found it. Your intellect was searching and searching for the secret, and one day intuition has ripened and the heart has known.

The intellect goes on thinking and thinking, and never knows. And the heart never thinks, it only knows. The heart is the faculty of real knowing. In the world of the heart, knowing means being; there is no difference between knowing and being.

The scientist knows the object *there*, separate from himself. The mystic knows God not as an object but as his own subjectivity – here, in himself, as himself.

Hakim Sanai says: The pure person, the meditator, knows the unity of two. And the lover knows the unity of three: of love, the lover, and the beloved. There comes a point in you where all is integrated. Thoughts keep you fragmentary and divided. When all thoughts have disappeared, how can you be divided, how can you be fragmentary? Integration arises; you are centered, you are one. And in that oneness, you have known; you have already known.

The heart comes to know, and then the heart informs the intellect, "Now there is no need, don't worry about it: it has happened. Now no need to inquire and search – stop! I have come to know."

It is always the heart that knows, remember it. Hence the emphasis on trust, on surrender. When you come to a master you have to be joined with the master through the heart, not through the intellect. If you join through the intellect then it is not much of a bridge, because the intellect does not know how to create a bridge – it knows how to create walls. And just small things will be enough to create walls.

A few days ago, a woman took sannyas. And just the other day she wrote a letter to me, saying, "Your criticism of the priests is ugly." Now, she does not know that she is creating a wall. Now it will be difficult for her to feel me, she has brought her own mind in. And she has been here for only a few days. Wait a little: if I have criticized the priests, there must be some reason. Wait a little, be patient, listen to what I am saying and why I am saying it. Don't be in such a hurry, otherwise you will start creating walls.

And if you create walls then there is no possibility of my being contacting your being. Then I cannot find you where you are. You will be hiding behind walls: I will come and knock, but you will not hear me – and for unnecessary reasons.

Now, what do you have to do with priests? Why should you be concerned about priests? Have you come here just to listen to me praise your priests? You have come here to be transformed: now, what has that got to do with the priests? And it is such a small thing!

And that woman has also written, saying, "Whenever you use the word 'ugly' it appears to me that the very use of the word is ugly."

Now, if you are in such a state of mind that my use of the word 'ugly' looks ugly to you, then you are not here. Then you are far away on some other planet: you are in your intellect. What is ugly in the word 'ugly'? It is very expressive and beautiful. Even the woman herself has to use the word 'ugly' – she says, "You use of the word 'ugly' is ugly." It is expressive; and that is the function of a word, that it should be expressive. And it *really* expresses, it fulfills its function!

But are you here to decide about my words? Are you here like some examiner? Then you are just functioning stupidly. Then you are the fool Hakim Sanai is talking about: you will miss. You will miss the whole message; you are more concerned with unnecessary things. And there must be a great ego behind this, who knows, and who believes she knows in a better way.

You will not be able to surrender, you will not be able to trust at all. And it is the heart, the trusting heart, which comes to realize reality – it is not the doubting mind.

THE PATH CONSISTS IN NEITHER WORDS
NOR DEEDS: ONLY DESOLATION CAN COME
FROM THESE...

Hakim Sanai says that there are three paths: *gyana* yoga, the path of knowledge; *karma* yoga, the path of action; and *bhakti* yoga, the path of love. He says:

THE PATH CONSISTS IN NEITHER WORDS
NOR DEEDS...

So neither is the path of knowledge going to help you, nor is the path of action going to help you, because action will come out of your mind, and knowledge will come out of your mind. Only the third thing can help you: love and silence, which are not part of your mind.

> THE PATH CONSISTS IN NEITHER WORDS
> NOR DEEDS: ONLY DESOLATION CAN COME
> FROM THESE, AND NEVER ANY LASTING EDIFICE.
> SWEETNESS AND LIFE ARE THE WORDS OF THE MAN
> WHO TREADS THIS ROAD IN SILENCE...

Neither words nor deeds but utter silence. And then your very life becomes a sweetness, and your very life becomes expressive, then your existence has a grace. And that is the song, that is your sermon.

> SWEETNESS AND LIFE ARE THE WORDS OF THE MAN
> WHO TREADS THIS ROAD IN SILENCE...

And one who penetrates into this inner silence, one who comes to know how to be in love and how to be in prayer and how to be in silence, and who drops all the mind and its ways, then the sweetness of his life is his expression. The aliveness of his life, the radiance of his life, are his words.

> ...WHEN HE SPEAKS IT IS NOT FROM IGNORANCE,
> AND WHEN HE IS SILENT IT IS NOT FROM SLOTH.

And such a man speaks sometimes, but his speech does not come from ignorance. Your speech comes from ignorance. You speak just to hide your ignorance, you speak to show your knowledge.

Now this woman has written me, saying, "Your criticism of the priests is ugly." She is trying to show her knowledge about priests. She thinks she knows better than me; she is advising me.

When you speak, remember, it should not be to show your knowledge, because any effort to show your knowledge is nothing but to cover your ignorance. Such a man who has known what silence is, and what love is, does not speak from ignorance, he speaks because he has known.

"He speaks" is not really a right expression – God speaks through him. He is no more. He is not the speaker, just a vehicle, a medium.

...AND WHEN HE IS SILENT IT IS NOT FROM SLOTH.

And when you are silent it is out of sloth, laziness, tiredness. When he is silent it is not out of sloth. He is silent out of prayer, out of love. He is silent, but tremendously alive in his silence. He is not dull, his silence is not unintelligent, his silence is not lazy, his silence is not mediocre.

His silence is full of songs, very pregnant. His silence is like a seed, and when he uses words those words are like flowers that come out of the seed. His silence is beautiful, his songs are beautiful, because those songs come from silence and those songs carry some fragrance of the silence.

When words speak in such a way that they carry silence, then you have come to know how to use words. Then you are no more dumb.

THE DUMB FIND TONGUES, WHEN THE SCENT
OF LIFE REACHES THEM FROM HIS SOUL.

But it all comes from him, from the beyond. Buddha, Bahauddin, Kabir, Christ, Mohammed, Mahavira, Sosan and Sanai – they don't speak on their own. They are hollow bamboos, flutes: they sing a song that comes through them but is not their own. The signature on their songs is that of God.

8 The Great Palace of Consciousness

The first question:

> CAN COWARDICE AND HYPOCRISY ALSO BE
> BEAUTIFUL? CAN I ACCEPT EVEN MY COWARDICE,
> MY HYPOCRISY, MY MISERLINESS AND A
> TENDENCY TOWARDS PRIVACY THAT YOU
> YOURSELF HAVE CALLED "IDIOCY"? AND IF I
> ACCEPT SUCH TENDENCIES, ALL OF WHICH TEND
> TO BOTTLE ME UP, HOW WILL I GET FREE?

Deva Ashoka, the very desire to be free keeps one unfree. Every desire is a chain, a bondage, an imprisonment. No desire can ever be fulfilled. By dropping the desire, its fulfillment happens.

Now, the greatest desire in the world is that of inner transformation. The desire for money is nothing, the desire for more power, prestige, is nothing. The greatest desire is the so-called spiritual desire. And once you are caught in that desire you will remain miserable forever.

Transformation is possible, but not by desiring it. Transformation is possible only by relaxing into that which is, whatsoever is. Unconditionally accepting yourself brings transformation.

We will have to go deeper into this phenomenon, because this is not only Ashoka's question, it is everybody's.

Man is in misery, man is in anguish. Hence everybody is searching for a state of bliss, a state of unity with existence. Man feels alienated, uprooted. Hence the desire is natural – to get roots into existence again, to be green again, to be blossoming again.

These few things have to be meditated upon. First: to establish that perfect unity, consciousness must first unify itself in terms of all its personal aspects by rejecting nothing which is experientially real in itself. This is the first thing to be understood.

You feel fear. Now the fear is an existential reality, an experiential reality; it is there. You can reject it: by rejecting it you will be repressing it. By repressing it you will create a wound in your being.

You feel cowardice. You can manage not to look at it. But it is a fact, a reality; just by not looking at it, it is not going to disappear. You are behaving like an ostrich: seeing the enemy, seeing the danger of death, the ostrich hides its head in the sand. But by hiding his head in the sand, by closing his eyes, the enemy does not disappear. In fact the ostrich becomes more vulnerable to the enemy. Thinking that now there is no enemy because nobody is seen, thinking that seeing the enemy is what gives it existence, now the ostrich is relieved of the fear. But he is more in danger: the enemy is more powerful because it has not been noticed.

Something can be done if the ostrich does not hide its head.

And that's what people are doing. You see cowardice, you try not to notice it. But it is a fact. By not noticing it, you have created a part of your being which you will not be able to see. You have divided yourself into segments. Now one day there is something else, anger, and you don't want to accept that there is anger in you. You stop looking at it. Then some other day there is greed, and so on and so forth. And whatsoever you stop looking at remains. But now you go on shrinking. Many more parts of your being become separate from you – you have separated them on your own. And the more fragmentary you are, the more miserable you will be.

The first step towards bliss is to be one. That's what Hakim Sanai is insisting again and again: to be one is so blissful, to be many is to be in hell. So whatsoever is experientially real, accept it. You cannot do anything by denying it. By denying it you create the problem, and the problem becomes more complex – it was simple.

You feel a coward – so what? So "I am a coward." Just see the point: if you can accept cowardice you have already become brave. Only a brave person can accept the fact of being a coward, no coward can do that. You are already on the way to transformation. So the first thing: nothing that is experienced as a fact has to be denied reality.

Second: in order to accomplish that, consciousness must first disidentify from all fixed conceptual selves with which it has identified itself, because if it holds to being some fixed and enduring conceptual self, there will be no tolerance for those experiential realities which are in contradiction with this fixed, conceptual, official self.

If you have a certain idea of how you should be, then you cannot accept the experiential truths of your being. If you have the idea that you have to be a brave man, that bravery is a value, then it is difficult to accept your cowardice. If you have the idea that you have to be a buddha-like person, compassionate, absolutely compassionate, then you cannot accept your anger. It is the ideal that creates the problem.

If you don't have any ideals then there is no problem at all. You are a coward, so you are a coward. And because there is no ideal of being a brave man, you don't condemn the fact – you don't reject it, you don't repress it, you don't throw it into the basement of your being so that there is no need for you ever to look at it.

But anything that you throw into your unconscious will go

on functioning from there, it will go on creating problems for you. It is like a disease that you have pushed inwards. It was coming to the surface, and from the surface there was a possibility that it might have disappeared. If a wound comes to the surface it is good, it is on the way to being healed, because it is only on the surface that it will be in contact with fresh air and the sun and can be healed. If you force it inwards, if you don't allow it to come to the surface, then it is going to become a cancer. Even a small disease, repressed, can become a dangerous disease. No disease should ever be repressed.

But the repression is natural if you have some ideal. Any ideal will do. If you have the ideal of being a celibate, a *brahmachari*, then sex becomes the problem. You can't watch it. If you don't have the ideal of becoming a *brahmachari*, a celibate, then sex is not rejected. Then there is no division between you and your sexuality. Then there is communion, and that communion brings joy. Self-communion is the base of all joy.

So the second thing to remember is: don't carry ideals. Just think, if you have an ideal that you have to have three eyes, a problem immediately arises because you have only two eyes and the ideal says you have to have three, if you don't have three something is missing. Now you hanker for the third. You have created an impossible problem for yourself; it will not be solved. At the most you can paint a third eye on your forehead. But the painted third eye is just a painted third eye; it is hypocrisy.

Ideals create hypocrisy in people. And now look at the absurdity: people have the ideal of not being hypocrites — and hypocrisy comes through ideals. If all ideals disappear there will be no hypocrisy. How can hypocrisy exist? It is the shadow of the ideal. The bigger the ideal, the bigger the hypocrisy.

Hence in India you will find more hypocrites than anywhere in the world, because India has lived for centuries with great ideals. Strange, berserk ideals...

For example, a Jaina *muni* cannot be satisfied unless he is capable, like the mythological Mahavira, of eating only once in a while. It is said that in twelve years Mahavira ate for only one year. That means once after twelve days: one day eating and twelve days fasting. Now, if this is your ideal you are going to remain in great misery. If this is not your ideal then there is no problem.

See it: the problem arises from the ideal. Now, a Christian monk is not puzzled by this, he has no problem with it. But the Jaina monk is continuously suffering because he cannot attain to the ideal; he falls short. If you are really pure, this is the Jaina idea, your body will not perspire. Now you have a stupid idea there. The body will continue to perspire, and you will continue to suffer.

The more ideals you have, the more will be your suffering and the more will be your hypocrisy, because if you cannot fulfill the ideals then at least you have to pretend. That's how hypocrisy comes in.

The world will not be hypocritical at all if we accept experiential facts without any judgment. Whatsoever is, is. If we live with the is-ness of existence and not with the oughts and the shoulds, how can hypocrisy arise?

Just the other day, somebody asked, "Beloved Master, are you not a hypocrite? Because you live comfortably, you live in a beautiful house, you move in a beautiful car, you live like a king."

Now, he does not understand what the word 'hypocrisy' means. This is my whole teaching – to live as beautifully as possible. I am not a hypocrite. In fact I am living the way I am teaching. If I was teaching to live in poverty, and I was living in a palace, that would be hypocrisy. But I am not teaching to live in poverty; poverty is not my goal.

You can go and tell Morarji Desai that he is a hypocrite. Or tell Sanjiva Reddy, the president of this country, "You are a hypocrite." You cannot say that to me. You can say to the president, Sanjiva Reddy, "You are a hypocrite, because you teach Gandhiism and you still go on eating meat. You talk about nonviolence and you go on eating meat! This is hypocrisy – pure hypocrisy, unpolluted hypocrisy!"

But you cannot say that to Jesus. He eats meat, but he has never propounded vegetarianism; he has never talked about that kind of nonviolence. You cannot tell him that he is a hypocrite. Jesus drinks wine; you cannot tell him that he is a hypocrite, unless he teaches otherwise.

My whole approach towards life is that of total acceptance, is that of celebration, not of renunciation. How can you tell me that I am a hypocrite? I may be the only person on this earth who is not a hypocrite, because I have no ideals.

The first necessity for the hypocrite is to have ideals. I have none; I am a nonidealist. I live naturally – and it is very natural to live in comfort and convenience. It is simply stupid, if comfort is available, not to live in it. If it is not available, that is another thing. Then whatsoever is available, live in it comfortably, manage to live in it comfortably.

I have lived in many kinds of situations but I have always lived comfortably. When I was a student I used to walk to the university, four miles every day. But I loved it. I walked those four miles every day with great comfort; I enjoyed it. When I was a teacher I used to go on a bicycle to the university; I enjoyed that too.

Whatsoever has been the situation, whether I have had only a bicycle or a Mercedes Benz, it doesn't make any difference: I have lived in comfort. Comfort is an attitude of mind, it is an approach towards life. I have lived in very very poor houses. When I became a teacher in a university, I started living in one single room with no windows, no ventilation. The rent was just twenty rupees per month. But I loved it, I enjoyed it, it was not a problem at all.

Whatsoever the moment allows, I have squeezed the moment to its totality. I have drunk fully of the moment, I have never repented and I have never desired for something else; if something else started happening I enjoyed that too.

You can never say to me that I am a hypocrite. It is impossible for me to be a hypocrite, because I have no ideals to fulfill, no oughts, no shoulds. The 'is' is all that is, and I live in it.

So the second thing to remember, Ashoka, is: don't have certain ideas about yourself. You must be carrying many ideas of how you should be. Hence the problem arises: CAN COWARDICE AND HYPOCRISY ALSO BE BEAUTIFUL?

Now if you have the idea to be a brave man then it looks ugly to be a coward. But cowardice is a fact, and the ideal is just an ideal, a fantasy of the mind.

Sacrifice fantasies to reality, drop all ideals, and then life starts becoming integrated. All the rejected fragments start coming back home, the repressed starts surfacing. For the first time you start feeling a kind of togetherness; you are no longer falling apart.

For example, if I hold myself to be a "kind" person, I will not be able to permit myself to recognize and accept angry feelings when they arise in consciousness, because kind people just don't get angry. Therefore, to bring about a personal unity in consciousness, I must first take my stand as being no thing fixed or enduring, but hold myself to be only the moment-to-moment experiential reality which arises in consciousness.

Thus some moments I am angry, then some moments I am sad, then some moments I am jealous, then some moments I am joyful. Moment-to-moment, whatsoever happens is accepted. Then you become one. And this oneness is the most fundamental thing to understand.

The master must help the disciple to confront and integrate with those rejected experiential aspects of self which he actually *is* at any given moment instead of trying to help him actualize its compensatory opposite or what the disciple feels that he *ought* to be, or that which he is trying to protect, enhance or affirm about himself.

My purpose here, my function here, is to take all ideals away from you. You have come here with ideals; you would like me to enhance your ideals, you would like me to support you and help you to become that which you want to become. That may be your motivation in coming here, but that is not my work here.

My work is just the opposite: to help you to accept that which is already the case and to forget all about your fantasies. I want you to become more realistic and pragmatic. I want to give you roots in the earth, and you are hankering for the sky and you have completely forgotten the earth.

Yes, the sky is also available, but only to those whose roots have gone deep into the earth. If a tree wants to rise high in the sky and whisper with the clouds and play with the winds and have some communion with the stars, then the tree will have to send deeper and deeper roots into the earth. The first thing is sending roots into the earth, the second thing happens of its own accord. The deeper the roots go, the higher the tree goes; there is no need to do anything else.

My effort here is to send your roots deep into the soil of truth. And the truth is that which you are. Then suddenly things will start happening: you will start rising. The ideals that you have always tried for and have never been able to achieve will start happening of their own accord.

If a person can accept his reality as it is, in that very acceptance all tension disappears. Anguish, anxiety, despair – they all simply evaporate. And when there is no anxiety, no tension, no fragmentariness, no division, no schizophrenia then suddenly there is joy, then suddenly there is love, then suddenly there is compassion. These are not ideals, these are very natural phenomena. All that is needed is to remove the ideals, because those ideals are functioning as blocks. The more idealistic a person is, the more blocked he is.

As peculiar and contradictory as it may sound, peace is to be found only in the midst of pain and never by struggling against or running away from what is considered to be the negative or painful.

Yes, cowardice gives you pain, fear gives you pain, anger gives you pain – these are negative emotions. But peace can be attained only by accepting and absorbing the painful, not by rejecting it. By rejecting it you will become smaller and smaller and smaller, and you will have less and less power. And you will be in a constant inner war, a civil war, in which one hand will fight with the other, in which you will simply dissipate your energy.

A very fundamental thing to be remembered: only communion with psychological pain opens the door for its liberation and transcendence – only communion with psychological pain. All that is painful has to be accepted; a dialogue has to be created with it. It is you. There is no other way to go beyond it, the only way is to absorb it.

And it has tremendous potential. Anger is energy, fear is energy, so is cowardice. All that happens to you has great momentum, a great quantity of energy hidden in it. Once you accept it, that energy becomes yours. You become stronger, you become wider, you start becoming more spacious. You have a bigger inner world then.

Only a yielding letting-be or full acceptance is its ending. Psychological pain ends only by accepting it in its totality. Psychological pain does not exist just because of the mere presence alone of some stimulus or reality termed "painful". Rather, the pain is produced by the interpretation of the fact or reality which produces the tendency to avoid or resist that fact.

Try to understand it: psychological pain is your own creation. Cowardice is not painful – only your idea that cowardice is wrong, your interpretation that cowardice should not be there.

Ashoka must be saying to himself, "Ashoka, you, a coward? No. How can you be a coward? You are a brave man."

You have a certain ego: that certain ego goes on condemning cowardice. It is because of that condemnation and interpretation that pain arises. And the cowardice is there, so it becomes a wound. You cannot accept it, and you cannot destroy it by rejecting it. Nothing is destroyed by being rejected; sooner or later you will have to cope with it. Again and again it will erupt, again and again it will disrupt your peace.

Only when the mind recoils from a fact or reality is there pain. You are recoiling from the facts of cowardice, fear, anger and sadness. Don't recoil. Recoiling from a fact creates pain.

Psychological pain is part and parcel of the process of escape and resistance. Pain is not inherent in any feeling but arises only after the intent to reject it arises. The moment you decide to reject something pain arises.

Watch it inside yourself, become a lab of great experimentation. Just see: you are feeling fear. It is dark and you are alone, and for miles there is nobody. You are lost in a jungle, sitting under a tree on a dark night, and lions are roaring – and fear is there.

Now there are two possibilities. One is, reject it. Hold yourself tight so you don't start trembling because of the fear. Then the fear becomes a painful thing: it is there and it hurts. Even when you are holding yourself very tight, it is there and it hurts.

The second is, enjoy it. Tremble. Let it become a meditation. It is natural – lions are roaring, the night is dark, danger is so close by, death can happen any moment. Enjoy it! Let the trembling become a dance. Once you accept it then trembling is a dance. Cooperate with the trembling and you will be surprised: if you cooperate with the trembling, if you *become* the trembling, all pain disappears.

In fact if you tremble, instead of pain you will find a great upsurge of energy arising in you. That's exactly what the body wanted to do. Why in fear does trembling arise? Trembling is a chemical process: it releases energy, it prepares you to fight or take flight. It gives you a great sudden upsurge – it is an emergency measure. When you start trembling you start warming up.

That's why when it is cold you tremble. There is no fear, so why do you tremble when it is cold? The body automatically trembles in the cold so that it becomes warm. It is a kind of natural exercise of the body. The inner tissues start trembling to become warmed up so they can face the cold.

Now, if you repress trembling when you are feeling cold it will become painful. That is exactly the case when you are in fear, the body is trying to prepare: it is releasing chemicals into the blood, it is preparing you to face some danger. Maybe you will need to have a fight, or maybe you will have to run away and take flight. Both will need energy.

See the beauty of fear, see the alchemical work of fear. It is simply trying to prepare you for the situation so that you can accept the challenge. But rather than accepting the challenge, rather than understanding fear, you start rejecting it. You say, "Ashoka, you are such a great man, a great sannyasin, and you are trembling? Remember what Osho used to say, that there is no death, that the soul is immortal. An immortal soul, and trembling? Remember what Krishna said: 'Death cannot destroy you, fire cannot burn you, weapons cannot penetrate you.' Remember! And don't tremble: hold yourself in control!"

Now you are creating a contradiction. Your natural process is that of fear, and you are bringing in an unnatural process to contradict fear. You are bringing ideals to interfere in the natural process. There will be pain, because there will be conflict.

Don't bother whether the soul is immortal or not. Right now the truth is that fear is there. Listen to this moment, and let this moment take you totally, allow this moment to possess you. And then there is no pain. Then the fear is a subtle dance of energies in you. And it prepares you – it is a friend, it is not your enemy. But your interpretations go on doing something wrong to you.

Essentially, the feeling of psychological pain is created by the attempt to separate consciousness from itself, the splitting of the unity of consciousness into the duality of a conceptual observing entity which tries to run away from distort or over-power the rejected feeling, and the observed feeling itself. If consciousness in duality is the cause of the pain, then only consciousness in unity can be the elimination of the pain. In unity is the ending of pain.

This split that you create between the feeling – the fear, the anger – and yourself makes you become two. You become the observer and the observed. You say, "I am here, the observer; and there is pain, the observed. And I am not the pain." Now this duality creates pain.

You are not the observed, you are not the observer, you are both. You are the observer and the observed, both.

Don't say, "I am feeling fear"; that is a wrong way of saying it. Don't say, "I am afraid"; that too is a wrong way of saying it. Simply say, "I am fear. In this moment I am fear." Don't create any division.

When you say, "I am feeling fear" you are keeping yourself separate from the feeling. You are there somewhere far away, and the feeling is around you. This is the basic disunity. Say, "I am fear." And watch – that's actually the case! When the fear is there, you *are* fear.

It is not that sometimes you feel love. When love is really there, you are love. And when anger is there, you are anger.

This is what Krishnamurti means when he says again and again, "The observer is the observed." The seer is the seen, and the experiencer is the experience. Don't create this divi-sion of subject and object. This is the root cause of all misery, of all split.

Thus, one must not judge good or bad, one must not label or have any kind of desire or goal in regard to what arises in consciousness. There must be no sense of avoidance, resistance, condemnation, justification, distortion or attachment in regard to what arises but only a choiceless awareness, and self-communion is established.

A choiceless awareness: that is the ultimate key to open the innermost mystery of your being. Don't say it is good, don't say it is bad. When you say something is good, attachment arises, attraction arises. When you say something is bad, repulsion arises. Fear is fear, neither good nor bad. Don't evaluate, just let it be. Let it be so.

When without condemnation or justification you are there, then in that choiceless awareness all psychological pain simply evaporates like dewdrops in the early morning sun. And left behind is a pure space, left behind is virgin space.

This is the One, the Tao, or you can call it God. This One that is left behind when all pain disappears, when you are not divided in any way, when the observer has become the observed, this is the experience of God, samadhi, or whatever you will.

And in this state there is no self as such, because there is no observer-controller-judger. One is only that which arises and changes from moment to moment. Some moments it may be elation, other moments it may be sadness, tenderness, destructiveness, fear, loneliness, et cetera.

One should not say, "I am sad," or "I have sadness," but "I *am* sadness" – because the first two statements imply a self separate from that which is. In reality there is no other self to whom the particular feeling is happening. There is only the feeling itself. Meditate over it: there is only the feeling itself.

There is no Ashoka feeling fear; Ashoka is fear in a certain moment. In certain other moments Ashoka is not fear, but Ashoka is not separate from the moment, from that which is arising. There is only the feeling itself. Thus, nothing can be done about what is experientially arising in the moment. There is nobody else to do anything.

This communion with pain does not bring greater pain but actually yields liberation and joy. In fact, consciousness in communion with *anything*, not just psychological pain of course, yields peace and joy. Be the truth and the truth will set you free.

I will repeat the question again: CAN COWARDICE AND HYPOCRISY ALSO BE BEAUTIFUL? Everything that is, is beautiful – even ugliness. CAN I ACCEPT EVEN MY COWARDICE, MY HYPOCRISY, MY MISERLINESS, AND A TENDENCY TOWARDS PRIVACY THAT YOU YOURSELF HAVE CALLED 'IDIOCY'?

Whatsoever is, is, whether you accept it or not. Your acceptance or rejection makes no difference at all. That which is, is. If you accept it you have joy arising in you, if you reject it you have pain. But the reality still remains the same. You may have pain, psychological pain: that is your creation because you were not able to accept and absorb something that was arising. You rejected truth; in rejection you became a prisoner. The truth liberates, but you rejected it. Hence you are in chains.

Reject truth, and you will remain more and more imprisoned.

The truth remains; it does not matter whether you reject it or accept it. It does not change the fact, it changes your psychological reality. And there are two possibilities: either pain or joy, either disease or health. If you reject it there will be disease, discomfort, because you are cutting a chunk of your being away from you; it will leave wounds and scars on you. If you accept, there will be celebration and health and wholeness. AND IF I ACCEPT SUCH TENDENCIES, ALL OF WHICH TEND TO BOTTLE ME UP, HOW WILL I GET FREE?

They are not bottling you up, it is your interpretation, Ashoka. No truth ever binds anybody; that is not the quality of truth. But when you reject it, in your rejection you become closed and you *are* bottled up. In that rejection you become a cripple, you become paralyzed. AND IF I ACCEPT SUCH TENDENCIES," YOU SAY, "ALL OF WHICH TEND TO BOTTLE ME UP, HOW WILL I GET FREE?

That very idea of getting free is again an ideal. Freedom is not an ideal, it is a by-product of accepting whosoever you are. Freedom is a by-product; it is not a goal of your endeavor and effort. It is not arrived at by great effort, it happens when you are relaxed.

And how can you be relaxed if you cannot accept your cowardice? If you cannot accept your fear, if you cannot accept your love, if you cannot accept your sadness, how can you be relaxed?

Why can't people relax? What is the basic cause of their constant chronic tension? This is the basic cause. Down the centuries, your so-called religions have been teaching you to reject and reject. They have been teaching you to renounce, they have been teaching you that all is wrong: you have to change this, you have to change that, only then will you be acceptable to God. They have created so much rejection that what to say about God? You are not even acceptable to yourself, you are not acceptable to the people you live with: how can you be accepted by God?

God already accepts you, that's why you are in existence. Otherwise you would not be here. This is my basic teaching to you: God already accepts you. You have not to earn it, you are already worthy. Relax, enjoy the way God has made you. If he has put cowardice in you, Ashoka, then there must be something in it. Trust and accept it. And what is wrong in being a coward? And what is wrong in being afraid? Only idiots don't feel fear, imbeciles are not afraid.

If a snake comes on the path you will jump immediately. Only the imbecile, the stupid, the idiot, will not be afraid of the snake. But if you are intelligent, the more intelligent you are, the faster you will jump. This is part of intelligence! This is perfectly good; this helps your life, it protects you.

But stupid ideologies have been given to man. and even now you are here, you go on persisting in your old patterns. You don't listen to me, to what I am saying. I am saying: Whatsoever you are, unconditionally accept it, and acceptance is the key to transformation.

I am not saying: accept yourself to be transformed – otherwise you have not accepted yourself at all, because deep down the desire is for transformation. You say, "Okay, if this brings transformation then I will accept myself." But this is not acceptance; you have missed the whole point. You are still desiring transformation. That's why in the end you ask: HOW WILL I GET FREE IF I ACCEPT...?

You are asking me, "Can you guarantee that if I accept myself, it will bring freedom?"

If I guarantee it to you, and you accept yourself because of the guarantee, where is the acceptance? You are using acceptance as a means – the goal is to be transformed, to be free, to attain to God, to nirvana. Where is the acceptance?

Acceptance has to be unconditional, for no reason at all, without any motivation. Only then does it free you. It brings tremendous joy, it brings great freedom, but the freedom does not come as an end. Acceptance itself is another name for freedom. If you have accepted truly, if you have understood what I mean by acceptance, there is freedom – immediately, instantly.

It is not that first you accept yourself, practice acceptance, and then one day there will be freedom – no. Accept yourself, and there is freedom, because psychological pain disappears immediately.

Try it. What I am saying is experimental. You can do it, it is not a question of believing me. You have been fighting with your fear – accept it, and see what happens. Just sit silently and accept it, and say, "I have fear, so I AM fear." In that very meditative state, "I am fear," freedom starts descending. When the acceptance is total, freedom has arrived.

The second question:

I AM VERY SUSPICIOUS OF MY WIFE, ALTHOUGH I
KNOW THAT SHE IS INNOCENT. WHAT CAN I DO TO
DROP MY SUSPICIONS?

There must be something in you that you are really suspicious of. Unless you can trust yourself you cannot trust your wife or anybody else. If you mistrust yourself you will project your mistrust on people who are around you. The thief thinks that everybody is a thief. It is natural, because he knows himself, and that is the only way of his knowing others.

What you think about others is basically a declaration of what you think about yourself. You know that if your wife is not constantly watching you, you will do something. You will start flirting with some women – you know it. Hence the fear: "If I am in the office, who knows? – the wife may be flirting with the neighbors." You know perfectly well what you are doing with the secretary; that is creating the problem.

That's why you say, "Though I know my wife is innocent, still I am suspicious." You will remain suspicious till something in you drops. It is not a question about the wife; all questions when they arise are really about you.

A traveling man went on the road for a short trip, but kept staying away. Every few weeks he'd send his wife a wire saying, "Can't come home, still buying." Every wire was the same, "Can't come home, still buying." This went on for three or four months, when his wife finally sent him a wire that said, "Better come home, I'm selling what you're buying!" That's how things happen in life.

The hungover couple talked about the wild party they held the night before. "Darling, this is rather embarrassing," said the husband, "but was it you I made love to in the library last night?" His wife looked at him reflectively and asked, "About what time?"

The basic mistrust must be about yourself. You are suspicious of yourself: maybe you are repressing too much? And whenever somebody represses something in him he starts projecting it on others. It almost always happens that the man who has a murderous instinct in him is always afraid that others are thinking to murder him; he becomes paranoid.

The person who is very violent is always afraid: "Other people are very violent and I have to be constantly on guard."

Because people don't trust themselves, hence they can't trust anybody else – wife, friend, father, mother, son, daughter. People are living in chronic suspicion. But the basic cause is that you have not been able to accept your facticity.

What I was just saying to Ashoka, I would like you to ponder over. Accept whatsoever you are: in that very acceptance you will accept others too. And yes, there is a possibility, if you sometimes become interested in seeing a woman, nothing is impossible, your wife may become interested in some man. But if you understand yourself and accept yourself you will accept your wife too.

If you can accept this, that "Sometimes I become attracted to a woman" then nothing is wrong, then your wife can also become attracted to some man. But if you reject it in your own being, if you condemn it in your own being, you will condemn it in others' beings too.

My criterion of a saint is one who is able to forgive all and everybody, because he knows himself. But your saints are incapable of forgiving. Your saints go on inventing more and more technologically perfect hells. Why? They have not yet been able to accept themselves.

They tell the story about the young good-looking attorney who claimed there never was a woman with whom he couldn't make it. One day the office hired a very good-looking secretary that for weeks every male tried to make and failed in the attempt.

The young attorney boasted that if enough money was bet,

he would succeed with her. When they questioned how he would prove it, he said he would record the entire action on his tape-recorder which he would hide under the bed.

When all the betting was made, he proceeded to make a date with her and by the end of the evening, not only was she in his apartment but eventually in his bed – whereupon he reached under and turned on the tape.

In a few moments, in support of his reputation, the secretary was in a state of violent lovemaking, and at its height cried out loudly, Keep kissing it honey, keep kissing it!"

Whereupon the attorney in his best courtroom manner leaned under the bed and dictated into the recorder, "Please let the record reflect, the lady indicated her left breast."

The mind of an attorney – constantly suspicious. Now he must have become afraid:"Keep kissing it honey, keep kissing it!"What? The record will not say anything and there may be suspicions.

But this is the mind of everybody. The mind is cunning, calculating, suspicious. The mind lives constantly in a kind of distrust, in doubt. The mind's whole climate is that of doubt.

So it is not a question of how to trust your wife, it is a question of how to *trust*. Mind lives in the climate of doubt, it feeds on doubt.And unless you know how to put the mind off when it is not needed and descend into the heart, you will not know how to trust.

The climate of the heart is trust. Mind cannot trust; mind is incapable of trusting. And we have all become hung-up in the head. Hence, even though we say that we trust, we don't trust. We insist that we trust, but our very insistence shows that we don't trust. We want to trust, we pretend to trust, we want the other to *believe* that we trust, be we don't trust.The head is impotent as far as trust is concerned. The head is the mechanism for doubt; the head is constantly a question-mark.

You will have to know how to come down to the heart, which has been bypassed by the society. The society does not teach you the ways of the heart, it only teaches you the ways of the mind. It teaches you mathematics and logic and it teaches you science, et cetera, et cetera – but they are all the cultivation of doubt.

Science has grown through doubt, doubt has been a blessing as far as science is concerned. But as science has grown more and more, man has shrunk. Humanity has disappeared, love has almost become a myth. Love is no more a reality on the earth. How *can* it be a reality? The heart itself has stopped beating.

Even when you love, you only *think* that you love; it comes through the head. And the head is not the faculty for love.

Start meditating. Start putting off the constant chattering of the head. Slowly slowly, the mind becomes quiet. Get into things where the mind is not needed – for example, dancing. Dance, and dance to abandon, because in dance the mind is not needed. You can lose yourself in a dance. In losing yourself in a dance, the heart will start functioning again.

Drown yourself in music. And slowly slowly you will see that there is a totally different world of the heart. And in the heart there is always trust. The heart does not know how to doubt, just as the mind does not know how to trust.

The third question:

WHAT IS SEXUAL PERVERSION?
WHY DO STRANGE SEXUAL HABITS EVOLVE,
AND FROM WHERE?
FOR EXAMPLE, SADO-MASOCHISM.

Man is not what he appears to be, he is far bigger. We know about man only in a very partial way.

You will have to understand these five categories: the first is the conscious mind. The conscious mind is a very tiny mind, just a little bit of you which can reason, think, rationalize, go through logical processes and is a little bit alert. It is a very tiny part of you, and we know man only from that tiny part.

We have looked into the great palace of human consciousness from a very tiny hole, maybe the keyhole. And whatsoever we have seen through the keyhole is not the whole reality.

Man is vast. Just hidden behind the conscious mind there is the unconscious mind. Its discovery is the great contribution of Sigmund Freud to humanity. The unconscious mind is nine times bigger than the conscious mind. It contains all your instincts, it contains all your inner functionings, body mechanisms, emotions and feelings. Except for logic, it contains all of you.

But that is deep in darkness. Freud has defined psychoanalysis as an effort to make the unconscious conscious, so that your consciousness becomes a little bigger. More light has to penetrate into the darkness of the unconscious, because the unconscious is nine times more powerful. Whatsoever you decide through the conscious will not be able to materialize unless it reaches to the unconscious.

That's why hypnosis goes far deeper than any other methodology. Hypnosis works directly on the unconscious. You may try for years to drop a certain habit, and you will not be able to, because you will try only from the conscious mind. And the conscious is very small; it has no power before the unconscious. And the unconscious has no way to know what the conscious is thinking.

But the hypnotist can help you to drop the habit within seconds, or at the most in a few sessions, because he will put the conscious to sleep and will start communicating directly with the unconscious. And if the unconscious agrees to drop the habit, then the habit is dropped. Then there is no way for the conscious to carry it any longer.

All realities change from the unconscious. But the unconscious itself is only a part. There is, still hidden behind, a collective unconscious which contains your whole past. And that is not a small thing. Because you have once been a lion and you have once been a snake and you have once been a tree.

The Eastern idea of passing through eighty-four million births is significant. It may not be exactly accurate but it is significant, it is meaningful. Eighty-four million births before you became a man, and all those births and their experiences are contained in the collective unconscious. It is almost the whole of history, from the very beginning – if there had ever been a beginning.

It goes to Karl Gustav Jung's credit that he brought the idea of the collective unconscious and introduced it to the world of psychology.

But these are only parts, even the collective unconscious is only a part. And Western psychology still has not started moving upwards. This is going downwards; the conscious, below it the unconscious, below that the collective unconscious.

Above the conscious there is the super-conscious, nine times bigger than the conscious. Above the conscious, parallel to the unconscious, there is the super-conscious. And still above the super-conscious there is the cosmic mind – you can call it the divine mind or the God mind or Tao. That means the ultimate in consciousness: all has become conscious and you are as big as the cosmos.

If you go deeper than the conscious you will be entering into darkness. If you go above the conscious you will be entering into light.

So there are five minds in you. And you are aware only of the small tiny part, the conscious mind.

Now, from the unconscious and from the collective unconscious many thing go on arising. Many things happen in your dreams, and sometimes you feel very puzzled about what kind of dream it was. You cannot make any head or tail of it, you cannot figure out what it was, the whole thing seems to be so absurd. It was from the collective unconscious that something arose and surfaced into the unconscious, and you had the dream.

But sometimes things start filtering from the collective unconscious into the conscious too. Then they are very bizarre, they are perversions. They only *look* like perversions – they are not really perversions, they are as natural as anything else, but they are very abnormal. FOR EXAMPLE, you ask, SADO-MASOCHISM.

There are people who enjoy torturing others, and there are people who enjoy torturing themselves, and particularly in relation to lovemaking. There are people who would like to torture the beloved person, or people who would like to be tortured by the beloved.

Sadism comes from the name of de Sade. He was incapable of getting into sexual arousal unless he beat the woman. So he used to carry a box with him, just like a doctor's box, with all the instruments of torture in it. And he was a very rich man, he was a duke, so all the women of his territory were available to him. Wherever he would see some beautiful woman he would simply give her a gesture and she had to come to his torture-chambers – they cannot be called love-chambers. And he had all kinds of instruments there in his chamber. The woman would immediately be made naked and he would beat her and do things to her which were very perverted. Unless blood started flowing from her body he would not get sexually aroused. Now, this is perversion. From where is it coming? It is coming from the deep deep collective unconscious, from those eighty-four million lives. Because there are animals....

For example, there is a certain African spider who is eaten by the woman while he is making love. He is just on top of the woman, the lady spider, and he is in great ecstasy, total orgasm, and abandoned, he has completely forgotten everything, and the lady starts eating him. And he has not yet even finished his....By the time orgasm is finished, the spider is also finished!

So he can make love only once. It is not perversion there, it is natural.

Just like de Sade, there was Masoch, from whose name comes the word 'masochism'. He was just the reverse of de Sade. He would force the woman to hit him, to beat him, to whip him. And unless he was whipped and beaten he would not have any sexual arousal.

Now, these people are suffering from the collective unconscious. Something is coming from the collecting unconscious. Something goes on surfacing into their conscious; they can't understand from where it comes. These are not criminals, they need treatment.

De Sade was forced to live in jail his whole life. That is ugly, that is unjust. He needed some deep hypnotic treatment. We should start feeling compassion for these people; they are sufferers from their past.

These things happen to everybody, but they come only to the unconscious in dreams. These other people are freaks; there is some passage between their unconscious and conscious open so easily that things start floating into their conscious and then they are possessed by them. They cannot avoid it.

And if you look into the habits of millions of animals you will be surprised. Do you know elephants make love in a certain way? The courtship continues for years. Now, if somebody has been an elephant in a past life, and the memory is there, somewhere in the collective unconscious, then the courtship can continue for years, on and on.

The woman elephant makes love only twice in a decade. Now, you will find many women who have that idea: twice in a decade. But it is natural as far as elephants are concerned, because the woman elephant will have to carry the pregnancy for twenty-two months. And it is some pregnancy! Twenty-two months carrying an elephant in your womb.... She becomes so afraid of the whole nonsense of lovemaking that for two or three years no playboy can persuade her to go into that trip again. Only after three, four, or five years, when the memory fades, can she be persuaded. So the courtship has to be very long.

And all these things are there inside the collective unconscious. And one thing may not be unnatural in a certain animal but will become unnatural in man. That's how perversions arise.

Do you know? There are such strange practices among animals that if you read about them you will be thrilled! You will not be able to believe what is going on in nature.

You know the common bedbug? The lady bedbug has no genitalia – NO genitalia. Each time the male bedbug has to make love to the woman he has to drill a hole. She has no entry. Now this is dangerous! But nature had given indications: there is a line on the belly of the lady bedbug, because if you drill anywhere else you will kill her! She can be drilled only on a particular line. You can turn over any lady bedbug and know whether she is a virgin or not, or how many times she has been made love to, because those holes will be there, scars will be there.

But if this type of thing surfaces in somebody's mind, if he starts drilling a hole into a woman, it will be a perversion. But this is how it is. There is a great collective unconscious of millions and millions of lives, and all kinds of experiences are stored there. Buddhists call it *alaya vigyan*: the storehouse of consciousness. It is infinite.

You ask me: WHAT IS SEXUAL PERVERSION?

It is something surfacing from the collective unconscious. AND WHY DO STRANGE SEXUAL HABITS EVOLVE, AND FROM WHERE?

They evolve from the collective unconscious. And a few people have openings; those openings are freak openings. It is as if a child is born with six fingers, or a child is born blind – these are exceptions, so are perverted people.

Just the other night, I was reading a book on Satya Sai

Baba, the name of the book is *Lord of the Air*. It is written by people who have lived with Satya Sai Baba for many years; it is based on their personal experience. They say that he is not only a homosexual, he is also a hermaphrodite. A hermaphrodite is a person who has the genitalia of both male and female.

Now, there are animals in which it is not a perversion, it is natural. There are earthworms which have both genitalia; you cannot decide wither one is male or female because each has both genitalia. So when earthworms make love it is a double-way affair. One functions as a male to the other, and also as a female; each makes love to the other in both the ways. The meeting has two points, so it is difficult to decide who is male. Both are male and both are female. So A makes love as a male to B's female parts, and B makes love as a male to A's female parts. It is a circular love affair, and both will become pregnant.

Nothing is wrong with earthworms, but if it is so with Satya Sai Baba then there is difficulty. And the way he walks, it seems these people must be right. Rarely it happens, but there is nothing to condemn — what can Satya Sai Baba do about it? There are a few children born with both genitalia, very rarely. But they live a very fearful life, afraid, hiding themselves; nobody should know about it.

Man is not yet so enlightened, otherwise there is nothing wrong in it. In fact Satya Sai Baba is far richer than anybody else, because he can enjoy love both the ways, as a man and as a woman.

Perversions can be in the body, perversions can be in the mind, but they both arise from the deep collective unconscious. And they both can be settled, but for that a tremendously deep hypnosis will be needed. No ordinary hypnosis will do; ordinary hypnosis can lead you only to the unconscious. To go to the collective unconscious a very deep hypnosis will be needed.

In the new commune I am going to give you methods to

go to the deep collective unconscious. But it is a very danger-
ous trip and great arrangements are needed before somebody
can enter the collective unconscious, because so much is there,
millions of experiences and they will suddenly explode.

A commune is needed. A closed commune is needed, the
closed Garden is needed – because it is not a question for the
ordinary masses to know about; they will not be able to un-
derstand. And that's why if something reaches to the masses,
some naked photographs reach to the masses, they are imme-
diately against me. They cannot understand what is happening
here.

We are trying to penetrate into the deepest layers of con-
sciousness. But this is an alchemical lab; the ordinary masses
will not be able to understand it. And if they do understand,
they will understand it according to themselves.

I am waiting for the new commune: much more has to be
done. But then things will become much more bizarre and
you will need a field, an energy-field, that surrounds you like a
soothing energy, that keeps you anchored with me so that you
are not lost into the collective unconscious. Only then can the
doors of the collective unconscious be opened.

They *can* be opened, and it is tremendously helpful if they
can be opened. If you can know your whole past, you will be
freed from it. Knowing something is to be free from it: know-
ing the truth liberates. If you can be allowed to go into your
past, to the very end, you will be finished with everything.
Because millions of times you have accumulated wealth, and
each time you have failed. If you can remember your past lives
and you can see that millions of times you have been playing
the same stupid game, to no point at all, then how can you go
on playing it in this life again? It will be impossible.

If you can see all your sexual experiences, it will be so
ridiculous to still go on playing the same game.

But for that, a totally secluded atmosphere and a great trust,
and absolute trust, will be needed. Hence I am trying to create

a commune which will be a world apart, and where we can go into the deepest possible experiments that have ever been done.

And once you have gone backwards, you become capable of going upwards and forwards, because the process is the same. Backwards, it is easier because it is a known path; you have forgotten about it but it is still a known path, you can go backwards.

Going upwards to super-consciousness and the cosmic mind is an unknown path. If you become capable of going backwards you will have learned how to penetrate the dangerous realms of your being. And then the next step higher can be taken: you can move from the conscious to the super-conscious.

It is the super-conscious in which all the experiences of angels and *devatas* and gods and kundalini and chakras and lotuses opening happen; they are all contained in the super-conscious. It is a beautiful world, it is psychedelic. Beyond that is the world of the cosmic mind where all experiences disappear – neither ugly nor beautiful, where the experiencer is left alone. Total, absolute aloneness. And that is the ultimate goal of consciousness, that is where evolution is moving towards.

But before you can take that quantum leap into the world that is above you, you will have to get deeper into the roots, into the dark roots of your unconscious and your past experiences.

Buddha and Mahavira both tried; they did great experiments. Those experiments are called *jati smaran*: remembering the past. And the past is vast – if you go on remembering it, it goes on revealing secrets.

The man who has gone into his whole past will come back absolutely healthy and psychologically whole. He will not have any perversions. His whole life will be transformed just by going there and coming back. Then all that he can ever imagine doing, he had done many times, and it was all futile and it was all in vain.

That very understanding, and all starts changing. And when you are free from the past you are capable of moving into the present: you can dive deep into the now and the here.

After some months of marriage, a girl wrote the following letter to her doctor. Dear Doctor,

Since I got married, my husband seems to have gone mad. He is after me at breakfast, coffee break, lunch time, even tea time – and then all night, every few hours. Is there anything I can do or give to help him? I await your kind reply. PS Please excuse my shaky handwriting.

So the husband is still after her. "There are many animals which make love that way. Now, something surfacing from those animal worlds...

A woman went to her doctor to complain that her husband's sexual feelings for her seemed to have declined.

The doctor, being an old friend of the family, gave the woman some pills to slip into her husband's tea so that at least the man wouldn't get a complex about being a bit under-powered.

Two days later, the woman was back in the doctor's surgery. "What happened?" asked the doctor. "Did the pills work?"

"Fantastic!" replied the woman. "I was so eager to see their effects on my husband that I tipped three of them into a cup of coffee, and within seconds of drinking it he got up, kicked the table and pulled me down on the floor and ravished me."

"Oh!" said the doctor. "I hope you weren't too surprised."

"Surprised?" said the woman. "I'll never be able to set foot in that restaurant again!"

That's how animals make love. You can lose your consciousness and you can behave like an animal.

Perversion means you are losing your consciousness and behaving like something below human beings. That capacity is man's: he can fall below the animals and he can rise above the gods. That is the glory of man and his misery too. That is the agony of man and his ecstasy too.

Man is the only animal in the world, the only being, who is capable of reaching to the deepest hell and rising to the highest heaven.

Perversion simply means you are falling backwards. Conversion means you are moving upwards, falling upwards. And if one is not converted towards the upward journey one remains perverted. Maybe your perversion is not very strange and you can adjust to it. Maybe it is a normal perversion, everybody has it; then it is okay, it can be tolerated. But a few people have exceptional perversions, private perversions, their own, and they cannot adjust to the society.

But remember, there are only two kinds of people: the perverted and the converted. There are only two categories: the perverted and the converted.

Be the converted: start rising above humanity. But the only way to rise above humanity is to accept all the animality that still exists in you and lurks in you.

One who is capable of accepting all that he is, becomes capable of receiving that which he can become.

9 A Wedding and a Wake

What is wisdom? It certainly is not knowledge. Knowledge is a pretender, it is a false coin. It looks like wisdom, and because it looks like wisdom it is very dangerous. One can be easily deceived by it.

Knowledge comes from without, wisdom arises within. Knowledge is a commodity, you can purchase it in the marketplace; it is sold, it is bought. Wisdom is not a commodity, you have to risk your life to find it. It is not a bargain, it is gambling.

Knowledge consists of all that you have known in the past. Wisdom has nothing to do with the past at all, it is of the present. It has nothing to do with the past and it has nothing to do with the future either, because the future is nothing but a projection of the past – modified, decorated, here and there a little bit changed, polished, painted – but it is the same old thing renovated.

Knowledge exists in time; time consists of the past and the future. Wisdom knows nothing of time, wisdom only knows eternity. Eternity consists only of now, this moment, the present. Eternity does not come, does not go, it is always here.

Wisdom brings peace, knowledge brings anxiety. Howsoever alike they appear, they are diametrically opposite. Wisdom brings contentment, utter contentment. Knowledge brings more and more discontent, because the mind exists only in the desire for more. The mind is nothing but another name for the desire of getting more and more and more. It is a constant hankering for more. If you have money, it desires MORE money; if you have power, it desires more power; if you have knowledge, it desires more knowledge. It is the same process, objects differ but the process remains the same.

Wisdom knows nothing of the 'more', it is utter contentment. And when the 'more' is there surrounding you, you are in a constant tension, a chronic tension, because nothing seems to be enough. You live in despair and anguish.

Knowledge gratifies the ego. In wisdom the ego simply disappears, it is not found at all. Knowledge knows of distinctions, knowledge depends on distinctions: this and that, here and there, now and then, good and bad, beautiful and ugly, the Devil and God. Knowledge is dualistic – 'I and thou', that's its form. It divides reality. Knowledge is schizophrenic, wisdom unites.

Wisdom means *unio mystica*. Then there is no God and no Devil, Only One is. What name you want to give to that One is just an arbitrary choice. You can call it God – but remember it is not God as opposed to the Devil. The God of wisdom is not opposed to the Devil, it contains the Devil in it. You can call it Tao, you can call it dharma, you can call it Logos, or whatever you will. But remember one thing: it contains the opposite. That is the essential thing to be remembered.

When a wise man asserts the word 'god', the devil is contained in it.

Do you know the original of the word 'devil'? It comes from a Sanskrit root *dev*, the same root from which the Sanskrit word *devata* comes; they both come from the same root. 'Devata' means God; 'devil' means Satan, but they originate in the same root, *dev*. It is from *dev* that the English word 'devil' comes, and also the word 'divine'. The divine and the devil are not two things.

Existence is one, utterly one, it is an organic unity. So when the wise man uses the word 'god' it contains the devil. When the wise man uses the word 'light' it contains all that is dark in it. It is comprehensive, it is inclusive, it does not exclude anything.

But when the man of knowledge uses the same words his connotation is different. When he uses the word 'god' it is against the devil. When he uses the word 'I' it is against thou, when he uses the word 'life' it is against death.

Wisdom knows no distinctions. All distinctions have to be dropped, only then does one become wise. The distinctions that morality creates, the distinctions upon which our mundane life exists and is built – all those distinctions have to be dropped. The distinction between man and woman is superficial, just on the surface. The distinction between matter and mind is also superficial, just on the surface. Matter is mind asleep, mind is matter become awake. The distinction between the body and the soul is superficial. The body is only the visible part of the soul, and the soul is the invisible part of the body; they are not two. Wisdom knows nothing of the two.

And this wisdom is not accumulated by accumulating information. It does not happen sitting in a library or in a university, it happens when you dissolve into your own core. It happens by going withinwards, it happens when you have touched your rock-bottom. When you have touched your very ground, it explodes. All distinctions disappear: suddenly life is one. Everything is connected with everything else, everything is dependent on everything else, everything is a member of everything else.

Then you don't see the tree separate from the earth – it is not. Then you don't see the tree separate from the sun, because it is not. Then the tree is joined with the sun with subtle rays. Without the sun the tree will disappear; it will not be green anymore, no flowers will come to it And without the earth there will be no juice in it, it will not be alive; and without the ocean it will also die. And if you go deep into the tree you will find it contains the whole existence.

Alfred Tennyson is right when he says, "If you can know a single flower, root and all, you will have known the whole existence." Why? Because even a single flower contains all. It has been part of the sun, part of the moon, part of the millions of stars, they have all poured themselves into this small flower. It has been contributed to by all – by the earth, and by things which you don't see as connected at all. A child playing by the rosebush has helped the rosebush to grow; without the child playing around it the rosebush would have been different.

Now there are scientific ways to know about it, that when a child is dancing around the rosebush, happy, singing, there is a connection with the rose. The rose feels the dance, the vibe, and grows faster. Now it is a well-established fact that if music is heard by roses they grow faster, they become bigger. If plants hear the music they grow faster, they bring bigger fruits, and they bring fruits sooner than they would have done otherwise.

If they are fed with noise, not with music, not with harmonious notes but with discordant noise, their growth suffers. They remain stunted. Flowers come, but not to their optimum; something remains retarded.

So everything contributes to everything else. You are whatsoever you are because the existence is whatsoever it is. You are an intrinsic part of this existence. Once you enter into your own being, you will become available to the whole and the whole will become available to you. You will be able to see in a new perspective.

So wisdom is not knowledge. Then what is it? Wisdom is meditation, wisdom is silence, wisdom is quietude, wisdom is *wu-wei*. Wisdom means a state of utter silence in absolute communion with existence. It is an orgasmic experience of being in tune with the whole.

The knowledgeable man is just like a donkey carrying the load of the past – of the scriptures, of theories, philosophies and theologies. He cannot answer a single real question, although he can answer millions of unreal questions.

A Hebrew driving a small cart drawn by a donkey came to a toll bridge. The toll collector came out of his house and said, "Here, you've got to pay toll before you can cross this bridge." "Vat! To pay toll?" "Yes, five cents to cross the bridge."

After an argument the Hebrew paid the five cents and went on. In the afternoon he came back again, but this time he had the donkey sitting on the seat and he was dragging the cart himself.

The toll man came out and said, "Here, you know you've got to pay five cents." The Hebrew shook his head, and pointing to the donkey, said, "Don't talk vit me – esk de driver."

The pundit, the scholar, the academician, is just like a donkey sitting in a cart pretending to be the driver. He is not a driver. He knows nothing. Although he has gathered much knowledge, still he knows nothing.

Knowing is a totally different phenomenon than knowledge.

The archbishop was visiting a small Catholic parish in a mining district for the purpose of administering confirmation. During the course of the exercises he asked one nervous little girl what matrimony was.

"It is a state of terrible torment which those who enter are compelled to undergo for a time to prepare them for a brighter and better world," she said. "No, no," remonstrated her rector. "That isn't matrimony. That's the definition of purgatory." "Leave her alone," said the archbishop. "Maybe she is right. What do you and I know about it?"

Knowing is through experiencing. Knowledge is not your own experience. You can know millions of things without knowing them – but then don't depend on it. It cannot be in communion with truth, it cannot reveal to you the mystery of life.

Two ladies in Boston heard the bishop give a rousing sermon on the beauties of married life. The ladies left the church feeling uplifted and contented.

"Twas a fine sermon His Reverence gave us this morning," observed one.

"That it was," agreed the other. "And I wish I knew as little about the matter as he does."

There is a way of knowing without knowing at all – that is knowledge. There is a way of knowing by really knowing – that is the way of wisdom. Wisdom is existential, knowledge is intellectual. In knowledge only part of your mind is involved, in wisdom your totality is immersed. And the difference is tremendous. The difference is incredible, immeasurable.

To know about reality is not really to know it. The 'about' takes you round and round, but never to the point. It is beating round the bush. You can go on beating, round and round, but it is almost futile.

Wisdom needs a direct approach. Wisdom needs to jump into the center of the thing, not go round and round. Going round and round you can become acquainted, but to be acquainted is not to know.

In the ordinary sense, whatsoever is called knowledge is a misnomer, because it is nothing but memory. It is not knowledge. Memory is not knowledge, it is parrot-like.

Knowledge is real only when you are an eye-witness to it: seeing is believing. But the people in the churches, in the temples, in the mosques, they say just the opposite. They say, "Believing is seeing." How can believing be seeing? Believing can only be deceiving. Believing can create a kind of hallucination around you: of you really believe too much in something you may start seeing it. But it is not there, it has been created by your mind. It is just your projection.

Never start with belief, otherwise you will never know the truth. Go empty into the search, with no belief, with no disbelief either. Just go open, not knowing this way or that. Go innocent, utterly naked.

Only one thing is needed for the disciple and that is openness and vulnerability – not belief. The real disciple is an agnostic. He says, "I don't know. I am *ready* to know but I don't know. And until I know, I am not going to believe. For or against, I am not going to believe either way. I will remain open for the truth to come and knock on my door. I will search."

But great courage is needed for that – to search without belief, without disbelief. The mind hankers to believe, because it can cling to the belief, it gives it great consolation. It starts feeling, "I know – a little bit, but at least I know. I am not utterly ignorant."

The disciple needs the courage to be utterly ignorant. In that ignorance, innocence arises. In that innocence you cannot find any ego in you. Ego needs beliefs – *or* disbeliefs, which are nothing but negative beliefs. One believes in God, one does not believe in God, but both are stubborn and dogmatic. Both have crutches to lean upon.

Throw away all your crutches. Only the is there a possibility of knowing the truth. And that is what I mean by "another kind of knowing": *being* the reality, not getting information about it.

Know love by being love, then it is wisdom. You can go to the British Museum and you can find all that has been written about love, and you can write a great PhD thesis about love, but you will not have known anything about love. You will not have tasted anything of love, not even a drop on your tongue. You may become very very clever about love, you may be able to talk about it, but you will be incapable of living it. And unless you are capable of living it, remember, you don't know it.

The real knowing comes by being that reality, by being one with or in unity or identity with that reality in its self-luminous state.

It is said in Zen that if you want to paint a bamboo, first go to the bamboo grove. Live with the bamboos in all kinds of seasons: let there be summer and winter and rains, and live with the bamboos so that you can feel how the bamboos feel. When it is dark and the night is silent and the stars are above, feel how the bamboos feel it. When the sun rises and there is great wind and the bamboos sway and dance, feel how the bamboos feel it. And when it is raining and the bamboos are delighted, let that delight enter into your being.

First become a bamboo if you want to paint a bamboo. Unless you have known the bamboo from its inside, unless you have become utterly identified with the bamboo, whatsoever you paint will be only a photograph, not a painting. That's the difference between a photograph and a painting. No camera will ever be able to do something like Van Gogh; no camera can do that.

Just the other night, a famous painter, Kelly, took sannyas. He has painted a painted of me without ever seeing me, but he has caught the feeling. It may not be exactly true about my face, because he had not seen me when he painted it. But it has the quality of my being.

He has painted me sitting surrounded by mountains. Not only has he caught my quality – even the mountains that are surrounding me have the same quality, the same meditativeness, the same stillness, the same calm, that same coolness. There is a tremendous harmony between me and the mountains. No camera could ever do it.

When for the first time the camera was invented, it was thought that now painting would soon become out of date, portraits would become out of date. What happened is just the opposite: painting has taken a new dimension because of the camera. All the bogus painters have disappeared, because their work can be done by the camera. Now only the true and authentic painters can exist.

Before the camera, the technician who knew how to paint the face in exact proportion was thought to be a great painter. Now that can be done by the camera, and more accurately. So that kind of technician-painter is no longer needed. Now only a meditative painter is needed, one who can function not from the without but from the within.

The other day, giving initiation to Kelly, I could feel he has that quality inside him which can participate with something, which can fall in tune with something. I have given him a new name, "Anand Nado": blissful soundless sound. That is the quality of meditation. There is no sound, it is soundlessness, yet there is great melody – unheard, unhearable, but the melody is there. There is no color specifically there, but it is very colorful. It is a paradox, that state. You are and you are not, and both are true. You are in *fana* and yet you are in *baqa*. You are utterly absent, *fana*, and you are utterly present, *baqa*: you are both together simultaneously.

Nado has that quality. Seeing him, looking into his eyes, I could see how he was able to paint me. From far away in America, without ever seeing me, he could catch the spirit. He must have fallen into a deep participation from that faraway land – a distance of thousands of miles, but he could commune with me.

Knowledge is about and about; it is not a communion. Wisdom is communion. that's why I say again and again that the artist is far closer to the mystic than the scientist, than the technician, than the professor; the artist is far closer. And in some moments the artist is almost a mystic – although they are only moments; they come and disappear, and he falls back to the mundane.

The mystic lives on the heights, he has made his house there. The artist sometimes reaches those heights; in some very precious moments he rises and soars there. But he is not capable of living on those heights; he falls back.

I hope Nado has the capacity to reach those peaks and will now become a permanent resident there.

That's what sannyas is all about. There is no need to come back to the mundane, one can remain in the sacred twenty-four hours. That is wisdom.

And that state is self-luminous. Whenever you are able to commune, if you can commune with bamboos swaying and dancing in the wind and in the rain, that experience of communion has a self-luminosity in it. It is self-evident, you need not have any other proofs.

If you can commune with a human being – your woman, your man, your friend, your child – that communion is self-evident. It is so powerful, it is so overwhelming, that you need not have any other proof. It is enough unto itself. That's why, though the whole world goes on saying there is no God, when Jesus comes to that communion he is ready to risk his life but he is not ready to say that there is no God.

The whole world says to Mansoor, "Stop declaring yourself a god!" The risk is great; Mansoor is made alert of it again and again. Even by his own master, Mansoor was told, "Stop asserting *'Anal haq*, I am God, I am truth!' because people are very fanatical, they will kill you."

Mansoor said, "That is acceptable, they can kill me. But what is happening in me is so self-evident – even if the whole world is against me it won't make any difference at all. I will still declare *'Anal haq*, I am truth' because I am!"

It is a self-luminous state. Wisdom is self-luminous. Knowledge is not self-luminous, knowledge needs supports.

Many times I receive letters from professors, academicians and pundits, saying, "In your books why don't you give footnotes or an appendix, so one can know from where these quotations have been taken and on what authority?"

What I am saying is self-luminous. It needs no footnotes, it needs no appendixes. It needs no support: I am enough unto myself. What I am saying is being said on my own authority. I am not trying to prove any hypothesis by supporting it with many arguments, by collecting data in support of it.

The Upanishads don't have any footnotes, the Koran is unaware of footnotes. Buddha has not given any sources – from where and on what authority he is speaking.

Whenever truth arrives it is self-luminous. It is the untruth that needs proofs, remember. It is the doubt inside you that collects proofs. Your statement is not a statement which can stand on its own; it needs props.

Knowledge gathers much information, data and argument. Wisdom is simply there: nude, innocent, available to all those who are ready to drink it.

In those moments of self-luminous wisdom there is the distinct realization that objects as such are never really directly related to or known, but rather it is only the knowledge of objects, as it takes place in consciousness, that is ever experienced or known. Therefore, all objects are essentially only objectifications of, and reducible to, pure consciousness, the one and only reality. In other words, what is known is not essentially different from the process of knowing or awareness of the known, and knowing is not essentially different from the knower, so that one realizes that the world is essentially the knower himself or pure consciousness, and so all is *one*.

When you are in that state of wisdom – self-luminous, silent, utterly relaxed, absolutely at home – this realization arises that consciousness is all, because whatsoever is known is known through consciousness. Whatsoever is known is nothing but a reflection in consciousness, whatsoever is known is nothing but a formation in consciousness. All forms arise in the ocean of consciousness and disappear. But the consciousness remains, abides, it is eternal.

For example, in the day when you open your eyes after the deep sleep of the night, you change from one world to another. Just a moment before, you were completely unaware of this world – the house, the wife, the children, the people, the neighborhood. You were lost in another world, the world of dreams, and you had completely forgotten this world. Now you open your eyes and the world of dreams starts disappearing. Within seconds it is gone and you become fully alert to this world, the waking world. The whole day you will live in it. In the night again you will fall asleep and this world will disappear and the dream world will unfold itself.

In the day you forget all about the dream world. In the dream world you forget all about the waking world. But one thing remains permanently there: the consciousness. The one who watches the waking world, and the one who watches the dreaming world. Only one thing remains constant; that constant thing is called your supreme self, *atman*, I-amness. It is not the ego, because the ego itself is a formation that comes and goes.

There are moments when you don't feel any ego. If you are watching a beautiful sunset you forget all about the ego – but you are there as a pure witness, with no idea of the ego. Listening to music, you forget all about your ego. You don't remember who you are, you become oblivious to it. But still the watcher is there.

In deep love, particularly in the peak moments of orgasmic release, you forget all about your ego. You are just a throbbing energy, a great pulsating energy, with no ego at all. But the witness is there. Your mirror goes on reflecting whatsoever is happening.

Wisdom means knowing this mirror that reflects all. It reflects good, it reflects bad, it reflects the ugly, it reflects the beautiful. But once you have understood that all those are reflections and you remain the same behind all the reflections, then what is the difference between the ugly and the beautiful, the good and the bad? They are both waves in you – one wave you call ugly, another wave you call beautiful, but both waves are your waves. It is just consciousness dancing.

This realization liberates. It liberates you from duality and makes you capable of becoming one with the nondual, the One. Now the sutras:

FOR THE WISE MAN EVIL AND GOOD ARE BOTH
EXCEEDINGLY GOOD. NO EVIL EVER COMES FROM

GOD; WHENEVER YOU THINK TO SEE EVIL
PROCEEDING FROM HIM, YOU WERE BETTER
TO LOOK ON IT AS GOOD.

For the wise man, evil and good are both exceedingly good. For the wise man, one who knows that all is one, how can there be a distinction between good and bad, between the saint and the sinner? There is no possibility of any distinction.

The moment you make the distinction you have already become a chooser, you have fallen back into the world of choice. You are no more a choiceless awareness – and that's what wisdom is all about.

...WHENEVER YOU THINK TO SEE EVIL PROCEEDING
FROM HIM...

And because the whole consists only of God, how can there be anything evil? But if sometimes you think that evil is happening...

YOU WERE BETTER TO LOOK ON IT AS GOOD.

Because you must be wrong somewhere; it must be your interpretation. For example, somebody is dying. Now death looks evil. Death is not evil – and if it looks like evil it is your misunderstanding, just your misunderstanding. You don't know what death is, hence it looks evil.

Death is nothing but a change of garments. If somebody is throwing away his old garments because he has got new ones, will you call it evil? Because you know that he is getting new garments and that's why he is throwing away the old ones, you will really congratulate him. You will not start feeling sorry for him. You will feel happy that the poor man at last has got new garments; the old were getting really rotten.

Exactly that is the case with death. The body is a composite phenomenon: one day it is born, one day it is young, one day it becomes old, and one day it has to die. It is just a preparation. Death is a preparation for a new birth. Those who know it will not say that death is evil. It is good, exceedingly good. But all depends on your interpretations.

It was a typical Holy Roller revival service, and the minister had just appealed to the pent-up audience to "hit the sawdust trail".

One buxom old dame who had been quivering convulsively all evening suddenly sprang to her feet and yelled, "Last night I was in the arms of the devil, but tonight I am in the arms of the Lord!"

A voice from the rear of the tabernacle called out, "Have you got a date for tomorrow night, sister?"

People have their own attitudes, choices, understandings, interpretations, inferences. They listen through that thick layer of many many thoughts. They see things through many-many-colored glasses, and then things look colored. And those colors are just projected by their glasses.

An Irishman at work on a building missed his footing on a scaffold, and fell from the ninth floor. He struck a telephone wire on the way down, whirled around, struck a clothes line, and landed in a pile of hay put there to feed the horses. The doctor who arrived decided that, by a miracle, no bones were broken. As the Irishman came to, the doctor was holding a glass of water to his lips to aid in reviving the patient.

"Phwat the devil happened – did the building fall?"

"No, but you did, my man; you had a very narrow escape from death." "Phwat's thot ye're givin'me to drink?" "Water, to revive you," answered the doctor.

"Givin' me wather, after fallin' nine stories! Faith, an' how far would I have to fall to git a drink of whiskey?"

Just look inside yourself: you have expectations, you have prejudices you have fixed, a priori ideas, and you are always looking through them.

The wise man drops all his thoughts, drops all his a priori conclusions. The wise man is one who lives without any conclusion. And once you can see reality without any conclusions, you will be surprised how much you have been missing. It is tremendously beautiful, it is absolutely good.

It is *satyam*, it is truth. It is *shivam*, it is good. It is *sunderam*, it is beautiful: *satyam shivam sunderam*.

But what we go on seeing is not that which is the case.

> I'M AFRAID THAT ON THE WAY OF FAITH,
> YOU ARE LIKE A SQUINTER SEEING DOUBLE,
> OR A FOOL QUARRELING WITH THE SHAPE
> OF A CAMEL.
> IF HE GIVES YOU POISON, DEEM IT HONEY;
> AND IF HE SHOWS YOU ANGER, DEEM IT MERCY.

Sanai says: Don't be like a squinter who goes on seeing double, and don't be like a fool who quarrels about the shape of a camel. There are people who think that the camel could have been made in a better way, more shapely. The camel is perfect as it is, the world is perfect as it is – and don't get into unnecessary arguments.

There are people who go on thinking that if *they* had made the world it would have been a better world. If they had made the world they would have done this and they would have done that. There would have been no disease, there would have been no death, there would have been no ugliness, there would have been no stupidity. And it looks so logical: yes, if a world is there where no disease exists, how beautiful it will be!

But do you know? – if there is no disease, there will be no health either. Do you know? – if there is no ugliness, there will be no beauty either. Do you know? – if there are no thorns, there will be no flowers either. Do you know? – if there is no death, there will be no life either. You cannot have a life without death. And if you could have a life without death it would be utterly boring; there would be no way to get rid of it.

A story is told of Alexander the Great when he came to the East. He had heard that in the desert there was a certain cave he was going to pass where there was a small pond of nectar. If you drank that nectar you would become immortal.

And the story is beautiful. Alexander reached there and entered the cave. He was so tremendously happy – just think of the happiness of you had been in his place! The nectar was there: just a moment more and he would be immortal. He cupped his hands, and just as he was going to drink, a crow who was sitting on the rock said, "Wait, just a minute!"

Alexander was surprised – a crow speaking? He asked, "What do you want to say?"

The crow said, "Just one thing, that's why I am sitting here. I have drunk from this pool: now I am here for millions of years. I want to die. The only idea that persists in me, twenty-four hours, is that of death. I want to get rid of this rotten body, but I cannot. I have tried but nothing succeeds. I have taken poison but it won't do. I have fallen from the mountains, it won't do. I have entered into fire, it won't burn. Now there is no way to die – and I am tired.

"Just think: for millions of years, I have to go on doing the same repetitive nonsense every day. And there is no hope even in the future. I will never be able to die, I cannot commit suicide, and I am tired of life! So now this is my mission: I sit here to prevent other people."

And it is said that Alexander thought for a moment, dropped the idea of drinking the nectar and rushed out of the cave – afraid that he might be tempted to drink it.

Without death, life would be an impossibly unbearable burden. Death relieves. And it is because of disease that you have the feeling of health. It is because of the dark night that the morning looks so beautiful.

Existence is dual, and existence is imperfect. But it is because of imperfection that there is growth. Just think, if everybody was perfect then there would be no growth. Then the world would be a graveyard; nothing would ever grow.

There are some modern paintings which are very horrible. They paint life as if life is something made of cement and concrete, as if all has stopped, nothing is growing. Just think of the nightmare if all stops, no tree grows, no child grows. If time stops and there is never any growth and everybody is stuck, that will be the state of a perfect world. It will be very very stale and dull and it will be unlivable.

Life is imperfect. Hence it has possibilities for growing. If you watch deeply, if you observe deeply, you will drop that foolish idea of improving upon it. It is good as it is.

This is the testimony of all the wise people of the world: the world is perfect in its imperfection, you cannot improve upon it. But our minds go on thinking that we are more clever. Our minds are cunning and we think we can use that cunningness to improve upon the very quality of life.

Our cunning minds succeed in the world, in the marketplace; they succeed in the universities, in the scientist's lab. But they cannot succeed in the world of meditation.

Muldoon was a man who lived by his wits, and his most famous talent was getting free drinks in strange pubs.

One night he went into a pub on the other side of town. The barman said, "What will you have?" "A small whiskey," said Muldoon. He got the whiskey, drank it but refused to pay for it. The barman called his boss but Muldoon said he had not asked for a drink – the barman had asked him what he was having. The boss, realizing he was dealing with a smart-aleck and not wishing to have any trouble, told the barman to let Muldoon get away with it but to see that it didn't happen again. Some months later, Muldoon again visited the pub.

"You're the fellow who got a drink here one night," said the barman, "and wouldn't pay for it." "Oh no – it wasn't me." "Then," said the barman, "you must have a double."

"Thanks very much – I will," said Muldoon.

Your cleverness may do in your world that *you* have cre-
ated, but your cleverness will not do in the world that God
has created. Your knowledge will be helpful to you in the
man-made world, but in God and his world only wisdom can
penetrate. Knowledge is clever, wisdom is innocent.

> I'M AFRAID THAT ON THE WAY OF FAITH, YOU ARE
> LIKE A SQUINTER SEEING DOUBLE, OR A FOOL
> QUARRELING WITH THE SHAPE OF A CAMEL.
> IF HE GIVES YOU POISON, DEEM IT HONEY;
> AND IF HE SHOWS YOU ANGER, DEEM IT MERCY.

Those who are following the path of faith, of trust, of love,
they will know it, that if God gives poison then it *must* be
honey, it can't be otherwise. We may not understand it right
now, because our understanding has limits. We may not be able
to see the point of it right now, because our vision is very
small, our perspective very narrow – and existence is vast. And
everything is linked with everything else.

Our situation is like those five blind men who went to see
the elephant and each touched a part of the elephant and
thought that he knew the whole of it. And they all started
quarreling.

That's how philosophers go on quarreling with each other.
Nobody has seen the elephant, and each seems to be very very
certain about his standpoint. And in a way he *has* seen a part,
he has at least felt a part. Somebody has touched the legs and
feels that an elephant is like a pillar. And he is not absolutely
wrong, true; he is partially right. But whenever any partial
truth starts claiming to be the whole, then there is danger –
and then it is more dangerous than a lie.

But that's what philosophical systems go on doing. Knowl-
edgeable people are blind people; they have not seen the ele-
phant, they have only specialized in a certain way. All those
five blind people were specialists, experts. One had touched

the leg, another had touched the ear, another one still had touched the trunk: they were all specialists, they knew only a part.

And this is the situation today. The chemist only knows about chemistry, and the physicist only knows about physics, and the psychologist knows only about the mind, and so on and so forth, and there seems to be no meeting ground. And there is a great quarrel amongst all these blind experts. The physicist does not know anything about chemistry, and the chemist knows nothing about poetry, and the poet knows nothing about music, and the musician knows nothing about mathematics, and they are all quarreling.

The quarrel is coming to bigger and bigger proportions. And each branch of knowledge is becoming so specialized, so narrow, that it seems almost impossible for any person to have contact with other specializations.

It is very difficult to find a man who is a poet and a mathematician and a physicist and a philosopher and a mystic; it is very difficult. And we need such people. Without such people, man will fall apart. Without such people there will be no possibility of a synthesis. Who will these people be? Is it possible for a man, is it feasible for a man, to know all that physics knows and chemistry and biology and geology and so on and so forth? It is humanly impossible. Nobody can know all the branches of knowledge that are available today.

Oxford University teaches three hundred and fifty subjects, and each subject has a tremendous amount of knowledge that has accumulated down the ages. They say the specialist is one who knows more and more about less and less. And the greatest specialist is one who knows nothing, or who knows *all* about nothing.

This is a very strange situation humanity is facing for the first time. Then who will become the bridge? Only the wise man can become the bridge. The wise man is not one who will know all these branches. The wise man will be one who will go deep into his own being and know the consciousness out of which all these branches have arisen. The wise man will get to the roots, will understand the roots. And by understanding the roots, all the branches and all the foliage and all the fruits and all the flowers are understood. The lover has died and left both belief and unbelief. Burning in love of the flame, the moth does not distinguish between the light of the mosque and the light of the monastery.

This is a Sufi saying. Wisdom arises when you die, when the ego disappears. The lover has died and left both belief and unbelief. Burning in love of the flame, the moth does not distinguish between the light of the mosque and the light of the monastery.

The moth will not be concerned whether the flame that has called it forth is burning in the mosque or in the temple. The moth recognizes only the flame; wherever it is, that is irrelevant. And so is the case with a lover, with a Sufi, with a disciple. He is not worried where the master is available, the flame is available – in the temple, in the mosque, in the church. He is not worried about that. Wherever he sees the flame he is ready to die in the flame, disappear into the flame. And in that very disappearance, wisdom arises. The death of the ego is the resurrection of wisdom in you. You are again a child, innocent, wondering, full of awe. And then the whole existence is a mystery.

Then it is fantastic. Then its beauty is unbelievable, then its joy is unbearable, then its ecstasy is overwhelming.

BE CONTENTED WITH YOUR LOT; BUT IF YOU HAVE
ANY COMPLAINTS, GO AND TAKE THEM TO THE
KAZI, AND OBTAIN SATISFACTION FROM HIM
– THAT'S HOW THE FOOL'S MIND WORKS!

If you dissolve your ego into your supreme self, then there will be great contentment. You will be contented with things as they are. Then there will be no desire to go anywhere else, to be somebody else. Then you will be utterly grateful, whatsoever you are. You will bow down immediately to God in great contentment, in great gratitude.

BE CONTENTED WITH YOUR LOT;
BUT IF YOU HAVE ANY COMPLAINTS...

And the wise man has no complaints, he knows nothing but contentment. And if you still have any complaints, then go to the priest, the Kazi; then go to the priest and obtain satisfaction from him, because that is his function.

Just see the difference between two words, 'contentment' and 'satisfaction'. Contentment arises out of wisdom, it is a fragrance of wisdom, and satisfaction is just imposed through knowledge. If you go to the priest he will satisfy you. If you go to the priest and say, "I am getting old and I am becoming afraid of death," he will say, "Don't be worried. Only the body dies, the soul is immortal." He will simply give you knowledge. He himself has not attained, otherwise he would not have been a priest.

The function of the priest is to console you. The function of the priest is somehow to keep you adjusted to the world. That has been the function of the priest up to now.

Now, particularly in the West, the function is being transferred to the psychotherapist. The priest has functioned as the psychotherapist is functioning today. The priest is the ancient-most psychotherapist, and the psychotherapist is the modern priest. Their function is to keep people satisfied, to help people remain adjusted to the society in which they are living.

This satisfaction is not contentment, this is just patchwork. Sooner or later, again the doubt will arise. The priest says the soul is immortal, but who knows? He may be wrong. He may be lying, he may be deceived – because you have also seen the priest in different situations.

I lived in Raipur for a few days. It happened, a professor's wife died, so I went to see him. There were many people and they were consoling him, saying, "Don't be worried." A man, a knowledgeable man, a brahmin scholar, was saying, "The soul is immortal, only the body dies."

A few days afterwards, just by coincidence, that scholar's wife died. I went there, just to see what the scholar was doing now. He was crying. I said, "This is absurd. You, and crying? And I have seen you consoling one professor whose wife had died, and you were telling him the soul is immortal. What happened to your knowledge?" He said, "Forget all about it. Who knows? I was just consoling the man. And please don't raise such uncomfortable questions at this moment. My wife is dead and you are bringing up some philosophical argument."

Your priest may say to you that the soul is immortal, but how long will you be able to trust it? One day you will see the priest behaving in just the opposite way. The priest says one thing, behaves in another way. It is not possible to attain contentment through the priest. But that is the priest's function, that he keeps you satisfied. Satisfaction is not contentment, satisfaction is a false coin again. Just as knowledge is a false coin compared to wisdom, satisfaction is a false coin compared to contentment. Contentment arises from your own understanding, satisfaction is given by others.

Always beware of the borrowed, the borrowed is always false. But that is the fool's mind, how it works. The fool's mind is more interested in consolation than in wisdom.

I had one old friend, his son died. He was seventy when his son died; the son was young, not more than forty. It was a great shock to the old man. I went to see him and I told him, "Stop crying and weeping, it is pointless. Now you know that even a young man, perfectly healthy, can die. And you are old, you are seventy, and you are no longer healthy either. So take a hint: don't waste your time in crying and weeping and suffering. It is an indication that *your* death is coming."

He said, "What?" He forgot all about his son – he was angry at me. Because these are the moments when people are searching for consolation. I said, "Yes, it is an indication that your death is coming. Now prepare for your death. God has simply made you aware: this is an alarm."

He became very angry with me. Who wants to hear about one's own death? He wanted me to say something nice about the son. And he said, "Can't you say anything nice?"

I said, "Nice things won't help; they will only console you, they will satisfy you. And many other people are doing it already. Let me do the real necessity. The real necessity is that you should not waste your time in crying and weeping and getting consoled and enjoying sympathy. The time has come to be shocked. Only such a shock can destroy your shock-absorbers. Look at the corpse of your son. Forty years old, perfectly young, healthy, and he can die within a moment.

"He was not ill. In the night suddenly he died, by the morning he was found dead in his bed. He had gone to bed perfectly healthy. Now think about you!"

He became so angry that he stopped coming to me. And within a year he did. But he didn't prepare. If he had been a little more intelligent he would have prepared – he would have met his death in a totally different way, he would have met his death meditatively. But the fool's mind works in a certain way. He is only worried about consolations and satis-factions.

The real thing is contentment. And contentment is possi-ble only when you have known your reality – when you have penetrated your innermost core of being and you have seen *there* that there is no death, and you have seen there that there is no disease and that you have seen there that it is eternal, it is beyond time.

Then all fear, all fear of death, all anguish, all anxiety, disappears. And there arises great contentment. That content-ment is prayer.

> WHATEVER BEFALLS YOU, MISFORTUNE OR
> FORTUNE, IS UNALLOYED BLESSING;
> THE ATTENDANT EVIL A FLEETING SHADOW.
> 'GOOD' AND 'EVIL' HAVE NO MEANING IN THE
> WORLD OF THE WORD: THEY ARE MERE NAMES,
> COINED IN THE WORLD OF 'ME' AND 'YOU'.

Whatever befalls you – if contentment has arisen in you, just a little taste of contentment, a little light of wisdom, just a little part of your being has become luminous – then...

> WHATEVER BEFALLS YOU, MISFORTUNE OR
> FORTUNE, IS UNALLOYED BLESSING.

Then all is blessing, all only *can* be blessing, because all comes from God. This whole existence is divine: how can evil happen?

But if you see the attendant evil, then know well, it is a fleeting shadow. Just as when you walk in the sun a shadow is created, but the shadow is nonexistential. Just as when you are in great ecstasy a shadow is created; that shadow is nonexistential. Know well that the nonexistential need not be worried about, it is just a shadow.

Evil is a shadow of good, and hate is a shadow of love, and anger is a shadow of compassion, and ugliness is a shadow of beauty, and sadness is a shadow of joy. Once you have seen it on your own – not because I say so but when you have seen it on your own – then the whole life is nothing but a constant showering of blessings.

> 'GOOD' AND 'EVIL' HAVE NO MEANING...

Then there is no question of good and evil. All is good, supremely good.

> ...IN THE WORLD OF THE WORD...

Logos, God, Tao. Good and bad are...

> ...MERE NAMES, COINED IN THE WORLD OF 'ME'
> AND 'YOU'.

There is no me and no you. This is *adab*, Sufis call it *adab*: being in the presence of the master, seeing and feeling that there is no me and no you.

Feel it right now! I am not here simply to talk to you on great things, I am here to give you a taste of those great things. Even if for a single moment you are not there as you, and you don't think of me as separate from you, just for a single moment we are bridged – in that very moment you will see great blessings descending. That is the grace of being with a master.

And it is easier to drop your 'me' and 'you' with a master than anywhere else. Why? Why can't you drop it anywhere else? Because anywhere else two persons will have to drop it, and it will become complicated. And two persons will have to drop it simultaneously, only then can there be a fleeting moment of joy. With the master it is possible because on one side, the master's side, there is no 'I', no 'you'. So half the work is already done. Now it is only on your side. So whenever you can drop your 'you', your 'I', immediately you are in contact, immediately you are bridged.

The master is an absence. Whenever you become an absence, two zeros dissolve into each other. Two zeros cannot remain separate. Two zeros are not two zeros; two zeros become one zero.

Just a few days ago, I said that from my side there is no relationship, the relationship between a master and a disciple is one-way traffic. Chetna wrote me a beautiful letter saying, "You told it very nicely, it was a sugar-coated pill, but it has stuck in my throat."

Chetna, drink a little more of me, so that it can go down

the throat. Drink a little more of me, drink a little more of this absence, drink a little more of one who is *not*. I can understand, it hurts. It is a bitter pill, even though sugar-coated. It hurts to feel that the relationship is only from your side and not from the master's side. You would like it that the master also needs you. You would like me to tell you, "I need you, I love you very much."

I can understand your need, but that will not be true. I can only say, "I don't need you, I love you." Need exists only with the ego. I cannot relate with you, because I am not. You can relate with me, because you are still there. Because you are there you can go on relating with me, but that relationship will remain only so-so, lukewarm.

If you also disappear the way I have disappeared, then there will be a meeting – no relationship, but a merging. And relationship cannot satisfy. You have known so many relationships: what has happened through them? You have loved, you have been friendly, you have loved your mother and father, your brother and sister, you have loved your woman, your husband, your wife. You have loved so many times, you have created relationships so many times. And you know, each relationship leaves a bitter taste in the mouth. It does not make you contented. It may satisfy for a moment, but again there is dissatisfaction. It may console you, but again you are left in the coldness of loneliness.

Relationship is not the true thing. The true thing is communion, the true thing is merger. When you relate you are separate, and in separation there is bound to remain the ugly, mischievous and agony-creating ego. It disappears only in the merger.

So, Chetna, drink a little more of my absence, drink a little more of my love which does not need you. And then the pill will go down the throat and you will be able to digest it. And one day will arise, the great day, when you will also love me and will not need me.

When two persons love and both have no need for each other, love takes wings. It is no more ordinary, it is no more of this world, it belongs to the beyond. It is transcendental.

> YOUR LIFE IS JUST A MORSEL IN HIS MOUTH;
> HIS FEAST IS BOTH A WEDDING AND A WAKE.
> WHY SHOULD DARKNESS GRIEVE THE HEART?
> — FOR NIGHT IS PREGNANT WITH NEW DAY.

We are all in God's mouth: a tremendously pregnant statement.

> YOUR LIFE IS JUST A MORSEL
> IN HIS MOUTH...

Be absorbed by him. Don't resist, don't fight: dissolve yourself in him.

> YOUR LIFE IS JUST A MORSEL IN HIS MOUTH...

Be eaten up by him. Don't fight, don't escape, because it is only if you absorb yourself in him that you will come to know what true life is.

> ...HIS FEAST IS BOTH A WEDDING AND A WAKE.

This is something beautiful: meditate over it. BOTH A WEDDING AND A WAKE — a wake means when somebody dies and you have to watch to corpse. A wedding and a wake, both together?

Yes, it is together, because your death is your resurrection. On the one hand, you die: it is a wake. On the other hand, you become married to him for ever and for ever: it is a wedding. It is a cross, a crucifixion, and a resurrection follows. And only those who are ready to die into God are born anew.

Then they have cosmic souls, then they have eternal beings.

WHY SHOULD DARKNESS GRIEVE THE HEART?

Don't be worried about death and darkness...

FOR NIGHT IS PREGNANT WITH NEW DAY.

Soon, as the night darkens and becomes more and more densely dark, the morning comes closer and closer. Die, learn to die, and you will be able to attain to life abundant.

YOU SAY YOU'VE UNROLLED THE CARPET OF TIME,
STEP THEN BEYOND LIFE ITSELF AND REASON, TILL
YOU ARRIVE AT GOD'S COMMAND.

How long have you lived in time? Millions of lives. If you trust the East, then eighty-four million lives. It is a long journey, you have unrolled the carpet of time long enough. Now be finished, now be a little more intelligent. Have you not learned any lesson? You have lived so long and you have done all that you can desire to do, and millions of times. And still you are not fed-up, not bored?

YOU SAY YOU'VE UNROLLED THE CARPET OF TIME,
STEP THEN BEYOND LIFE ITSELF AND REASON...

Now the moment has come. Step beyond life: die into God. And of course, if you want to die into God you will have to step beyond reason, because reason will say, "What are you going to do? Death? Who knows? Resurrection may follow, may not follow. Who knows? The seed may die and there may come no sprout and no tree in its place. How can it be guaranteed?" Reason will create a thousand and one doubts.

But you have been reasoning and reasoning for millions of

lives, and reason has not given you a single conclusion, it has not made you a little bit more intelligent. It keeps you in the old rut. If you have seen that it keeps you in the old rut, be courageous — trust. Courage means trust, trust means courage. Take the risk: go beyond reason and go beyond life...

TILL YOU ARRIVE AT GOD'S COMMAND.

And if you can go beyond reason and beyond your so-called life, suddenly you are taken up, possessed by God. Then he starts living through you. Then you become a flute, a hollow bamboo, then he sings the song.

YOU CANNOT SEE ANYTHING, BEING BLIND BY
NIGHT, AND BY DAY ONE-EYED WITH YOUR
FOOLISH WISDOM!

In the night you cannot see because it is dark. In ignorance you cannot see because you are ignorant, and in knowledge you cannot see because your knowledge covers your eyes. The ignorant is suffering because he is ignorant, and the knowledgeable is suffering because he is knowledgeable.

Drop both! — ignorance and knowledge. Simply be utterly clean of both, knowledge and ignorance: just be an opening.

And in that opening comes the great guest, in that opening you become the host. God is ready to penetrate you, but either your ignorance prevents him or your knowledge prevents him.

Remember, innocence is the absence of *both*, ignorance and knowledge. The innocent man is not aware that he knows, is not aware that he does not know. He is simply a pure mirror, reflecting whatsoever is the case.

Become a pure mirror: that's what meditation is all about.

10
Something to be Remembered

The first question:

THE MASSES WERE AGAINST JESUS,
THEY WERE AGAINST BUDDHA,
THEY ARE AGAINST YOU. WHY?

The masses live in a kind of non-individual existence. They live like sheep. So whenever a man like Jesus or Buddha is there, asserting his individuality, his rebellion, his freedom, he is naturally disliked. The masses become afraid; their foundations are shaken. If Jesus is right, then the whole life pattern of the masses will have to be changed. It is too much work, and people have invested too much in their slavery.

The presence of Jesus makes people feel bankrupt. The moment you come across a buddha, you are reduced to a very ugly kind of inhuman being. You lose all dignity, you feel humiliated. If you are intelligent you will rise to the occasion: you will see the point that up to now you have lived in ignorance, in sleep. And you will feel grateful to the Buddha that his presence has become a ray of light into your dark night of the soul.

But that much intelligence is very rare. People are stupid and stubborn, they immediately react. Rather than rising higher and taking the challenge of the peak the Buddha is, they destroy Buddha, they destroy Jesus, so that they can again fall asleep and dream their so-called sweet dreams.

That's why they are against me: I am a kind of disturbance. My presence cannot be ignored: either you have to be with me, or you have to be against me. Whenever you cannot ignore the presence of a certain person and you have to choose, great turmoil arises in your being – because no choice is easy. Choice means change.

You have lived for fifty years in a certain way: those habits have become settled. Now, suddenly I am here calling you forth out of your grave that you have believed was real life. I am here condemning all that you have lived for – all your values, all your so-called morality, all your knowledge, all your religion. Only very courageous people, very few chosen ones, will be able to rise to the occasion and risk all that they have for something that is not visible, for something which you can only trust.

Now, this is difficult for the ordinary masses; they decide for the known. Jesus is something of the unknown, Buddha is something from the beyond. Now the question is whether to choose the known, the familiar, the safe, the comfortable, the convenient, or to choose this adventure and go with Buddha into something uncharted and unmapped, into something one can never be certain about, whether it is or it is not.

Buddha himself may be deceived or may be a deceiver. There is no way, this way or that, to be totally certain about it. In deep hesitation, in deep confusion, in deep trembling, one has to go with the Buddha. Only those who are still young, whose minds have not yet gathered too much dust, who are still capable of wondering, feeling the awe of life, who are still not absolutely settled, closed, finished, who are not yet dead – only those few people will be able to go with me, with Jesus, with Buddha. Others are bound to be against them. And then there are many other reasons too.

People like to belong to groups. It gives a kind of consolation, satisfaction: "I am on the right track." If you are a

Christian then millions of Christians are with you; you belong to them, you are not alone.

If you are with me, you are almost alone. You will be uprooted from the crowd to which you had belonged up to now. For a few moments you will be nowhere, no one. You will become anonymous. You will not be a Christian or a Hindu or a Mohammedan – and that has become your identity.

You have been a Christian or a Hindu or a Jew, and that is your identity, that's what you know about yourself. If somebody asks, "Who are you?" you can say, "I am a Catholic." It gives you a certain false feeling that you know yourself. People go on living in the world of "as if". But when you live in the world of "as if" long enough it starts looking real; you start believing it.

The child is born: he is not Christian nor Jew nor Hindu. And he is perfectly happy without being a Hindu. But soon he will become a Hindu or a Mohammedan or somebody else. He will have to be taught; he will be given an identity, a label – and that label means much to you, because behind the label is emptiness.

Once the label is taken away, you will fall into an abysmal emptiness. Unless you are really courageous, unless you have real guts to go into that emptiness, you will want to cling to the label.

Some experiments by Henry Tajfel at Bristol University have produced unexpected results. Parties of schoolboys aged fourteen to fifteen were subjected to a quick, and bogus, psychological test; then each boy was told that he was either a "Julius person" or an "Augustus person". No explanation was given of the characteristics of the Julius or Augustus people, nor did the boys know who the other members of their group were. Nevertheless, they promptly identified with their fictitious group, proud to be a Julius person or an Augustus person to such an extent that they were willing to make financial sacrifices to benefit their anonymous group brothers and to cause discomfort in the other camp. Tajfel says that you can alter a person's behavior predictably, just by telling him he belongs to a group – even a group of which he has never heard before. Almost automatically the participant in these experiments favors anonymous members of his own group and, given the opportunity, he is likely to go out of his way to put members of another group at a disadvantage. People will stick up for a group to which they happen to be assigned, without any indoctrination about who else is in the group or what its qualities are supposed to be.

Only by grasping the full import of the positive and quick propensity of human beings to identify with any group they find themselves in can one make a firm base from which to search out the origin of hostility.

These experiments of Henry Tajfel are of tremendous import. People love to *belong*. And when a man like Jesus comes, he uproots you from your group. Jesus comes and he takes you out of your community of the Jews. He starts something new, which has no past, no history, no respectability. He simply begins things from ABC.

Now, those few people who followed Jesus must have been of some integrity, otherwise they would not have followed him – because following Jesus meant that they would no more be part of the Jewish community in which they had been born and indoctrinated, and to which they had always belonged. And they had always been proud that they were Jews, the chosen people of God. They had always believed they were special people.

Now here comes the son of a carpenter, Jesus, with nothing in his past to support him, a vagabond, and he starts gathering a group of people. This group is so new, it will take time for people to belong to it; it will happen only when Jesus is gone. But when Jesus is gone it is pointless.

After Jesus died, nearabout two hundred, three hundred

years afterwards, Christianity itself started becoming a special group. Then people were happy to belong to it. Now millions are happy to belong to Christianity.

People like to belong. Now, if you come to me you will be losing your belonging. You will be becoming alone. And you will be going with somebody who has no past, no traditional support. It will be an absolutely new enterprise, risky. It is a gamble. And people even like to belong to fictitious groups – what to say about religions?

Arthur Koestler says: I found these experiments of Henry Tajfel extremely revealing, not only on theoretical grounds but also for personal reasons, related to a childhood episode which has never ceased to puzzle and amuse me.

On my first day at school, aged five, in Budapest, Hungary, I was asked by my future classmates the crucial question: 'Are you an MTK or an FTC?' These were the initials of two leading soccer teams, perpetual rivals for the league championship, as every schoolboy knew – except little me, who had never been to a football match. However, to confess such abysmal ignorance was unthinkable, so I replied with haughty assurance: MTK, of course!

And thus the die was cast: for the rest of my childhood in Hungary, and even when my family moved to Vienna, I remained an ardent and loyal supporter of MTK; and my heart still goes out to them, all the way across the Iron Curtain. Moreover, their glamorous blue-and-white striped shirts never lost their magic, whereas the vulgar green-and-white stripes of their unworthy rivals still fill me with revulsion.

I am even inclined to believe that this early conversion played a part in making blue my favorite color. After all, the sky is blue, a primary color, whereas green is merely the product of its adulteration with yellow. I may laugh at myself, but the emotive attachment, the magic bond, is still there, and to shift my loyalty from the blue-white MTK to the green-white FTC would be downright blasphemy.

UNIO MYSTICA

Truly, we pick up our allegiances like infectious germs. Even worse, we walk through life unaware of this pathological disposition, which lures man from one historic disaster into the next.

You come to me – you have already belonged to a group for your whole life. You have been a Hindu, a Mohammedan, a Christian, a Jew. And these groups are not ordinary groups like football teams – they indoctrinate, from the very beginning they start conditioning you. A great conditioning exists in you.

So whenever a man like Jesus or Buddha is there, your conditioning goes against him. He wants to create an unconditional mind, that's the problem. He wants you to get rid of all your pathological attachments, that's the problem. You are too much attached to your disease, your pathology, and anybody who wants to see you healthy and whole will look like the enemy. See the point.

Another new sannyasin, Dwabha, has just written to me saying, "I am feeling very good here, but when I go out there are Christians who hand out pamphlets to me about Christianity, about Jesus, and they tell me that you are an anti-Christ. So what should I do?"

It is natural. Christians are becoming afraid, because so many Christians are coming to me. The fear is natural, they have a vested interest. Hindus are afraid, Jainas are afraid; their fear is understandable. To take anybody from any group to which he has belonged is to offend the group, because their number is reduced. And number means power. In this world, the more people belong to your group, the more powerful you are. In the name of religion, much power politics goes on.

So they will tell you that I am anti-Christ. They were telling Jesus' followers that Jesus was anti-Moses, they were telling Buddha's followers that Buddha was anti-Veda. That has been an old story; it is nothing new.

Truth cannot be accepted by the masses because the masses live in lies. And they have lived so long in their lies that those

299

lies are not longer lies to them, they really believe in them. Whenever you say something different from their beliefs you create confusion in them, and nobody wants to be confused. You create an inner trembling, a doubt in them, and nobody wants to be in doubt. But doubt is there. If they had known the truth there would have been no fear. They have not known the truth, they have only believed. Doubt is there, deep down in their souls, so whenever you say something that goes against them their doubt starts rising and surfacing. And they are afraid to be in doubt. Everybody wants certainty. Why? Because certainty gives you security, certainty gives you confidence. Doubt makes you shaky.

And I am going to create much doubt in you — because in my vision, unless doubt destroys your false certainties, there is no possibility of attaining to true certainty. True certainty is not out of belief; it comes out of experience, it comes out of your own realization.

I am not anti-Jesus, I am certainly anti-Christianity. I am not anti-Buddha, I am certainly anti-Buddhist. I am not anti-Krishna but I am certainly anti-Hindu.

Whatever I am saying and doing is the work of Jesus, the work of Krishna and Buddha. Certainly not in the same language — how can it be in the same language? How can I speak Aramaic to you, how can I use the metaphors Jesus used? Those metaphors are out of date, they don't belong to this century. I will have to be more scientific, I will have to be more logical. Even so I want you to go beyond logic, I will have to lead you to the extreme point of logic first; only from there you can take the jump into the illogical.

I cannot talk with you the way Buddha talked. He was talking to a different audience. So my words will be different, my approaches will be different, my methodology will be different. But the moon that I am pointing to is the same. My finger is different, it's bound to be so. If you compare my finger with Jesus' finger, they are different. But the moon that we

are pointing to is the same. Look at the moon and don't be
bothered too much by the fingers.

The second question:

> I HAVE BEEN THINKING OF BECOMING A
> SANNYASIN FOR AT LEAST SEVEN YEARS.
> WHY AM I NOT ABLE TO TAKE THE JUMP?

It seems you are not aware of death at all. If you are aware
of death you cannot postpone like that. And now, because you
have been postponing for seven years, postponement must
have become a habit. You have practiced it long; you have
become too attached to postponing.

Postponement gives you a good feeling. First, it is not risky;
you need not change. You are always going to change tomor-
row, and the tomorrow never comes. So meanwhile you can
remain the same as you are. The tomorrow becomes a protec-
tion: "Tomorrow I will become a sannyasin. So today, what-
soever I am, I *have* to be. It is only the question of one day:
tomorrow I will become a sannyasin and I will take the jump."
And when tomorrow comes, it always comes as today.

Now, for seven years you have been practicing postpone-
ment. It must have become a kind of addiction. Remember,
death can happen any moment. Those who are aware of death,
they drop postponement, because tomorrow is not certain.
Only this moment is certain, the moment that is already in
your hands. Even the next moment is not certain.

So if you see something valuable in a thing, do it! And do it
NOW. Remember it: now or never. If you don't want to do it,
who is telling you to do it? Forget all about it. But please
don't postpone. Either decide "I am not going to take sann-
yas" – and that's perfectly good. At least decisiveness will be
there, your worry will be dropped. Decide "I am not going to

take sannyas" and be finished with it. Or take the jump and be finished with it.

A male dinosaur and a female dinosaur were having an affair. For ten million years they walked around, talking and looking into each other's eyes. Then they would sometimes hold hands, and this continued for twenty million years more.

For the next fifteen million years they would kiss and touch each other all over. Then finally the male said to the female, "Dear, we have been together for so many years, how do you feel about...you know, I think it is time we made love!"

"I want to but I can't" she answered. "I have now got my period for the next seventy million years."

You are not a dinosaur, time is very short. Life is very small. Out of a seventy-year life span, almost thirty-five years are lost in sleep. And then eating, drinking, dressing, going to the office, coming to the house...then earning the bread – and the friends and the clubs and the hotels and the movies and the TV. Just count, and you will not find even one year to live. You will not find even one year left to live. You will not even find one year out of seventy years to meditate, to search, to be.

It is already too much that you have spent seven years thinking of sannyas. Either take it or forget all about it, but be decisive. To remain so indecisive for so long is dangerous because then indecisiveness becomes your nature.

The third question:

BELOVED MASTER,
I FINALLY REALIZED THAT I AM NEVER GOING TO
GET ENLIGHTENED. BUT THERE IS NO WAY TO DIE.
WHAT TO DO?

Pratima, this is a great realization. No one is going to get enlightened, because enlightenment is not something that has to happen. It has already happened, you *are* enlightened. You just have to look into yourself and find it. It is already the case.

That's my whole theme that I am preaching to you, day in and day out, year in and year out. Enlightenment is not something like an achievement that will happen some day. It has already happened, you *are* enlightened, there is nobody who is not enlightened.

But man has the capacity to remember or to forget, and you have forgotten it. You have decided to forget about it; you are keeping it behind your back. It is there; you can keep it behind your back for millions of lives, but it is there, and it will remain there. And any moment you decide to turn, a one-hundred-and-eighty-degree turn, you will be surprised: it has always been there waiting, waiting for you to come home.

Pratima, you are not going to get enlightened because you *are* enlightened. I am here not to *make* you enlightened, but just to remind you. Just to remind you: that's the function of the master, to shake you into wakefulness.

God is your treasure. All that you need, all that you can *ever* need, is already given. It is already provided for. But you have not searched within yourself, you have not opened the treasures within yourself. And you go on looking all over the earth. You can go on looking and you will not find it, because it is not something to be found, it is something to be remembered. See the distinction, the difference: it is vast. It is a difference that makes a great difference.

It is as if you have money in your pocket but you have forgotten. And then one day suddenly you remember and it is there. One day suddenly, searching for something else, you find it.

Enlightenment is not something in the future, it is your presentness. Become aware of it now. This is it.

The fourth question:

MORARJI DESAI SAID IN AN INTERVIEW GIVEN
TO "SUNDAY": "OSHO PUTS EMPHASIS
ON THE SOCIALIZATION OF WOMAN."
HE SAID, "JUST AS PROSTITUTES ARE SOCIALIZED,
HE WANTS ALL WOMEN TO BE SOCIALIZED."
HE ALSO SAID, "OSHO GOES EVEN FURTHER AND
SAYS THAT THERE IS NO NEED OF MARRIAGE.
OSHO ALSO ADVOCATES FREE SEX."
WHAT DO YOU SAY ABOUT IT, BELOVED MASTER?

Morarji Desai is a male chauvinist. Women are not property, so how can they be public or private? What is a man, public or private? If men need not be public property or private property, then why should women be either Public property or private property? The whole idea is based in male chauvinistic attitudes.

Morarji Desai represents all that is rotten in the human past. These are the two attitudes that have been taken by men about women; both are wrong.

Karl Marx and Engels have some insight about it. They say that as the ownership of things arose, the ownership of women arose simultaneously. The husband/wife relationship came as a by-product of private property. Hence Marx and Engels were in favor of making women socialized. That is going from one stupidity to another; but the basic idea is the same, that the woman is a property. Either she belongs to a particular man for his whole life, then she is a wife. Or she is possessed by a man for one single night, then she is a prostitute.

What is the difference between a prostitute and a wife? One is a temporary arrangement, the other is a little more permanent. Marriage is a permanent kind of prostitution; deep down, it is not different. Hence marriage and prostitution have both existed together.

If you go into it, it is marriage that has created prostitution. And prostitution will never disappear from the world unless marriage disappears; it is the shadow of marriage. In fact prostitutes have been saving marriage. It is a safety measure: the man can go once in a while, just for a change, to some other woman, a prostitute, and save his marriage and its permanency.

That's what has been done, down the ages. The prostitute was there to save you and your marriage. So whenever your marriage was on the rocks you could always go to the prostitute. Whenever you were bored with your woman, tired of her, just to be refreshed you could go to the prostitute, and things would start flowing again with your own woman. The prostitute was a kind of holiday.

People think prostitution is against marriage, they are utterly wrong. Prostitution is the other side of the same coin: on one side it is marriage, on the other side it is prostitution.

That's why marriage has existed for at least five thousand years, but people have not been able to get rid of prostitution – they cannot. There is a logical relationship, they are interdependent. If prostitution is simply stopped, marriages will start falling apart. The prostitute is like a glue, she helps you to remain not bored with your woman. But both are based on the idea of property.

In China, for centuries, it was the rule that if a man killed his woman he was not thought to be a murderer. He could not be punished by the court, because the woman was his property. It is your right to destroy your chair, or if you want to demolish your house it is nobody else's business to interfere.

For centuries the woman has been thought of as property. In India, even the words are there: the woman is known as *nari sampatti*, the female property. When a girl is married, the father is said to give the girl as a gift: *kanyadan*.

The woman has been treated as a thing. I am against it.

Who told Morarji Desai that I want women to be socialized? That must have been his inference. I have never said it. There is no need to socialize, because that will again be treating women in an inhuman way.

That was the idea of Engels and Marx, because they were reactionaries. They were reacting against private property. So just as factories had to be nationalized, socialized and state-owned, in exactly the same way, everything private should be owned by the society. They made this proposal that the woman should be owned by the society. Everything that had been owned by persons now had to be owned by the state or by the society.

I am not a Communist, I am an anti-Communist. My whole approach is that the woman is not a thing, the woman is a human being, as much as Morarji Desai. Nobody needs to own anybody else. Neither the husband needs to own the woman, nor does the woman need to own the husband. The whole idea of ownership is ugly, violent and degrading. I have never said this.

But there are a thousand and one rumors in this country about me, what I say, what I am doing here. This seems to be really strange. These people never come here to see what is happening; they go on believing in the rumors.

The first thing: the woman is different from the man, but not unequal. She has equal rights. The difference is there, and the difference is beautiful and the difference should be maintained.

Now there is a tendency in the West to destroy the difference. And whenever something starts happening in the mind, it immediately affects the body. The Western woman is losing much femininity. Particularly because of women's lib, the idea is: destroy differences, only then can you be equal.

That's nonsense. You can be different *and* equal. The rose is different from the lotus, but they have an equal right to be in the sun and to be in the wind and to be in the rain; they have an equal right to exist. They are different, and their difference is beautiful; it makes life rich, it gives variety.

Men and women *are* different, and they should remain different, because that is the whole reason for their attraction to each other. If they become too much alike they will lose that attraction. They should be diametrically opposite, they should be as far away from each other as possible, so that the mystery continues and the desire to explore each other continues.

The Western woman is losing something. The Eastern woman is not yet a human being; she is thought of as property. People like Morarji Desai still go on thinking of women as property, private property. In the East the woman still remains a thing, a commodity to be sold and purchased; either permanently, then it becomes marriage, or temporarily, then it is prostitution. The difference between prostitution and your so-called marriage is only of degrees – not of quality, only of quantity.

In the West, because of women's lib, the idea is arising that the woman has to be just like the man, only then will she be equal. That's again another foolishness. Equality need not be similarity. And if the woman becomes similar to the man she will lose all her charm, all her grace, all her beauty.

Even her body is adjusting and becoming more like a man's. She is losing her curves, she is losing softness, becoming a little hard. She is becoming aggressive, losing her receptivity, and she is pretending to be like a man. If the woman starts pretending to be like a man she will always remain a second-rate man: she can never become first-rate, she will be a copy. How can a woman become a first-rate man? That is impossible. It is as impossible as a man trying to become a first-rate woman; he will just be a copy, an actor, a pretender. And all pretension is to be condemned.

The woman has to remain a woman, the woman has to keep her distance. The woman has to grow those differences, because those differences are of immense value. It is in those differences that the whole poetry of life exists. Those differences are the magnetic force: bring men and women too close, make them too alike, too similar, and you will have destroyed something of immense value. The natural attraction will be gone.

I am neither for that, nor for the Eastern stupidity that the woman should be treated as a commodity. Why can't men and women exist as friends, equal although utterly different? What is the need of there being either private property, a private ownership of women, or a social ownership? The very idea of ownership is wrong. Nobody can own anybody else.

If understanding grows in the world, parents will not even own their children. They should not, because the idea of ownership is dehumanizing. Children come through you but you don't own them, they are not your property. Love them because you have given birth to them, but don't try to make them imitators. Don't use and exploit them for your own ambitions, don't claim that they belong to you. They only belong to existence and nobody else.

You ask: MORARJI DESAI SAID IN AN INTERVIEW GIVEN TO "SUNDAY": "OSHO PUTS EMPHASIS ON THE SOCIALIZATION OF WOMEN. JUST AS PROSTI-TUTES ARE SOCIALIZED, HE WANTS WOMEN TO BE SOCIALIZED."

That is utterly false, I have never said anything like that. And one would hope that a responsible person like the prime minister of a country would have a little more sense, would go into facts and see what I have said and what I have not said. HE ALSO SAID, "OSHO GOES EVEN FURTHER AND SAYS THAT THERE IS NO NEED OF MARRIAGE."

That's true, there is no need of marriage, friendship is enough. Marriage came into existence only because man was incapable of love and friendship; it was a poor substitute. If you love somebody there is no need to make it a legal contract. And the legal contract cannot make it a certainty that you will love the person always. The legal contract has no power over love. Marriage is a legal contract; it is ownership, private ownership. It is a license to own the woman. Just as you have dog licenses, it is a license – you are the owner.

This simply shows that there is no love. Law comes in only

when there is no love; otherwise, love is enough unto itself.

Love should be the primary phenomenon, and then you can bee together. The togetherness should be a friendship and a responsibility. When two persons love each other they are responsible, they care for each other. No law is needed to create that caring and that responsibility; no law is capable of creating it, either. At the most, it can impose a certain formal structure on you which will destroy your love, your friendship.

As the society becomes more and more alert and more and more conscious, as it is becoming every day, marriage is going to disappear. Instead of marriage there will be friendship. Just as in the past 'husband' and 'wife' were beautiful words, in the future 'girlfriend' and 'boyfriend' will take a very respectable place.

Meanwhile, because you have to live in a society, you can go into marriage, but marriage should remain secondary. It should be only because you have loved each other; it should come out of your love, not vice versa. In the past it has been tried: first get married and then love each other. That is impossible; nobody can manage love, it is in nobody's power to create love. It happens when it happens.

You can put two persons together. And that's what has been done, down the ages. Marry two persons: they *have* to be together. And when two persons are together they start liking each other, just as brothers like their sisters, and sisters like their brothers. It is a forced arrangement. And when two persons are together, a liking, a certain kind of liking arises, and they depend on each other, they use each other. But love – that's a totally different affair.

If marriage comes first, there is almost no possibility of love ever happening. In fact, marriage was invented to prevent love, because love is dangerous. It takes you to such high peaks of joy, ecstasy, romance and poetry that it is dangerous for the society to allow people to soar so high, to see something of that height and depth. Because if a person has known love, nothing will ever satisfy him. Then you cannot satisfy him by just giving him a big bank allowance, no. A big bank balance will not help; now he knows something about real richness.

If a man has loved and lived those ecstatic moments, you will not be able to attract him towards power politics. Who cares? You will not be able to force him into ugly inhuman jobs. He would like to remain a poor man, but his love flowing. Once you kill love – and marriage is an effort to kill it – once you kill love, then the energy of the person that is no longer moving into love is available for the society to exploit.

You can make him a soldier, and he will be a dangerous soldier. He will be ready to kill – any excuse, and he will be ready to kill, or to be killed. He will be boiling with frustration, with anger: you can force him into any ambitious direction. He will become a politician. He will become like Morarji Desai, his whole life only thinking of only one thing: how to become the prime minister of the country.

Now at the age of eighty-three he HAS become the prime minister. And just the other day I was reading in the newspapers that he has asked people to pray for his long life. Long life – still? Will you ever leave this poor country, or not? Long life for himself and his colleagues so they can serve the country. Will you not give the chance of serving the country to a few other people? Now, how long does he want to torture us?

These are the people who have not known love. Love frustrated becomes a great greed, love frustrated becomes great violence, love frustrated leads you into the world of ambitions. Love frustrated is very destructive.

But the society needs destructive people. It needs great armies: it needs armies of politicians, it needs armies of clerks, stationmasters, et cetera, et cetera. It needs people who are ready to do anything, because they have not known anything higher in life. They have never touched any poetic moment in their life; they can go on counting money their whole life and thinking this is all there is. Love is dangerous.

I would like love to become available to each and all. And if marriage happens at all, it should be a by-product of love and it should remain secondary. If love disappears one day, no hindrances should be created in dissolving the marriage. If two persons want to get married, both should have to agree to it. But for divorce, even if one person wants to divorce, that should be enough reason. Two persons need not agree to divorce.

Right now, no hindrances are created for marriage. Any two fools can go to the registry office and get married. But a thousand and one hindrances are created for divorce. This is a very insane approach.

In my vision, all kinds of hindrances should be created when people are getting married. They should be told, "Wait for two years. Live together for two years. And after two years, if you still want to get married, come back."

People should be allowed to live together so that they can know what kind of people they are and whether they are suited or not, whether they mix or not, whether the can create a harmony in their life or not.

But anybody can go to the marriage office and get married, and nobody creates any disturbance. This is absurd. And when you want to get separated, then the whole court and the law and the police and everybody, is there to prevent you. The society is for marriage and against divorce.

I am neither for marriage nor for divorce. In my vision there should be only a kind of friendship between people, a responsibility, a caring. And if that day is far away, then meanwhile marriage should not be allowed so easily. People should be given a chance to test each other, to live in all kinds of situations. Just out of a poetic vision, just out of a first-sight love, marriage should not be allowed.

Let things cool down, let things become ordinary. Let them see whether they can manage with ordinary life, with day-to-day problems, and only then allow them to get married.

That too should be temporary. Maybe every two years they have to come back to renew it; if they don't come, it is finished. The license should be renewed every two years, and whenever they want to separate, no problem should be created. AND HE SAID, "OSHO ALSO ADVOCATES FREE SEX." WHAT DO YOU SAY ABOUT IT?

It is very difficult for Morarji Desai and people like him to understand what I am saying. What I am saying really means transcendence of sex. I am not teaching sex, I am teaching love. But in people's minds there is no difference between love and sex. In their minds love means sex, because they have not known love, they have only known sex.

Love and sex are far apart. Sex is a biological phenomenon, love is a human phenomenon. And what is the difference?

Biologically, nature is interested in you reproducing, so that life continues. Sex is a reproductory system. So in nature sex has no other significance than reproduction. It is only *man's* glory, his dignity and freedom, that sex is, by and by, becoming free from biological hangovers.

Sex is becoming play, fun, celebration. When sex becomes play, fun, and celebration it starts moving towards a new quality, that is love.

Love is not needed for reproduction. Love is an *art* like music, like poetry, like painting.

The difference is such: animals eat, man also eats; as far as eating is concerned there is no difference. But watch closely: whenever animals eat, they move into a place where nobody can see them eating because they are always afraid that that the other may start taking something from their food. Animals eat alone. It is only man who likes to eat with people, who invites people, who makes a celebration out of eating. That is new, that is something utterly new; it doesn't exist in the animal world.

Animals eat just to fulfill their bodily needs. Man brings some aesthetics to his eating habits. He will prepare food: he will prepare it in beautiful shapes and colors, he will give beautiful flavors to the food. And he will have eating manners: he will arrange the table and the lights and music and incense, and he will have friends gather, talking and gossiping, and then he will eat. Now eating has taken a totally different turn. It has become an art.

So is the case with sex. In animals it is only a reproductive phenomenon.

Morarji Desai's guru, Mahatma Gandhi, used to say, "Make sexual contact only when you want to reproduce." Now, that is animal, that is below human. He thought he was teaching something great, spiritual. That was not spiritual at all; that is below human dignity.

What he was teaching is utterly animalistic. He was saying that sex is allowed only when you want to reproduce a child, otherwise not. Then there is no possibility of love.

Love is the aesthetics of sex. Love is an effort to free it from its biological past. You love woman, not because you are basically interested in producing a child; you love a woman for her own sake. You love a woman for the sheer joy of being with her, you love a man for the sheer joy of sharing your energy with him. Sex may come into it, may not come into it.

If love is there and the climate of love is there and sex comes into it, even sex is ordinary sex no more. It is transformed by the love climate.

But it is not necessary that it should come. Two lovers can simply sit holding hands, looking at the full moon. There is not necessarily any need for sex to enter it. It is enough, it is immensely satisfying. Two lovers can read poems to each other, sing a song together, dance, hug, hold each other. Sex is not a necessity. If it happens, it is good. If it does not happen, there is no hankering for it to happen. Love is its own fulfillment. Love goes higher than sex.

I teach love. And if you know love, you will slowly slowly start moving beyond sex.

Mahatma Gandhi had no vision of love. And Morarji Desai

learnt all that he knows from Mahatma Gandhi. He has no vision of love. I don't think he has ever loved anybody; I don't think he knows anything of love. All that he knows is ambition, greed and power-politics.

Sex, he must have known, because he has reproduced children. But that sex must have been something ugly, animalistic, mechanical, just for the sake of reproduction. He has been so much against any human warmth and contact that he even advised Mahatma Gandhi, his guru, against it.

Mahatma Gandhi, in his old age, used to walk with two girls, one on either side, just for support. He would put his hands on those two girls' shoulders and walk. He used to call them his walking-sticks.

You will be surprised that Morarji Desai brags about this very much: he says that he even advised Mahatma Gandhi, "This is not right, you should not touch women. And you should not walk with girls, your hands on their shoulders; it is not good." Now, this man knows nothing of human warmth. This man is constantly obsessed with sex. He has known only very very rudimentary animal sex in his life.

And he goes on projecting his ideas on me. I am not teaching free sex, I am teaching love. Love certainly brings love to a higher plane; it helps sex to move beyond biology towards spirituality.

And then there is one step more. If you go on loving, non-possessive love, without becoming each other's property; if your love goes on growing into deep friendship, accepting the other as the other is, without making any demands on how he should be, without becoming each other's dominators; if your love goes on growing into friendship, prayer arises.

In love, sometimes sex will be a part. In prayer, sex will disappear completely. Love is the bridge between sex and prayer. Don't get stuck on the bridge: go beyond sex.

But all going beyond is always going through. Hence I say don't reject sex, otherwise you will never be able to know love. Transform sex, don't reject it. Anything rejected remains hanging around you like a lodestone.

Morarji is just a male-chauvinistic, traditionalist, obscurantist fascist.

The fifth question:

BLESSED ONE, IS IT NECESSARY TO COMMUNICATE
IN DETAIL A PROBLEM I HAD WHICH I IN MY MIND
HAVE ALREADY TURNED OVER TO YOU AS MY
LOVING MASTER, FOR HELP AND GUIDANCE?
CAN I NOW CONSIDER IT YOUR PROBLEM RATHER
THAN MINE?

Subuddha, You can absolutely trust me. Forget all about your problem, I have taken it. It may raise its head again and again: you will have to remember constantly that you have given it to me, that you are not to think about it any longer, any more, that it has nothing to do with you.

And when you can do this with *this* problem you will be able to find a key. Then you can do it with *all* your problems. Problems are never solved, they are always dissolved. They are not worth solving either; one has to go beyond them.

This is one of the essential parts of *adab*: surrender your problems to your master and forget about them. Then you are finished, then it is none of you business.

And remember, it is not that it becomes my problem – I don't know even what your problem is. And it is not that I will be troubled by your problem and I will be worried by it and I will lose my sleep over it – nothing! I am just an excuse so that you can drop your problem. By dropping it, you go beyond it. In that very dropping, something happens within you: in that very dropping, trust happens, intelligence happens. In that very dropping, the energy that was getting hooked into the problem is released. You become more vital, you pulsate with new energy, and you can rise higher.

Problems are never solved but one can go beyond them. And when one has gone beyond them they are no longer material, they are irrelevant.

I am just an excuse, I don't do a thing. But you can do miracles through me. And Subuddha can do it, he *has* that quality. It is not in everybody's capacity to do it, but I have looked in Subuddha's eyes and I have felt it, that he knows how to surrender. And I am not asking for your money to be surrendered to me. I am simply asking: Surrender your problems to me, surrender all your diseases to me, surrender all your pathologies to me. And in that very surrendering you will be unburdened, you will be free.

The last question:

BELOVED MASTER, YOU SAY UNENLIGHTENED
PERSONS CANNOT BE COMPARED.
BUT I COMPARE AND EVALUATE MYSELF
CONSTANTLY WITH OTHER PEOPLE.
I FEEL THIS CONSTANTLY BRINGS CLOUDS
AND A DISTANCE BETWEEN ME AND THEM.
WHAT CAN BE DONE ABOUT IT?

Veetdharma, I have said that unenlightened people cannot be compared, because they are utterly different from each other. Their histories are different, their biographies are different, their pasts are different. They have moved through different terrains, different lives, in different ways; their karmas are different. They cannot be compared.

It will be like comparing a stone with a roseflower, or a roseflower with a star. People are so different from each other, they cannot be compared.

Only unenlightened persons can be compared, because they are no longer different at all, because they *are* no more. Emptiness can have only one taste

When two rooms are utterly empty, what is there to compare? They are so alike. If you want to compare, you can compare; you can say both are empty. Otherwise there is nothing in them to compare. When both the rooms are full of different furniture and paintings, there is much to compare; they are different.

The unenlightened person is utterly unique, there is nobody like him. He has his own pathology, his own neurosis, and nobody else has it. You can compare him in a way.

Two unenlightened persons are so alike, you can compare only that they are alike. But the paradox has to be understood: two enlightened persons are so alike, how will you compare them? And the other side of the paradox: two unenlightened persons are so unalike that the mind tends to compare them. One has this much money, the other has more. One has this quality, the other has something else; the temptation is there to compare.

From where comes the temptation to compare? It comes from your own ego. You are constantly comparing where you are on the scale. Somebody is poorer than you and you feel good, and somebody is richer than you and you feel bad. Seeing the poor man you feel very good – sometimes out of that feeling you may even want to help the poor man a little bit. Seeing the rich man you feel jealous, you feel very bad, hurt. Seeing the rich man a great desire arises in you how to become that rich, to prove yourself.

And it is a multidimensional phenomenon. You see an ugly man and you feel good, and you see a beautiful man and you feel bad: it is a constant comparing, because the ego can exist only between this comparison. If you drop this comparison, if you simply say "I am what I am, and they are what they are" then the ego will immediately lose its roots in you. Then it cannot exist. It exists between inferiority and superiority: this has to be understood.

Ego is sandwiched between inferiority and superiority, it is a thin layer between the two. And because it is sandwiched between inferiority and superiority it is constantly in trouble. misery and tension. Everybody is sandwiched.

If you watch yourself you will always see who is behind you and who is ahead of you, and that you are sandwiched. And the person who is behind you is trying to get ahead of you, so he has to be stopped. And the person who is ahead of you is trying to go still further ahead: he has to be stopped too. You have to get ahead and you have to gain speed and you have to put more energy into conflict and competition.

This how the whole world of ego continues. Watch and see the ways of the ego, and then it is not very difficult to drop it. Just seeing it, understanding it, your grip loosens. What is the point? There are millions of people in the world – if you go on comparing with everybody, your whole life will just remain miserable.

Somebody has beautiful eyes, and you don't, and somebody has something else, and you don't. And both ways it is bad, then too it puffs up your ego. And the puffed up ego becomes very sensitive, very touchy, anybody can hurt it.

You ask me: YOU SAY UNENLIGHTENED PEOPLE CANNOT BE COMPARED.

In a way they cannot be compared, because they are unique. In a way they can be compared, because their uniqueness only consists of quantitative differences. Enlightened people can be compared in a way, because they are all alike. And they cannot be compared, because they are so alike.

If you understand me rightly, comparison as such is meaningless. It is meaningless with unenlightened people, it is meaningless with enlightened people. Comparison itself is wrong, and the comparing mind is an egoistic mind.

Just go inside – because when you compare you have to go

outside, you have to focus on others. Just go inside and see who you are. Uncomparing, just see who you are. Just see what is your reality, not in reference to somebody else.

You are something authentic in your own right. Why not see it? Why compare? Comparison will give you a false identity. And that false identity is what is called ego.

When the false has been dropped, the real arises. And that real is incomparable. Because the real is not any self, it is open sky.

They tell the story of the rich old man who picked up a young girl and took her to his penthouse apartment. It was a very hot summer night and eventually they reached the bed, which had been his original objective.

Unfortunately he had figuratively bitten off more than he could chew and while lying on top of her, with the sweat pouring off his face, nothing else was happening. Finally the beautiful young girl impatiently reached behind her and extracted from her pillow a large feather and proceeded to brush his head with it.

The old man exclaimed, "What the hell are you doing? I am having enough trouble as it is!" She looked up and murmured sweetly, "Well, comparatively speaking, I am beating your brains out!"

The mind is continuously thinking in comparisons, it is constantly comparing. The mind lives in relativity, the mind is a by-product, an epiphenomenon of relativity. And you are not part of relativity. You are something beyond Albert Einstein's world of relativity. You are neither time nor space, you are something beyond: you are the witness. And the witness is not confined by any time or space, the witness is beyond all relativity. The witness is absolutely there; its existence is absolute.

Albert Einstein says there is nothing like an absolute. He is right as far as science is concerned, but he is wrong because he has not looked withinwards.

Outside, all is relative. Inside, nothing is relative. Outside

everything is moving. Inside, nothing is moving. Outside every-
thing is flux. Inside, everything is eternity.

But he has not looked inside, he has not looked at the
center of the cyclone.

Have you heard the old story of the little ten-year old boy
who went to the zoo with his mother?

When they came to the elephant, the little boy asked his
mother what that was that was hanging from the elephant.
"That's its tail, son" replied the mother.

"No, the other thing hanging" said the kid. "That's his
trunk" said the mother. "No, the other thing that is hanging"
insisted the little boy. "It's nothing, son, nothing at all" replied
the embarrassed mother.

A few weeks later, the little boy went to the circus with his
father and when they came to the elephant, the kid started
with his father.

"What's that hanging from the elephant?" asked the boy.

"Its tail, son" replied the father. "No, the other thing" asked
the son. "That's his trunk, son." "No, the other thing hanging
from the elephant" the son persisted.

"Well, son, I think by now you are old enough to know"
and the father began to explain the facts of life to him. When
he had finished, the kid turned to his father and said "How
come when I asked mother what it was, she said it was noth-
ing at all?"

"Well, my son" said the father "your mother just happens to
be a little spoiled."

You get it? That's how the mind continues to compare and
compare and compare.

Drop comparisons and just be and just see that which is,
not in reference to something else. And once you have looked
within yourself and seen that which is, without any reference
to anything else, you will be surprised how much you have
been missing. Then open your eyes and look at things without
any comparison.

A roseflower does not have to be compared with other roseflowers, it exists in its own right. It has no reference to any other rose that has been on the earth or will ever be on the earth. It is individual, authentically individual.

Then look at each person as authentically individual. And then life looks so rich, infinitely rich, because it exists of tremendous uniqueness. Our comparison dulls our mind, our comparison gathers dust on the mirror of our consciousness.

Veetdharma, drop this old habit of comparing. But the beginning has to be done inside. Old habits die hard but if you become alert they can be dropped. It will take a little time, but as the habits start disappearing, you will start entering into the world or reality which is non-comparative. And the world that is non-comparative is the world of the absolute, the world of god.

That's what we are searching for here. Science searches for the world of relativity, religion for the world of the absolute.

about osho

Osho is a modern-day buddha whose wisdom, clarity and humor have touched the lives of millions of people around the world. He is creating the conditions for the emergence of what he calls the "New Man" – a completely new kind of human being who is aware, life-affirmative and free.

According to Osho, the spiritual traditions of the past have made a deep split within the individual, reflected in all the institutions of society. His way is to heal this split, to restore the unity of body and spirit, earth and sky.

After his enlightenment in 1953, the evolution of this New Man became his dream. In 1966, Osho left the academic world and his post as a philosophy professor at the University of Jabalpur and began touring India intensively and speaking to many hundreds of thousands of people. At the same time, Osho was developing practical tools for man's self-transformation.

By the late 1960s, Osho had begun to create his unique dynamic meditation techniques. He says that modern man is so burdened with the traditions from the past and the anxieties of modern-day living, that he must go through a deep cleansing process before he can begin to discover the thought-free, relaxed state of meditation.

By 1974, a commune had been established around Osho in Pune, India, and the trickle of visitors from the West had become a flood. Today, his Commune is the largest spiritual growth center in the world. Each year it attracts thousands of international visitors to its meditation, therapy, bodywork and creative programs.

Osho speaks on virtually every aspect of the development of human consciousness. His talks cover a staggering range – from the meaning of life and death, to the struggles of power and politics, from the challenges of love and creativity, to the significance of science and education. These talks, given over thirty years, have been recorded on audio cassette and video-tape, and published in hundreds of books in every major language of the world. He belongs to no tradition and says, "My message is not a doctrine, not a philosophy. My message is a certain alchemy, a science of transformation."

Osho left his body in 1990 as a result of poisoning by U.S. government agents, while being held in custody for technical immigration violations in 1985. He asks always to be referred to in the present tense. The words on his Samadhi, which Osho himself dictated, read:

OSHO
Never Born Never Died
Only Visited this Planet Earth between
December 11, 1931 – January 19, 1990

further information

Osho Commune International in Pune, India, is a place to relax from the outward stresses of life and nourish the soul. Osho describes the Commune as a laboratory, an experiment in creating a "New Man" – a human being who lives in harmony with the inner and the outer, with himself and his environment,and who is free from all ideologies and conditionings that now divide humanity.

Set in 31 acres in the tree-lined suburb of Koregaon Park, this meditation resort receives thousands of visitors every year from all countries and from all walks of life.Visitors generally spend from three weeks to three months and stay in nearby hotels and apartments.

The Commune houses the unique Osho Multiversity, which offers hundreds of personal growth and self-discovery programs and professional trainings throughout the year, all of which are designed to help people find the knack of meditation: the passive witnessing of thoughts, emotions and actions, without judgment or identification.

Unlike many traditional Eastern disciplines, meditation at Osho Commune is an inseparable part of daily life, whether working, relating, or just being. The result is that people do not renounce the world but bring to it a spirit of awareness, celebration, and a deep reverence for life.

At the center of the Commune is Gautama the Buddha

Auditorium, where seven different one-hour-long meditations are offered every day, including:

Osho Dynamic Meditation*: Osho's technique designed to release tensions and repressed emotions, opening the way to a new vitality and an experience of profound silence.

Osho Kundalini Meditation*: Shaking free dormant energies, and through spontaneous dance and silent sitting, allowing these energies to be redirected inwards.

Osho Nataraj Meditation*: The inner alchemy of dancing so totally, that the dancer disappears and only the dance remains.

Osho Nadabrahma Meditation*: Based on an ancient Tibetan humming technique to harmonize the energy flow.

Osho No-dimensions: A powerful method for centering the energy, based on a Gurdjieff technique.

Osho Vipassana Meditation: Gautam Buddha's technique of dissolving mental chatter through the awareness of breath.

The highlight of the day at the Commune is the evening meeting of the Osho White Robe Brotherhood. This two-hour celebration of music, dance and silence, followed by a videotape discourse from Osho, is unique – a deep and complete meditation where thousands of seekers, in Osho's words, "...dissolve into a sea of consciousness."

*Service mark Osho International Foundation

further information

For information about visiting the Commune,
your nearest Osho Meditation Center and general
information, contact:
osho commune international
17 Koregaon Park, Pune 411 001 (MS), India
Tel: +91 (0)20 613 6655 Fax: +91 (0)20 613 9955
e-mail: osho-commune@osho.com

For publishing and copyright information
regarding Osho's books, contact:
osho international
570 Lexington Ave, New York, NY 10022, USA
Tel: +1 212 588 9888 Fax: +1 212 588 1977
e-mail: osho-int@osho.com

www.osho.com
A comprehensive web site in different languages
featuring Osho's meditations, books and tapes,
an online tour of Osho Commune International,
a list of Osho Information Centers worldwide, and a
selection of Osho's talks.